Nietzsche and Philosophy

European Perspectives:
A Series of the Columbia University Press

Nietzsche and Philosophy

Gilles Deleuze

Translated by Hugh Tomlinson

New York
Columbia University Press

Clothbound editions of Columbia University Press books are Smyth-sewn and printed on permanent and durable acid-free paper.

Originally published in France in 1962 as *Nietzsche et la philosophie* by Presses Universitaires de France.

The publishers acknowledge the financial assistance of
the French Ministry of Culture and Communication
in the translation of this work

Library of Congress Cataloging in Publication Data

Deleuze, Gilles.
Nietzsche and Philosophy.

(European perspectives)
Translation of: Nietzsche et la philosophie
1. Nietzsche, Friedrich Wilhelm, 1844–1900.
I. Title. II. Series.
B3317.D413 1983 193   82–17676
ISBN 0–231–05668–0
ISBN 0–231–05669–9 pbk.

p 10 9 8 7 6 5 4
c 10 9 8 7 6 5 4 3 2

Contents

Preface to the English Translation

to Hugh Tomlinson

It is always exciting for a French book to be translated into English. It is an opportunity for the author, after so many years, to consider the impression he would like to make on a prospective reader, whom he feels both very close to and very cut off from.

Nietzsche's posthumous fate has been burdened by two ambiguities: was his thought a forerunner of fascist thinking? And was this thought itself really philosophy or was it an over-violent poetry, made up of capricious aphorisms and pathological fragments? It is perhaps in England that Nietzsche has been most misunderstood. Tomlinson suggests that the major themes which Nietzsche confronts and battles against – French rationalism and German dialectics – have never been of central importance to English thought. The English had at their theoretical disposal an empiricism and a pragmatism which meant that the detour through Nietzsche was of no great value to them. They did not need the detour through Nietzsche's very special empiricism and pragmatism which ran counter to their "good sense". In England therefore Nietzsche was only able to influence novelists, poets and dramatists: this was a practical, emotional influence rather than a philosophical one, lyrical rather than theoretical.

Nevertheless Nietzsche is one of the greatest philosophers of the nineteenth century. And he alters both the theory and the practice of philosophy. He compares the thinker to an arrow shot by Nature that another thinker picks up where it has fallen so that he can shoot it somewhere else. According to him, the philosopher is neither eternal nor historical but "untimely", always untimely. Nietzsche has hardly any predecessors. Apart from the Pre-Socratics of long ago he recognised only one predecessor – Spinoza.

Nietzsche's philosophy is organised along two great axes. The first is concerned with force, with forces, and forms of general semeiology. Phenomena, things, organisms, societies, consciousness and spirits are signs, or rather symptoms, and themselves reflect states of forces. This is the origin of the conception of the philosopher as "physiologist and physician". We can ask, for any given thing, what state of exterior and interior forces it presupposes. Nietzsche was responsible for creating a whole typology to distinguish active, acted and reactive forces and to analyse their varying combinations. In particular, the delineation of a genuinely reactive type of forces constitutes one of the most original points of Nietzschean thought. This book attempts to define and analyse the different forces. This kind of general semeiology includes linguistics, or rather philology, as one of its parts. For any proposition is itself a set of symptoms expressing a way of being or a mode of existence of the speaker, that is to say the state of forces that he maintains or tries to maintain with himself and others (consider the role of conjunctions in this connection). In this sense a proposition always reflects a mode of existence, a "type". What is the mode of existence of the person who utters any given proposition, what mode of existence is needed in order to be able to utter it? The mode of existence is the state of forces insofar as it forms a type which can be expressed by signs or symptoms.

   The two great human reactive concepts, as "diagnosed" by Nietzsche, are those of *ressentiment* and bad conscience. *Ressentiment* and bad conscience are expressions of the triumph of reactive forces in man and even of the constitution of man by reactive forces: the man-slave. This shows the extent to which the Nietzschean notion of the slave does not necessarily stand for someone dominated, by fate or social condition, but also characterises the dominators as much as the dominated once the regime of domination comes under the sway of forces which are reactive and not active. Totalitarian regimes are in this sense regimes of slaves, not merely because of the people that they subjugate, but above all because of the type of "masters" they set up. A universal history of *ressentiment* and bad conscience – from the Jewish and Christian priests to the secular priest of the present – is a fundamental component of Nietzsche's historical perspectivism (Nietzsche's supposedly anti-semitic texts are in fact texts on the original priestly type).

   The second axis is concerned with power and forms an ethics and an ontology. Nietzsche is most misunderstood in relation to the question of power. Every time we interpret will to power as "wanting or seeking power" we encounter platitudes which have nothing to do with Nietzsche's thought. If it is true that all things reflect a state of forces then power designates the element, or rather the differential relationship, of forces which directly confront one another. This relationship expresses itself in the dynamic qualities of types such as "affirmation" and "negation". Power is therefore not what the will wants, but on the contrary, the one that wants in the will. And "to want or seek power" is only the lowest degree of the will to power, its negative form, the guise it assumes when reactive forces prevail in the state of things. One of the most original characteristics of Nietzsche's philosophy is the transformation of the question "what is . . .?" into "which one is . . .?" For example, for any given proposition he asks "which one is capable of uttering it?" Here we must rid ourselves of all "personalist" references. The one that . . . does not refer to an individual, to a person, but rather to an event, that is, to the forces in their various relationships in a proposition or a phenomenon, and to the genetic relationship which determines these forces (power). "The one that" is always Dionysus, a mask or a guise of Dionysus, a flash of lightning.

The eternal return is as badly misunderstood as the will to power. Every time we understand the eternal return as the return of a particular arrangement of things after all the other arrangements have been realised, every time we interpret the eternal return as the return of the identical or the same, we replace Nietzsche's thought with childish hypotheses. No one extended the critique of all forms of identity further than Nietzsche. On two occasions in *Zarathustra* Nietzsche explicitly denies that the eternal return is a circle which makes the same return. The eternal return is the strict opposite of this since it cannot be separated from a selection, from a double selection. Firstly, there is the selection of willing or of thought which constitutes Nietzsche's ethics: only will that of which one also wills the eternal return (to eliminate all half-willing, everything which can only be willed with the proviso "once, only once"). Secondly, there is the selection of being which constitutes Nietzsche's ontology: only that which *becomes* in the fullest sense of the word can return, is fit to return. Only action and affirmation return: becoming has being and only becoming has being. That which is opposed to becoming, the same or the identical, strictly speaking, *is* not. The negative as the lowest degree of power, the reactive as the lowest degree of force, do not return because they are the opposite of becoming and only becoming has being. We can thus see how the eternal return is linked, not to a repetition of the same, but on the contrary, to a transmutation. It is the moment or the eternity of becoming which eliminates all that resists it. It releases, indeed it creates, the purely active and pure affirmation. And this is the sole content of the Overman; he is the joint product of the will to power and the eternal return, Dionysus and Ariadne. This is why Nietzsche says that the will to power is not wanting, coveting or seeking power, but only "giving" or "creating". This book sets out, primarily, to analyse what Nietzsche calls becoming.

But the difficulty of Nietzsche depends less on conceptual analysis than on practical evaluations which evoke a whole atmosphere, all kinds of emotional dispositions in the reader. Like Spinoza, Nietzsche always maintained that there is the deepest relationship between concept and affect. Conceptual analyses are indispensable and Nietzsche takes them further than anyone else. But they will always be ineffective if the reader grasps them in an atmosphere which is not that of Nietzsche. As long as the reader persists in: 1) seeing the Nietzschean "slave" as someone who finds himself dominated by a master, and deserves to be; 2) understanding the will to power as a will which wants and seeks power; 3) conceiving the eternal return as the tedious return of the same; 4) imagining the Overman as a given master race – no positive relationship between Nietzsche and his reader will be possible. Nietzsche will appear a nihilist, or worse, a fascist and at best as an obscure and terrifying prophet. Nietzsche knew this, he knew the fate that lay in store for him, he who gave Zarathustra an "ape" or "buffoon" as a double, foretelling that Zarathustra would be confused with his ape (a prophet, a fascist or a madman . . .). This is why a book about Nietzsche must try hard to correct the practical or emotional misunderstanding as well as re-establishing the conceptual analysis.

And it is indeed true that Nietzsche diagnosed nihilism as the movement which carries history forward. No one has analysed the concept of nihilism better than he did, he invented the concept. But it is important to see that he defined it in terms of the triumph of reactive forces or the negative in the will to power. To nihilism he opposed transmutation, that is the becoming which is simultaneously the only action of force and the only affirmation of power, the transhistoric element of man, the Overman (and not the superman). The Overman is the focal point, where the reactive (*ressentiment* and bad conscience) is conquered, and where the negative gives way to affirmation. Nietzsche remains inseparable, at every moment, from the forces of the future, from the forces yet to come that his prayers invoke, that his thought outlines, that his art prefigures. He not only diagnoses, as Kafka put it, the diabolical forces already knocking at the door, but he exorcises them by raising the last Power capable of struggling with them, against them, and of ousting them both within us and outside us. A Nietzschean "aphorism" is not a mere fragment, a morsel of thought: it is a proposition which only makes sense in relation to the state of forces that it expresses, and which changes sense, which must change sense, according to the new forces which it is "capable" (has the power) of attracting.

And without doubt this is the most important point of Nietzsche's philosophy: the radical transformation of the image of thought that we create for ourselves. Nietzsche snatches thought from the element of truth and falsity. He turns it into an interpretation and an evaluation, interpretation of forces, evaluation of power. – It is a thought-movement, not merely in the sense that Nietzsche wants to reconcile thought and concrete movement, but in the sense that thought itself must produce movements, bursts of extraordinary speed and slowness (here again we can see the role of the aphorism, with its variable speeds and its "projectile-like" movement). As a result philosophy has a new relationship to the arts of movement: theatre, dance and music. Nietzsche was never satisfied with the discourse or the dissertation (*logos*) as an expression of philosophical thought, although he wrote the finest dissertations – notably the *Genealogy of Morals*, to which all modern ethnology owes an inexhaustible "debt". But a book like *Zarathustra* can only be read as a modern opera and seen and heard as such. It is not that Nietzsche produces a philosophical opera or a piece of allegorical theatre, but he creates a piece of theatre or an opera which directly expresses thought as experience and movement. And when Nietzsche says that the Overman resembles a Borgia rather than a Parsifal, or that he is a member of both the order of Jesuits and the Prussian officer corps, it would be wrong to see these as protofascist statements, since they are the remarks of a director indicating how the Overman should be "played" (rather like Kierkegaard saying that the knight of the faith is like a bourgeois in his Sunday best). – To think is to create: this is Nietzsche's greatest lesson. To think, to cast the dice . . .: this was already the sense of the eternal return.

Translator's Note

The translator of a work of philosophy must, above all, be scrupulous in his rendering of the philosophical "content" of the original. I have sought to be as consistent and accurate as possible in my rendering of Deleuzian philosophical terms and have received some valuable advice from M. Deleuze himself on the translation of some important expressions. I have occasionally given further explanations in translator's notes, marked with an asterisk.

But content can never be completely separated from style. I have not, however, attempted to transpose the precise classical discursive style of the original into some hypothetical English equivalent. Instead I have sought to convey something of the "force" of the original by sticking closer to the rhythms of the French than is, perhaps, usual. Thus I have retained much of M. Deleuze's clause structure and his division into paragraphs and sub-paragraphs. The latter are indicated by the use of the dash (–).

I have used the most widely available English translations of Nietzsche's works. Most of the references to these have been included in the text following the abbreviations given overleaf. The standard English translations of Nietzsche sometimes differ significantly from the older French versions cited in the original and I have sometimes had to modify the English accordingly. Such modifications are indicated by an asterisk after the reference. Unfortunately the only French translation of Nietzsche's *Nachlass* available until recently was one of a little known selection by F. Würzbach. This is not available in English and has not been fully collated with the standard arrangement which is also known as the *Will to Power* and which has been translated. I have given references to the *Will to Power* where possible (WP) alongside references to Würzbach's selection (VP).

I would like to acknowledge the help and advice of Linda Zuck (whose idea it was in the first place), Barbara Habberjam, Peter Dews and many other friends and colleagues. The translation is dedicated to Jill.

H.T.

Abbreviations of Nietzsche's Works

1

The Tragic

1. The Concept of Genealogy

Nietzsche's most general project is the introduction of the concepts of sense and value into philosophy. It is clear that modern philosophy has largely lived off Nietzsche. But not perhaps in the way in which he would have wished. Nietzsche made no secret of the fact that the philosophy of sense and values had to be a critique. One of the principal motifs of Nietzsche's work is that Kant had not carried out a true critique because he was not able to pose the problem of critique in terms of values. And what has happened in modern philosophy is that the theory of values has given rise to a new conformism and new forms of submission. Even the phenomenological apparatus has contributed to placing the Nietzschean inspiration, which is often present in phenomenology, at the service of modern conformism. But, with Nietzsche, we must begin from the fact that the philosophy of values as envisaged and established by him is the true realisation of critique and the only way in which a total critique may be realised, the only way to "philosophise with a hammer". In fact, the notion of value implies a *critical* reversal. On the one hand, values appear or are given as principles: and evaluation presupposes values on the basis of which phenomena are appraised. But, on the other hand and more profoundly, it is values which presuppose evaluations, "perspectives of appraisal", from which their own value is derived. The problem of critique is that of the value of values, of the evaluation from which their value arises, thus the problem of their *creation*. Evaluation is defined as the differential element of corresponding values, an element which is both critical and creative.[1]* Evaluations, in essence, are not values but ways of being, modes of existence of those who judge and evaluate, serving as principles for the values on the basis of which they judge. This is why we always have the beliefs, feelings and thoughts that we deserve given our way of being or our style of life.

There are things that can only be said, felt or conceived, values which can only be adhered to, on condition of "base" evaluation, "base" living and thinking. This is the crucial point; *high* and *low*, *noble* and *base*, are not values but represent the differential element from which the value of values themselves derives.

Critical philosophy has two inseparable moments: the referring back of all things and any kind of origin to values, but also the reffering back of these values to something which is, as it were, their origin and determines their value. This is Nietzsche's twofold struggle: against those who remove values from criticism, contenting themselves with producing inventories of existing values or with criticising things in the name of established values (the "philosophical labourers", Kant and Schopenhauer, BGE 211); but also against those who criticise, or respect, values by deriving them from simple facts, from so-called "objective facts" (the utilitarians, the "scholars", BGE Part 6). In both cases philosophy moves in the *indifferent* element of the valuable in itself or the valuable for all. Nietzsche attacks both the "high" idea of foundation which leaves values indifferent to their own origin and the idea of a simple causal derivation or smooth beginning which suggests an indifferent origin for values. Nietzsche creates the new concept of genealogy. The philosopher is a genealogist rather than a Kantian tribunal judge or a utilitarian mechanic. Hesiod is such a philosopher. Nietzsche substitutes the pathos of difference or distance (the differential element) for both the Kantian principle of universality and the principle of resemblance dear to the utilitarians. "It was from the height of this *pathos of distance* that they first seized the right to create values and to coin names for them; what did utility matter?" (GM I 2 p. 26*).

Genealogy means both the value of origin and the origin of values. Genealogy is as opposed to absolute values as it is to relative or utilitarian ones. Genealogy signifies the differential element of values from which their value itself derives. Genealogy thus means origin or birth, but also difference or distance in the origin. Genealogy means nobility and baseness, nobility and vulgarity, nobility and decadence in the origin. The noble and the vulgar, the high and the low – this is the truly genealogical and critical element. But, understood in this way, critique is also at its most positive. The differential element is both a critique of the value of values and the positive element of a creation. This is why critique is never conceived by Nietzsche as a

reaction but as an *action*. Nietzsche contrasts the activity of critique
with revenge, grudge or *ressentiment*.[2]* Zarathustra will be followed
from one end of the book to the other by his ape, his "buffoon", his
"demon"; but the ape is as different from Zarathustra as revenge and
ressentiment are from critique itself. To be confused with his ape; this
is what Zarathustra feels as one of the frightful temptations held out to
him (Z III "Of Passing By"). Critique is not a re-action of *re-sentiment*
but the active expression of an active mode of existence; attack and not
revenge, the natural aggression of a way of being, the divine wickedness without which perfection could not be imagined (EH I 6–7). This
way of being is that of the philosopher precisely because he intends to
wield the differential element as critic and creator and therefore as a
hammer. Nietzsche says that his adversaries think "basely".
Nietzsche has high expectations of this conception of genealogy: a
new organisation of the sciences, a new organisation of philosophy, a
determination of the values of the future.

2. Sense

We will never find the sense of something (of a human, a biological or
even a physical phenomenon) if we do not know the force[3]* which
appropriates the thing, which exploits it, which takes possession of it
or is expressed in it. A phenomenon is not an appearance or even an
apparition but a sign, a symptom which finds its meaning in an
existing force. The whole of philosophy is a symptomatology, and a
semeiology. The sciences are a symptomatological and semeiological
system. Nietzsche substitutes the correlation of sense and phenomenon for the metaphysical duality of appearance and essence and for the
scientific relation of cause and effect. All force is appropriation,
domination, exploitation of a quantity of reality. Even perception, in
its divers aspects, is the expression of forces which appropriate
nature. That is to say that nature itself has a history. The history of a
thing, in general, is the succession of forces which take possession of it
and the co-existence of the forces which struggle for possession. The
same object, the same phenomenon, changes sense depending on the
force which appropriates it. History is the variation of senses, that is to
say "the succession of more or less profound, more or less mutually
independent processes of subduing" (GM II 12 p. 78). Sense is
therefore a complex notion; there is always a plurality of senses, a
constellation, a complex of successions but also of coexistences which

make interpretation an art. "All subjugation, all domination amounts to a new interpretation."

Nietzsche's philosophy cannot be understood without taking his essential pluralism into account. And, in fact, pluralism (otherwise known as empiricism) is almost indistinguishable from philosophy itself. Pluralism is the properly philosophical way of thinking, the one invented by philosophy; the only guarantor of freedom in the concrete spirit, the only principle of a violent atheism. The Gods are dead but they have died from laughing, on hearing one God claim to be the only one, "Is not precisely this godliness, that there are gods but no God?" (Z III 'Of the Apostates', p. 201). And the death of this God, who claimed to be the only one, is itself plural; the death of God is an event with a multiple sense. This is why Nietzsche does not believe in resounding "great events", but in the silent plurality of senses of each event (Z II "Of Great Events"). There is no event, no phenomenon, word or thought which does not have a multiple sense. A thing is sometimes this, sometimes that, sometimes something more complicated – depending on the forces (the gods) which take possession of it. Hegel wanted to ridicule pluralism, identifying it with a naive consciousness which would be happy to say "this, that, here, now" – like a child stuttering out its most humble needs. The pluralist idea that a thing has many senses, the idea that there are many things and one thing can be seen as "this and then that" is philosophy's greatest achievement, the conquest of the true concept, its maturity and not its renunciation or infancy. For the evaluation of this and that, the delicate weighing of each thing and its sense, the estimation of the forces which define the aspects of a thing and its relations with others at every instant – all this (or all that) depends on philosophy's highest art – that of interpretation. To interpret and even to evaluate is always to weigh. The notion of essence does not disappear here but takes on a new significance, for not every sense has the same value. A thing has as many senses as there are forces capable of taking possession of it. But the thing itself is not neutral and will have more or less affinity with the force in current possession. There are forces which can only get a grip on something by giving it a restrictive sense and a negative value. Essence, on the other hand, will be defined as that one, among all the senses of a thing, which gives it the force with which it has the most affinity. Thus, in a favourite example of Nietzsche's, religion does not have a unique sense, it serves many forces. But which force has the maximum affinity with religion? Which is the one where we can no longer know who dominates, it dominating religion or religion dominating it?[4] For all things all this is a question of weighing, the delicate but rigorous art of philosophy, of pluralist interpretation.

Interpretation reveals its complexity when we realise that a new force can only appear and appropriate an object by first of all putting on the mask of the forces which are already in possession of the object. The mask or the trick are laws of nature and therefore something more than mere mask or trick. To begin with life must imitate matter merely in order to survive. A force would not survive if it did not first of all borrow the feature of the forces with which it struggles (GM III 8, 9, 10). Thus the philosopher can only be born and grow with any chance of survival by having the contemplative air of the priest, of the ascetic and religious man who dominated the world before he appeared. The fact that we are burdened by such a necessity not only shows what a ridiculous image philosophy has (the image of the philosopher-sage, friend of wisdom and ascesis) but also that philosophy itself does not throw off its ascetic mask as it grows up: in a way it must believe in this mask, it can only conquer its mask by giving it a new sense which finally expresses its true anti-religious force (GM III 10). We see that the art of interpreting must also be an art of piercing masks, of discovering the one that masks himself, why he does it and the point of keeping up the mask while it is being reshaped. That is to say that genealogy does not appear on the first night and that we risk serious misunderstanding if we look for the child's father at the birth. The difference *in* the origin does not appear *at* the origin – except perhaps to a particularly practised eye, the eye which sees from afar, the eye of the far-sighted, the eye of the genealogist. Only when philosophy has grown up can we grasp its essence or its genealogy and distinguish it from everything that it originally had too great a stake in being mistaken for. It is the same for every thing. "In *all things* only the higher degrees matter!" (PTG). The problem is one of origin but origin conceived as genealogy can only be determined in relation to higher degrees

Nietzsche says that there is no need to wonder what the Greeks owe to the East (PTG). Philosophy is Greek insofar as it is in Greece that it attains its higher form for the first time, that it first shows its true force and its goals – these are not the same as those of the Eastern priest even when they are made use of. *Philosophos* does not mean "wise man" but "friend of wisdom". But "friend" must be interpreted in a strange way: the friend, says Zarathustra, is always a third person in between "I" and "me" who pushes me to overcome myself and to be overcome in order to live (Z I "Of the Friend" p. 82). The friend of wisdom is the one who appeals to wisdom, but in the way that one appeals to a mask without which one would not survive, the one who makes use of wisdom for new, bizarre and dangerous ends – ends which are, in fact, hardly wise at all. He wants wisdom to overcome itself and to be overcome. The people are certainly not always wrong: they have a foreboding of the essence of the philosopher, his anti-wisdom, his immoralism, *his* conception of friendship. Humility, poverty, chastity – we can guess the sense that these wise and ascetic values take on when they are revived by philosophy, by a new force (GM III 8).

3. *The Philosophy of the Will*

Genealogy does not only interpret, it also evaluates. Up to now we have presented things as if different forces struggled over and took successive possession of an almost inert object. But the object itself is force, expression of a force. This is why there is more or less affinity between the object and the force which takes possession of it. There is no object (phenomenon) which is not already possessed since in itself it is not an appearance but the apparition of a force. Every force is thus essentially related to another force. The being of force is plural, it would be absolutely absurd to think about force in the singular. A force is domination, but also the object on which domination is exercised. A plurality of forces acting and being affected at distance, distance being the differential element included in each force and by which each is related to others – this is the principle of Nietzsche's philosophy of nature. The critique of atomism must be understood in terms of this principle. It consists in showing that atomism attempts to impart to matter an essential plurality and distance which in fact belong only to force. Only force can be related to another force. (As Marx says when he interprets atomism, "Atoms are their own unique objects and can relate only to themselves" – Marx "Difference Between the Democritean and Epicurean Philosophy of Nature". But the question is; can the basic notion of atom accommodate the essential relation which is attempted to it? The concept only becomes coherent if one thinks of force instead of atom. For the notion of atom cannot in itself contain the difference necessary for the affirmation of such a relation, difference in and according to the essence. Thus atomism would be a mask for an incipient dynamism.)

Nietzsche's concept of force is therefore that of a force which is related to another force: in this form force is called will. The will (will to power) is the differential element of force. A new conception of the philosophy of the will follows from this. For the will is not exercised mysteriously on muscles or nerves, still less on "matter in general", but is necessarily exercised on another will. The real problem is not that of the relation of will to the involuntary but rather of the relation of a will that commands to a will that obeys – that obeys to a greater or lesser extent. " 'Will' can of course operate only on 'will' – and not on 'matter' (not on 'nerves' for example): enough, one must venture the hypothesis that wherever 'effects' are recognised, will is operating on will" (BGE 36 p. 49). The will is called a complex thing because insofar as it wills it wills obedience – but only a will can obey commands. Thus pluralism finds its immediate corroboration and its chosen ground in the philosophy of the will. And Nietzsche's break with Schopenhauer rests on one precise point; it is a matter of knowing whether the will is unitary or multiple. Everything else flows from this. Indeed, if Schopenhauer is led to deny the will it is primarily because he believes in the unity of willing. Because the will, according to Schopenhauer, is essentially unitary, the executioner comes to understand that he is one with his own victim. The consciousness of the identity of the will in all its manifestations leads the will to deny itself, to suppress itself in pity, morality and ascetism (Schopenhauer *The World as Will and Idea*, Book 4). Nietzsche discovers what seems to him the authentically Schopenhauerian mystification; when we posit the unity, the identity, of the will we must necessarily repudiate the will itself.

Nietzsche denounces the soul, the "ego" and egoism as the last refuges of atomism. Psychic atomism is more valid than physical atomism: "In all willing it is absolutely a question of commanding and obeying, on the basis of a social structure composed of many 'souls' " (BGE 19 p. 31). When Nietzsche praises egoism it is always in an aggressive or polemical way, against the virtues, against the virtue of disinterestedness (Z III "Of the Three Evil Things"). But in fact egoism is a bad interpretation of will, just as atomism is a bad interpretation of force. In order for there to be egoism it is necessary for there to be an *ego*. What directs us towards the origin is the fact that every force is related to another, whether in order to command or to obey. The origin is the difference in the origin, difference in the origin is *hierarchy*, that is to say the relation of a dominant to a dominated force, of an obeyed to an obeying will. The inseparability of hierarchy and genealogy is what Nietzsche calls "our problem" (HH Preface 7). Hierarchy is the originary fact, the identity of difference and origin. We will understand later why the problem of hierarchy is precisely the problem of "free spirits". Be that as it may, we can note the progression from sense to value, from interpretation to evaluation as tasks for genealogy. The sense of something is its relation to the force which takes possession of it, the value of something is the hierarchy of forces which are expressed in it as a complex phenomenon.

4. Against the Dialectic

Is Nietzsche a "dialectician"? Not all relations between "same" and "other" are sufficient to form a dialectic, even essential ones: everything depends on the role of the negative in this relation. Nietzsche emphasises the fact that force has another force as its object. But it is important to see that forces enter into relations with other forces. Life struggles with *another kind* of life. Pluralism sometimes appears to be dialectical – but it is its most ferocious enemy, its only profound enemy. This is why we must take seriously the resolutely anti-dialectical character of Nietzsche's philosophy. It has been said that Nietzsche did not know his Hegel. In the sense that one does not know one's opponent well. On the other hand we believe that the Hegelian movement, the different Hegelian factions were familiar to him. Like Marx he found his habitual targets there. If we do not discover its target the whole of Nietzsche's philosophy remains abstract and barely comprehensible. The question "against whom" itself calls for several replies. But a particularly important one is that the concept of the Overman is directed against the dialectical conception of man, and transvaluation is directed against the dialectic of appropriation or the suppression of alienation. Anti-Hegelianism runs through Nietzsche's work as its cutting edge. We can already feel it in the theory of forces.

In Nietzsche the essential relation of one force to another is never conceived of as a negative element in the essence. In its relation with the other the force which makes itself obeyed does not deny the other or that which it is not, it affirms its own difference and enjoys this difference. The negative is not present in the essence as that from which force draws its activity: on the contrary it is a result of activity, of the existence of an active force and the affirmation of its difference. The negative is a product of existence itself: the aggression necessarily linked to an active existence, the aggression of an affirmation. As for the negative concept (that is to say, negation as a concept) "it is only a subsequently-invented pale contrasting image in relation to its positive basic concept – filled with life and passion through and through" (GM I 10 p. 37). For the speculative element of negation, opposition or contradiction Nietzsche substitutes the practical element of *difference*, the object of affirmation and enjoyment. It is in this sense that there is a Nietzschean empiricism. The question which Nietzsche constantly repeats, "what does a will want, what does this one or that one want?", must not be understood as the search for a goal, a motive or an object for this will. What a will wants is to affirm its difference. In its essential relation with the "other" a will makes its difference an object of affirmation. "The pleasure of knowing oneself different", the enjoyment of difference (BGE 260); this is the new, aggressive and elevated conceptual element that empiricism substitutes for the heavy notions of the dialectic and above all, as the dialectician puts it, for the *labour* of the negative. It is sufficient to say that dialectic is a labour and empiricism an enjoyment. And who says that there is more thought in labour than in enjoyment? Difference is the object of a practical affirmation inseparable from essence and constitutive of existence. Nietzsche's "yes" is opposed to the dialectical "no"; affirmation to dialectical negation; difference to dialectical contradiction; joy, enjoyment, to dialectical labour; lightness, dance, to dialectical responsibilities. The empirical feeling of difference, in short hierarchy, is the essential motor of the concept, deeper and more effective than all thought about contradiction.

Furthermore, we must ask what does the dialectician himself want? What does this will which wills the dialectic want? It is an exhausted force which does not have the strength to affirm its difference, a force which no longer acts but rather reacts to the forces which dominate it – only such a force brings to the foreground the negative element in its relation to the other. Such a force denies all that it is not and makes this negation its own essence and the principle of its existence. "While every noble morality develops from a triumphant affirmation of itself, slave morality from the outset says No to what is 'outside', what is 'different' what is 'not itself' and *this* No is its creative deed" (GM I 10 p. 36). This is why Nietzsche presents the dialectic as the speculation of the pleb, as the way of thinking of the slave:[5] the abstract thought of contradiction then prevails over the concrete feeling of positive difference, reaction over action, revenge and *ressentiment* take the place of aggression. And, conversely, Nietzsche shows that what is negative in the master is always a secondary and derivative product of his existence. Moreover the relation of master and slave is not, in itself, dialectical. Who is the dialectician, who dialectises the relationship? It is the slave, the slave's perspective, the way of thinking belonging to the slave's perspective. The famous dialectical aspect of the master-slave relationship depends on the fact that power is conceived not as will to power but as representation of power, representation of superiority, recognition by "the one" of the superiority of "the other". What the wills in Hegel want is to have their power *recognised*, to *represent* their power. According to Nietzsche we have here a wholly erroneous conception of the will to power and its nature. This is the slave's conception, it is the image that the man of *ressentiment* has of power. *The slave only conceives of power as the object of a recognition, the content of a representation, the stake in a competition, and therefore makes it depend, at the end of a fight, on a simple attribution of established values.*[6] If the master-slave relationship can easily take on the dialectical form, to the point where it has become an archetype or a school-exercise for every young Hegelian, it is because the portrait of the master that Hegel offers us is, from the start, a portrait which represents the slave, at least as he is in his dreams, as at best a successful slave. Underneath the Hegelian image of the master we always find the slave.

5. The Problem of Tragedy

A commentator on Nietzsche must, above all, avoid any kind of pretext for dialectising his thought. The pretext is nevertheless ready made. It is that of the tragic culture, thought and philosophy which runs through Nietzsche's work. But what does Nietzsche really mean by "tragic"? He opposes the tragic vision of the world to two others: the dialectical and the Christian. Or rather, more accurately, tragedy has three ways of dying. It dies a first time by Socrates' dialectic, this is its "Euripidean" death. It dies a second time by Christianity and a third time under the combined blows of the modern dialectic and Wagner himself. Nietzsche insists on the fundamentally Christian character of the dialectic and of German philosophy (AC 10) and on the congenital incapacity of Christianity and the dialectic to live, understand or think the tragic. "It is I who discovered the tragic", even the Greeks misinterpreted it (VP IV 534).

The dialectic proposes a certain conception of the tragic: linking it to the negative, to opposition and to contradiction. The contradiction of suffering and life, of finite and infinite in life itself, of particular destiny and universal spirit in the idea, the movement of contradiction and its resolution – this is how tragedy is represented. Now, if one looks at the *Birth of Tragedy* it is quite clear that Nietzsche wrote it not as a dialectician but as a disciple of Schopenhauer. We must also remember that Schopenhauer himself did not value the dialectic very highly. And yet, in his first book, the schema that Nietzsche offers us under Schopenhauer's influence is only distinguishable from the dialectic by the *way* in which contradiction and its resolution are conceived. This is what allows Nietzsche to say later of the *Birth of Tragedy*, "It smells offensively Hegelian" (EH III "The Birth of Tragedy" 1 p. 270). For contradiction and its resolution still play the role of essential principles; "one sees there antithesis transforming itself into unity". We must follow the movement of this difficult book in order to understand how Nietzsche will later establish a new conception of the tragic:

1) The contradiction in the *Birth of Tragedy* is between primitive unity and individuation, willing and appearance, life and suffering. This "original" contradiction bears witness against life, it accuses life. Life needs to be justified, that is to say redeemed from suffering and contradiction. The *Birth of Tragedy* is developed in the shadow of the Christian dialectic; justification, redemption and reconciliation.

2) The contradiction is reflected in the opposition of Dionysus and Apollo. Apollo is the divine incarnation of the principle of individuation. He constructs the appearance of appearance, the beautiful appearance, the dream or the plastic image and is thus freed from suffering: "Apollo overcomes the suffering of the individual by the radiant glorification of the eternity of the phenomenon" (BT 16 p. 104), he *obliterates* pain. Dionysus, on the contrary, returns to primitive unity, he shatters the individual, drags him into the great shipwreck and absorbs him into original being. Thus he reproduces the contradiction as the pain of individuation but resolves them in a

higher pleasure, by making us participate in the superabundance of unique being or universal willing. The Dionysus and Apollo are therefore not opposed as the terms of a contradiction but rather as two antithetical ways of resolving it; Apollo mediately, in the contemplation of the plastic image, Dionysus immediately in the reproduction, in the musical symbol of the will.[7] Dionysus is like the background on which Apollo ,embroiders beautiful appearances; but beneath Apollo Dionysus rumbles. The antithesis of the two must therefore be resolved, "transformed into a unity".[8]

3) *Tragedy is this reconciliation*, this wonderful and precarious alliance dominated by Dionysus. For in tragedy Dionysus is the essence of the tragic. Dionysus is the only tragic character, "the suffering and glorified God", his sufferings are the only tragic subject, the sufferings of individuation absorbed in the joy of original being, and the chorus is the only tragic spectator because it is Dionysian, because it sees Dionysus as its lord and master (BT 8 and 10). But, on the other hand, the Apollonian contribution is as follows: in the tragedy it is Apollo who develops the tragic into *drama*, who expresses the tragic in a drama. "We must understand Greek tragedy as the Dionysian chorus which ever anew discharges itself in an Apollonian world of images . . . In several successive discharges this primal ground of tragedy radiates this vision of the drama which is by all means a dream apparition . . . Thus the drama is the Dionysian embodiment of Dionysian insights and effects" (BT 8), the objectivation of Dionysus beneath an Apollonian form and in an Apollonian world.

6. Nietzsche's Evolution

In the *Birth of Tragedy* the tragic in its totality is thus defined as original contradiction, its Dionysian solution and the dramatic expression of this solution. It is characteristic of *tragic culture* and its modern representatives – Kant, Schopenhauer and Wagner – to reproduce and resolve the contradiction, to resolve it in reproducing it, to resolve it on the original basis. "Its most important characteristic is that wisdom takes the place of science as the highest end – wisdom that, uninfluenced by the seductive distractions of the sciences, turns with unmoved eyes to a comprehensive view of the world and seeks to grasp, with sympathetic feelings of love, the eternal suffering as its own" (BT 18 p. 112). But even in the *Birth of Tragedy* a thousand pointers make us sense the approach of a new conception which has little to do with this schema. From the outset Dionysus is insistently presented as the *affirmative and affirming* god. He is not content with "resolving" pain in a higher and suprapersonal pleasure but rather he affirms it and turns it into someone's pleasure. This is why Dionysus is himself *transformed* in multiple affirmations, rather than being dissolved in original being or reabsorbing multiplicity into primeval depths. He affirms the pains *of growth* rather than reproducing the sufferings *of individuation*. He is the god who affirms life, for whom life must be affirmed, but not justified or redeemed. But what prevents this second Dionysus from getting the better of the first is the fact that the suprapersonal element always accompanies the affirming element and finally takes on its benefits. There is, for example, a premonition of the eternal return when Demeter learns that she will give birth to Dionysus once again; but this resurrection of Dionysus is only interpreted as the "end of individuation" (BT 10). Under Schopenhauer and Wagner's influence the affirmation of life is still only conceived in terms of resolution of the suffering at the heart of the universal and of a pleasure which transcends the individual. "The individual must be transformed into an impersonal being, superior to the person. This is what tragedy proposes" (UM III "Schopenhauer Educator" cf. 3–4).

When, at the end of his work, Nietzsche went back to the *Birth of Tragedy* he recognised two essential innovations surpassing the semi-dialectical, semi-Schopenhauerian framework (EH III "The Birth of Tragedy" 1–4). The first is precisely the affirmative character of Dionysus, the affirmation of life instead of its higher solution or justification. Secondly Nietzsche congratulates himself on having discovered an opposition which was only fully developed later. For, after the *Birth of Tragedy*, the true opposition is not the wholly dialectical one between Dionysus and Apollo but the deeper one between Dionysus and Socrates. It is not Apollo who is opposed to the tragic or through whom the tragic dies, it is Socrates: and Socrates is as little Apollonian as Dionysian (BT 12). Socrates is defined by a strange reversal, "while in all productive men it is instinct that it is the creative-affirmative force, and consciousness acts critically and dissuasively, in Socrates it is the instinct that becomes the critic and consciousness that becomes the creator" (BT 13 p. 88). Socrates is the first genius of decadence. He opposes the idea to life, he judges life in terms of the idea, he posits life as something which should be judged, justified and redeemed by the idea. He asks us to feel that life, crushed by the weight of the negative, is unworthy of being desired for itself, experienced in itself. Socrates is "the theoretical man", the only true opposite of the tragic man (BT 15).

But once again there is something preventing this second theme from developing freely. For the opposition of Socrates and tragedy to gain its full importance, for it really to become the opposition of "no" and "yes", of the negation of life and its affirmation, it was first of all necessary for the affirmative element in tragedy itself to be released, exposed for itself and freed from all subordination. Once on this road Nietzsche will no longer be able to stop. The Dionysus/Apollo anti-thesis will also have to give up first place, become blurred or even disappear in favour of the true opposition. Finally, the true opposition itself will have to change. It can no longer be content with Socrates as its typical hero, for Socrates is too Greek, a little too Apollonian at the outset because of his clarity, a little too Dionysian in the end, "Socrates the student of music" (BT 15). Socrates does not give the negation of life its full force; the negation of life has not yet found its essence. It will therefore be necessary for the tragic man, at the same time as he discovers his own element in pure affirmation, to discover his deepest enemy as the one who carries out the enterprise of negation in a true, definitive and essential manner. Nietzsche rigorously real-ises this programme. For the Dionysus-Apollo antithesis – gods who are reconciled in order to resolve pain – is substituted the more mysterious complementarity of Dionysus-Ariadne; for a woman, a fiancée, is necessary where affirming is concerned. For the Dionysus/Socrates opposition is substituted the true opposition: "Have I been understood? – Dionysus versus the crucified" (EH IV 9; VP III 413, IV 464). Nietzsche notes that the *Birth of Tragedy* remains silent about Christianity, it has not *identified* Christianity. And it is Christianity which is neither Apollonian nor Dionysian; "It negates aesthetic values, the only values recognised by the *Birth of Tragedy*; it is nihilist in the most profound sense, whereas in the Dionysian symbol the ultimate limit of affirmation is attained" (EH III "The Birth of Tragedy" 1 p. 271).

7. Dionysus and Christ

In Dionysus and in Christ the martyr is the same, the passion is the same. It is the same phenomenon but in two opposed senses (VP IV 464). On the one hand, the life that justifies suffering, that affirms suffering; on the other hand the suffering that accuses life, that testifies against it, that makes life something that must be justified. For Christianity the fact of suffering in life means primarily that life is not just, that it is even essentially unjust, that it pays for an essential injustice by suffering, it is blameworthy because it suffers. The result of this is that life must be justified, that is to say, redeemed of its injustice or saved. Saved by that suffering which a little while ago accused it: it must suffer since it is blameworthy. These two aspects of Christianity form what Nietzsche calls "bad conscience" or the *internalisation of pain* (GM II). They define truly Christian nihilism, that is to say the way in which Christianity denies life; on the one side the machine for manufacturing guilt, the horrible pain-punishment equation, on the other side the machine to multiply pain, the justification by pain, the dark workshop.[9] Even when Christianity sings the praises of love and life what curses there are in these songs, what hatred beneath this love! It loves life like the bird of prey loves the lamb; tender, mutilated and dying. The dialectician posits Christian love as an antithesis, for example as the antithesis of Judaic hatred. But it is the profession and mission of the dialectician to establish *antitheses* everywhere where there are more delicate evaluations to be made, *coordinations* to be interpreted. That the flower is the antithesis of the leaf, that it "refutes" the leaf – this is a celebrated discovery dear to the dialectic. This is also the way in which the flower of Christian love "refutes" hate – that is to say, in an entirely fictitious manner. "One should not imagine that love . . . grew up . . . as the opposite of Jewish hatred! No, the reverse is true! That love grew out of it as its crown, as its triumphant crown spreading itself farther and farther into the purest brightness and sunlight, driven as it were into the domain of light and the heights in the pursuit of the goals of that hatred – victory, spoil and seduction" (GM I 8 p. 35*).[10] Christian joy is the joy of "resolving" pain in this way, pain is internalised, offered to God, carried to God, "that ghastly paradox of a 'God on the cross', that mystery of an unimaginable and ultimate cruelty" (GM I 8 p. 35), this is truly Christian mania, a mania which is already wholly dialectical.

How different this aspect is from the true Dionysus! The Dionysus of the *Birth of Tragedy* still "resolved" pain, the joy that he experienced was still the joy of resolving it and also of bearing this resolution in the primeval unity. But now Dionysus has seized the sense and value of his own transformations, he is the god for whom life does not have to be justified, for whom life is essentially just. Moreover it is life which takes charge of justification, "it affirms even the harshest suffering" (VP IV 464). We must be clear, it does not resolve pain by internalising it, it affirms it in the element of its exteriority. And, from this, the opposition of Dionysus and Christ is developed point by point as that of the affirmation of life (its extreme valuation) and the negation of life (its extreme depreciation). Dionysian *mania* is opposed to Christian mania; Dionysian intoxication to Christian intoxication; Dionysian laceration to crucifixion; Dionysian resurrection to Christian resurrection; Dionysian transvaluation to Christian transubstantiation. For there are two kinds of suffering and sufferers. "Those who suffer from the superabundance of life" make suffering an affirmation in the same way as they make intoxication an activity; in the laceration of Dionysus they recognise the extreme form of affirmation, with no possibility of subtraction, exception or choice. "Those who suffer, on the contrary, from an impoverishment of life" make intoxication a convulsion, a numbness; they make suffering a means of accusing life, of contradicting it and also a means of justifying life, of resolving the contradiction.[11] All this in fact goes into the idea of a saviour; there is no more beautiful saviour than the one who would be simultaneously executioner, victim and comforter, the Holy Trinity, the wonderful dream of bad conscience. From the point of view of a saviour, "life must be the path which leads to sainthood". From the point of view of Dionysus, "existence seems holy enough by itself to justify a further immensity of suffering" (VP IV 464). Dionysian laceration is the immediate symbol of multiple affirmation; Christ's cross, the sign of the cross, is the image of contradiction and its solution, life submits to the labour of the negative. "Developed contradiction, solution of the contradiction, reconciliation of the contradictories" – all these notions become foreign to Nietzsche. It is Zarathustra who exclaims, "*Something higher than all reconciliation*" (Z II "Of Redemption") – affirmation. Something higher than all developed, resolved and suppressed contradiction – transvaluation. This is the common ground between Zarathustra and Dionysus: "Into all abysses I still carry the blessings of my saying Yes (Zarathustra) . . . *But this is the concept of Dionysus once again*" (EH III

"Thus spoke Zarathustra" 6 p. 306). The opposition of Dionysus or Zarathustra to Christ is not a dialectical opposition, but opposition to the dialectic itself: differential affirmation against dialectical negation, against all nihilism and against this particular form of it. Nothing is further from the Nietzschean interpretation of Dionysus than that presented later by Otto: a Hegelian Dionysus, dialectical and dialectician!

8. The Essence of the Tragic

Dionysus affirms all that appears, "even the most bitter suffering", and appears in all that is affirmed. Multiple and pluralist affirmation – this is the essence of the tragic. This will become clearer if we consider the difficulties of making *everything* an object of affirmation. Here the effort and the genius of pluralism are necessary, the power of transformations, Dionysian laceration. When anguish and disgust appear in Nietzsche it is always at this point: can everything become an object of affirmation, *that is to say of joy?* We must find, for each thing in turn, the special means by which it is affirmed, by which it ceases to be negative.[12] The tragic is not to be found in this anguish or disgust, nor in a nostalgia for lost unity. The tragic is only to be found in multiplicity, in the diversity of affirmation *as such*. What defines the tragic is the joy of multiplicity, plural joy. This joy is not the result of a sublimation, a purging, a compensation, a resignation or a reconciliation. Nietzsche can attack all theories of the tragic for failing to recognise tragedy as an aesthetic phenomenon. *The tragic* is the aesthetic form of joy, not a medical phrase or a moral solution to pain, fear or pity.[13] It is joy that is tragic. But this means that tragedy is immediately joyful, that it only calls forth the fear and pity of the obtuse spectator, the pathological and moralising listener who counts on it to ensure the proper functioning of his moral sublimations and medical purgings. "Thus the artistic listener is also reborn with the rebirth of tragedy. In his place in the theatre a curious *quid pro quo* used to sit with half moral, half scholarly pretensions – the 'critic' " (BT 22 p. 133). And indeed, a true renaissance is needed in order to liberate the tragic from all the fear or pity of the bad listeners who gave it a mediocre sense born of bad conscience. The anti-dialectical and anti-religious dream which runs through the whole of Nietzsche's philosophy is a logic of multiple affirmation and therefore a logic of pure affirmation and a corresponding ethic of joy. The tragic is not founded on a relation of life and the negative but on the essential relation of joy and multiplicity, of the positivity and multiplicity, of affirmation and multiplicity. "The hero is joyful, this is what has, up to now, escaped the authors of tragedies" (VP IV 50). Tragedy – frank, dynamic, gaiety.

This is why Nietzsche renounces the conception of drama which he upheld in the *Birth of Tragedy*; drama is still a pathos, a Christian pathos of contradiction. Nietzsche reproaches Wagner for this very reason, for having produced a dramatic music, for repudiating the affirmative character of music, "I suffer from the fact that it is a music of decadence and no longer the flute of Dionysus" (EH III "The Case of Wagner" 1 p. 317). In the same way Nietzsche demands the rights of *heroic* expression against the dramatic expression of tragedy; the joyful, graceful, dancing and gambling hero (VP III 191, 220, 221; IV 17-60). It is Dionysus' task to make us graceful, to teach us to dance, to give us the instinct of play. Even a historian hostile or indifferent to Nietzschean themes recognises joy, buoyant gracefulness, mobility and ubiquity as characteristic of Dionysus.[14] Dionysus carries Ariadne up to the sky; the jewels in Ariadne's crown are the stars. Is this the secret of Ariadne? The bursting constellation of a famous dicethrow? It is Dionysus who throws the dice. It is he who dances and transforms himself, who is called "Polygethes", the god of a thousand joys.

Dialectics in general are not a tragic vision of the world but, on the contrary, the death of tragedy, the replacement of the tragic vision by a theoretical conception (with Socrates) or a Christian conception (with Hegel). What has been discovered in Hegel's early writings is in fact the final truth of the dialectic: modern dialectic is the truly Christian ideology. It wants to justify life and submit it to the labour of the negative. But nevertheless Christian ideology and tragic thinking still have something in common – the problem of the meaning of existence. "Has existence a meaning?" is, according to Nietzsche, the highest question of philosophy, the most empirical and even the most "experimental" because it poses at one and the same time the problems of interpretation and evaluation. Strictly speaking it means "what is justice?" and Nietzsche can say without exaggeration that the whole of his work is an effort to understand this properly. There are, of course, bad ways of understanding the question: for a long time the sense of existence has only been looked for by positing it as something faulty or blameworthy, something unjust which ought to be justified.

A god was needed to interpret existence. It was necessary to accuse life
in order to redeem it, to redeem it in order to justify it. Existence was
evaluated but always from the standpoint of bad conscience. This is
the Christian inspiration which compromises philosophy as a whole.
Hegel interprets existence from the standpoint of the unhappy consciousness but the unhappy consciousness is only the Hegelian version of the bad conscience. Even Schopenhauer . . . Schopenhauer
made the question of existence or justice reverberate as never before,
but he found, in suffering, a way of denying life and, in the negation of
life, the only way of justifying it. "As a philosopher, Schopenhauer
was the *first* admitted and inexorable atheist among us Germans:
This was the background of his enmity against Hegel. The ungodli-
ness of existence was for him something given, palpable, indisputable
. . . As we thus reject the Christian interpretation and condemn its
'meaning' like counterfeit, *Schopenhauer's* question immediately
comes to us in a terrifying way: Has existence any meaning at all? *It
will require a few centuries before this question can even be heard completely and in its full depth*. What Schopenhauer himself said in answer
to this question was – forgive me – hasty, youthful, only a compromise, a way of remaining stuck, in precisely those Christian-ascetic
moral perspectives in which one had *renounced faith* along with the
faith in God" (GS 357 pp. 307 and 308). What therefore is the other way
of understanding the question, the truly tragic way, in which existence *justifies* all that it affirms, including suffering, instead of being
itself justified by suffering, or in other words, sanctified and deified?

9. The Problem of Existence

The story of the meaning of existence is a long one. Its origins are
Greek, pre-Christian. As we have seen suffering was used as a way of
proving the *injustice* of existence, but at the same time as a way of
finding a higher and divine *justification* for it. (It is blameworthy
because it suffers, but because it suffers it is atoned for and
redeemed.) The Greeks themselves interpreted and evaluated existence as excess. The Titanic image ("the necessity of the crime which
is imposed on the Titanic individual") is historically the first sense
given to existence. An interpretation which is so seductive that
Nietzsche, in the *Birth of Tragedy*, was not yet able to resist it and uses
it to help Dionysus (BT 9). But he only had to discover the true
Dionysus in order to see the trap it hides or the end it served: it made

existence a moral and religious phenomenon! Existence seems to be given so much by being made a crime, an excess. It gains a double nature – an immense injustice and a justifying atonement. It is Titanised by crime, it is made divine by the expiation of crime.[15] And what is there at the end of all this if not a subtle way of depreciating existence, of subjecting it to judgment, moral judgment and above all God's judgment? According to Nietzsche Anaximander is the philosopher who gave perfect expression to this conception of existence. He said "Beings must pay penance and be judged for their injustices, in accordance with the ordinance of time" (cf. PTG 4 p. 45). This means; 1) that becoming is an injustice (*adikia*) and the plurality of things that come into existence is a sum of injustices; 2) that things struggle between themselves and mutually expiate their injustice by the *phtora*; 3) that things all derive from an original being ("Apeiron") which falls into becoming, into plurality, into a blameworthy act of generation, the injustice of which it redeems eternally by destroying them ("Theodicy") (PTG).

Schopenhauer is a kind of modern Anaximander. What attracts Nietzsche so much to them both and thus explains why, in the *Birth of Tragedy*, he is still in general faithful to their interpretation? It is undoubtedly their difference from Christianity. They see existence as criminal and blameworthy but not yet as something faulty and responsible. Even the Titans do not yet know the incredible semitic and Christian inventions, bad conscience, fault and responsibility. At the time of the *Birth of Tragedy* Nietzsche opposes the Titan and Promethean crime to original sin. But he does it in dark and symbolic terms, because this opposition is his negative secret like the mystery of Ariadne is his positive one. He writes that, "in original sin, curiosity, mendacious deception, susceptibility to seduction, lust – in short a series of pre-eminently feminine affects was considered the origin of evil . . . Thus the Aryans understand sacrilege as something masculine; while the Semites understand sin as feminine" (BT 9 p. 71). This is not Nietzschean misogyny; Ariadne is Nietzsche's first secret, the first feminine power, the anima, the inseparable fiancée of Dionysian affirmation.[16] But the infernal feminine power is altogether different; negative and moralising, the terrible mother, the mother of good and evil, she who depreciates and denies life. "There is no longer any other way of restoring honour to philosophy; we must begin by stringing up the moralists. However much they speak of happiness and virtue they will only convert old women to philosophy. Let us face up to all these sages, illustrious for millenia; all of them old women or mature women, to speak like Faust, mothers. Mothers, mothers! frightful word" (VP III 408). Mothers and sisters; this second feminine power has the function of accusing us, of making us responsible. "It is your fault," says the mother, "your fault if I don't have a better son, more respectful of his mother and more conscious of his crime." "It is your fault," says the sister, "your fault if I am not more beautiful, more rich and more loved." The imputation of wrongs and responsibilities, the bitter recrimination, the perpetual accusation, the *ressentiment* – this is the pious interpretation of existence. "It's your fault, it's your fault", until the accused, in turn, says, "it's my fault" and the desolated world resounds with all these moans and their echoes. "Everywhere where responsibilities have been sought it is the instinct of revenge that has sought them. This instinct of revenge has gained such a hold on humanity through the centuries that all of metaphysics, psychology, history and above all morality bear its imprint. As soon as man began thinking he introduced the bacillus of revenge into things" (VP III 458). Nietzsche does not see *ressentiment* (it's your fault) and bad conscience (it's my fault) and their common fruit (responsibility) as simple psychological events but rather as the fundamental categories of semitic and Christian thought, of our way of thinking and interpreting existence in general. Nietzsche takes on the tasks of providing a new ideal, a new interpretation and another way of thinking (GM II 23). *"To give irresponsibility its positive sense"*, "I wished to conquer the feeling of a full irresponsibility, to make myself independent of praise and blame, of present and past" (VP III 383, 465). Irresponsibility – Nietzsche's most noble and beautiful secret.

In comparison with Christianity the Greeks are children. Their way of depreciating existence, their "nihilism", does not have the perfection of the Christian way. They judged existence blameworthy but they had not yet invented the refinement which consists in judging it faulty and responsible. When the Greeks spoke of existence as criminal and "hubric" they thought that the gods had driven men mad; existence is blameworthy *but it is the gods who take upon themselves the responsibility for the fault*. This is the great difference between the Greek interpretation of crime and the Christian interpretation of sin. This is the reason why, in the *Birth of Tragedy*, Nietzsche still believed in the criminal character of existence, since the crime at least did not imply the responsibility of the criminal. " 'Foolishness', 'folly', a little 'disturbance in the head', this much even the Greeks of the strongest, bravest age conceded of themselves as the reason for much that was bad and calamitous – foolishness, *not* sin! do you grasp that? . . . 'He must have been deluded by a *god*' they concluded finally, shaking their heads . . . In this way the gods served in those days to justify man to a certain extent even in his wickedness, they served as originators of evil – in those days they took upon themselves not the punishment but, what is *nobler*, the guilt" (GM II 23 p. 94). But Nietzsche came to realise that this great difference was whittled down by reflection. When existence is posited as blameworthy only one step is needed in order to make it responsible. All that is needed is a change of sex, Eve instead of the Titans, a change in the gods, a single God, actor and lover of justice, in place of spectator-gods and "olympian judges". That a god takes upon himself the responsibility for the folly he inspires in men, or that men are responsible for the folly of God who puts himself on the cross; these two solutions are not very different – although the first is incomparably more beautiful. In fact the question is not: is blameworthy existence responsible or not? *But is existence blameworthy . . . or innocent?* At this point Dionysus has found his multiple truth: innocence, the innocence of plurality, the innocence of becoming and of all that is.[17]

10. Existence and Innocence

What does "innocence" mean? When Nietzsche denounces our deplorable mania for accusing, for seeking out those responsible outside, or even inside, ourselves, he bases this critique on five grounds. The first of these is that "nothing exists outside of the whole".[18] But the last and deepest is that "there is no whole": "It is necessary to disperse the universe, to lose respect for the whole" (VP III 489). Innocence is the truth of multiplicity. It derives immediately from the principles of the philosophy of force and will. Every thing is referred to a force capable of interpreting it; every force is referred to what it is able to do, from which it is inseparable. It is this way of being referred, of affirming and being affirmed, which is particularly inno- cent. Whatever does not let itself be interpreted by a force nor evaluated by a will calls out for *another* will capable of evaluating it, another force capable of interpreting it. But *we* prefer to save the interpretation which corresponds to our forces and to deny the thing which does not correspond to our interpretation. We create grotesque representations of force and will, we separate force from what it can do, setting it up in ourselves as "worthy" because it holds back from what it cannot do, but as "blameworthy" in the thing where it manifests precisely the force that it has. We split the will in two, inventing a neutral subject endowed with free will to which we give the capacity to act and refrain from action (GM I 13). Our situation in relation to existence is such that we have not even recognised the will which is capable of evaluating the Earth (of "weighing" it), nor the force capable of interpreting existence. Then we deny existence itself, we replace interpretation by depreciation, we invent depreciation as a way of interpreting and evaluating. "One interpretation among others was shipwrecked, but as it passed for the only possible interpretation it seems that existence no longer has meaning, that everything is in vain" (VP III 8). *Alas, we are bad players*. Innocence is the game of existence, of force and of will. Existence affirmed and appreciated, force not separated, the will not divided in two – this is the first approximation to innocence (VP III 457–496).

Heraclitus is the tragic thinker. The problem of justice runs through his entire work. Heraclitus is the one for whom life is radically innocent and just. He understands existence on the basis of an *instinct of play*. He makes existence an *aesthetic phenomenon* rather than a moral or religious one. Thus Nietzsche opposes him point by point to Anaximander, just as Nietzsche himself is opposed to Schopenhauer.[19] Heraclitus denied the duality of worlds, "he denied being itself". Moreover *he made an affirmation of becoming*. We have to reflect for a long time to understand what it means to make an affirmation of becoming. In the first place it is doubtless to say that there is only becoming. No doubt it is also to affirm becoming. But we also affirm the being of becoming, we say that becoming affirms being or that being is affirmed in becoming. Heraclitus has two thoughts which are like ciphers: according to one there is no being, everything is becoming; according to the other, being is the being of becoming as such. A working thought which affirms becoming and a contemplative thought which affirms the being of becoming. These two ways of thinking are inseparable, they are the thought of a single element, as Fire and Dike, as Physis and Logos. For there is no being beyond becoming, nothing beyond multiplicity; neither multiplicity nor becoming are appearances or illusions. But neither are there multiple or eternal realities which would be, in turn, like essences beyond appearance. Multiplicity is the inseparable manifestation, essential transformation and constant symptom of unity. Multiplicity is the affirmation of unity; becoming is the affirmation of being. The affirmation of becoming is itself being, the affirmation of multiplicity is itself one. Multiple affirmation is the way in which the one affirms itself. "The one is the many, unity is multiplicity." And indeed, how would multiplicity come forth from unity and how would it continue to come forth from it after an eternity of time if unity was not *actually* affirmed in multiplicity? "If Heraclitus only perceives a single element it is nevertheless, in a sense, diametrically opposed to that of Parmenides (or of Anaximander) . . . The unique must be affirmed in generation and destruction." Heraclitus had taken a deep look, he had seen no chastisement of multiplicity, no expiation of becoming, no culpability of existence. He saw no negativity in becoming, he saw precisely the opposite: the double affirmation of becoming and of the being of becoming – in short the justification of being. Heraclitus is obscure because he leads us to the threshold of the obscure: what is the being of becoming? What is the being inseparable from that which is becoming? *Return is the being of that which becomes*. Return is the being of becoming itself, the being which is affirmed in becoming. The eternal return as law of becoming, as justice and as being.[20]

It follows that existence is not responsible or even blameworthy. Heraclitus went as far as proclaiming "the struggle of the many is pure justice itself! In fact the one is the many!" (PTG 6 p. 57). The correlation of many and one, of becoming and being forms a *game*. Affirming becoming and affirming the being of becoming are the two moments of a game which are compounded with a third term, the player, the artist or the child.[21] The player-artist-child, Zeus-child: Dionysus, who the myth presents to us surrounded by his divine toys. The player temporarily abandons himself to life and temporarily fixes his gaze upon it; the artist places himself provisionally in his work and provisionally above it; the child plays, withdraws from the game and returns to it. In this game of becoming, the being of becoming also plays the game with itself; the *aeon* (time), says Heraclitus, is a child who plays, plays at draughts (*Diels* 53). The being of becoming, the eternal return, is the second moment of the game, but also the third term, identical to the two moments and valid for the whole. For the eternal return is the distinct return of the outward movement, the distinct contemplation of the action, but also the return of the outward movement itself and the return of the action; at once moment and cycle of time. We must understand the secret of Heraclitus interpretation; he opposes the instinct of the game to hubris; "It is not guilty pride but the ceaselessly reawoken instinct of the game which calls forth new worlds." Not a theodicy but a cosmodicy, not a sum of injustices to be expiated but justice as the law of this world; not hubris but play, innocence. "That dangerous word hubris is indeed the touchstone for every Heraclitean. Here he must show whether he has understood or failed to recognise his master" (PTG 7 p. 61).

11. The Dicethrow

The game has two moments which are those of a dicethrow – the dice that is thrown and the dice that falls back. Nietzsche presents the dicethrow as taking place on two distinct tables, the earth and the sky. The earth where the dice are thrown and the sky where the dice fall back: "if ever I have played dice with the gods at their table, the earth, so that the earth trembled and broke open and streams of fire snorted forth; for the earth is a table of the gods, and trembling with creative new words and the dice throws of the gods" (Z III "The Seven Seals" 3 p. 245). "O sky above me, you pure and lofty sky! This is now your purity to me, that there is no eternal reason-spider and spider's web in you; that you are to me a dance floor for divine chances, that you are to me a god's table for divine dice and dicers" (Z III "Before Sunrise" p. 186). But these two tables are not two worlds. They are the two hours of a single world, the two moments of a single world, midnight and midday, the hour when the dice are thrown, the hour when the dice fall back. Nietzsche insists on the two tables of life which are also the two moments of the player or the artist; "We temporarily abandon life, in order to then temporarily fix our gaze upon it." The dicethrow affirms becoming and it affirms the being of becoming.

It is not a matter of several dicethrows which, because of their number, finally reproduce the same combination. On the contrary, it is a matter of a single dicethrow which, due to the number of the combination produced, comes to reproduce itself as such. It is not that a large number of throws produce the repetition of a combination but rather the number of the combination which produces the repetition of the dicethrow. The dice which are thrown once are the affirmation of *chance*, the combination which they form on falling is the affirmation of *necessity*. Necessity is affirmed of chance in exactly the sense that being is affirmed of becoming and unity is affirmed of multiplicity. It will be replied, in vain, that thrown to chance, the dice do not necessarily produce the winning combination, the double six which brings back the dicethrow. This is true, but only insofar as the player did not know how to *affirm* chance from the outset. For, just as unity does not suppress or deny multiplicity, necessity does not suppress or abolish chance. Nietzsche identifies chance with multiplicity, with fragments, with parts, with chaos: the chaos of the dice that are shaken and then thrown. *Nietzsche turns chance into an affirmation*. The sky itself is called "chance-sky", "innocence-sky" (Z III "Before Sunrise"); the reign of Zarathustra is called "great chance" (Z IV "The Honey Offering" and III "Of Old and New Law Tables"; Zarathustra calls himself the "redeemer of chance"). "*By chance*, he is the world's oldest nobility, which I have given back to all things; I have released them from their servitude under purpose . . . I have found this happy certainty in all things: that they prefer to *dance* on the feet of chance" (Z III "Before Sunrise" p. 186); "My doctrine is 'Let chance come to me: it is as innocent as a little child!' " (Z III "On the Mount of Olives" p. 194). What Nietzsche calls *necessity* (destiny) is thus never the abolition but rather the combination of chance itself. Necessity is affirmed of chance in as much as chance itself affirmed. For there is only a single combination of chance as such, a single way of combining all the parts of chance, a way which is like the unity of multiplicity, that is to say number or necessity. There are many numbers with increasing or decreasing probabilities, but only one number of chance as such, one fatal number which reunites all the fragments of chance, like midday gathers together the scattered parts of midnight. This is why it is sufficient for the player to affirm chance once in order to produce the number which brings back the dicethrow.[22]

To know how to affirm chance is to know how to play. But we do not know how to play, "Timid, ashamed, awkward, like a tiger whose leap has failed. But what of that you dicethrowers! You have not learned to play and mock as a man ought to play and mock!" (Z IV "Of the Higher Man" 14 p. 303). The bad player counts on several throws of the dice, on a great number of throws. In this way he makes use of causality and probability to produce a combination that he sees as desirable. He posits this combination itself as an end to be obtained, hidden behind causality. This is what Nietzsche means when he speaks of the eternal spider, of the spider's web of reason, "A kind of spider of imperative and finality hidden behind the great web, the great net of causality – we could say, with Charles the Bold when he opposed Louis XI, "I fight the universal spider" (GM III 9). To abolish chance by holding it in the grip of causality and finality, to count on the repetition of throws rather than affirming chance, to anticipate a result instead of affirming necessity – these are all the operations of a bad player. They have their root in reason, but what is the root of reason? The spirit of revenge, nothing but the spirit of revenge, the spider (Z II "Of the Tarantulas"). *Ressentiment* in the repetition of throws, bad conscience in the belief in a purpose. But, in this way, all that will ever be obtained are more or less probable relative numbers. That the universe has no purpose, that it has no end to hope for any more than it has causes to be known – this is the certainty necessary to play well (VP III 465). The dicethrow fails because chance has not been affirmed enough in one throw. It has not been affirmed enough in order to produce the fatal number which necessarily reunites all the fragments and brings back the dicethrow. We must therefore attach the greatest importance to the following conclusion: for the couple causality-finality, probability-finality, for the opposition and the synthesis of these terms, for the web of these terms, Nietzsche substitutes the Dionysian correlation of chance-necessity, the Dionysian couple chance-destiny. Not a probability distributed over several throws but all chance at once; not a final, desired, willed combination, but the fatal combination, fatal and loved, *amor fati*; not the return of a combination by the number of throws, but the repetition of a dicethrow by the nature of the fatally obtained number.[23]

12. Consequences for the Eternal Return

Whereas the thrown dice affirm chance once and for all, the dice which fall back necessarily affirm the number or the destiny which brings the dice back. It is in this sense that the second moment of the game is also the two moments together or the player who equals the whole. The eternal return is the second moment, the result of the dicethrow, the affirmation of necessity, the number which brings together all the parts of chance. But it is also the return of the first moment, the repetition of the dicethrow, the reproduction and re-affirmation of chance itself. Destiny in the eternal return is also the "welcoming" of chance, "I cook every chance in *my* pot. And only when it is quite cooked do I welcome it as *my* food. And truly, many a chance came imperiously to me; but my *will* spoke to it even more imperiously, then it went down imploringly on its knees – imploring shelter and love with me, urging in wheedling tones; 'Just see, O Zarathustra, how a friend comes to a friend!' " (Z III "Of the Virtue that makes small" 3 p. 191). This means that there are fragments of chance which claim to be valid in themselves, they appeal to their probability, each solicits several throws of the dice from the player; divided among several throws, having become simple probabilities, the fragments of chance are slaves who want to speak as masters.[24] But Zarathustra knows that one must not play or let oneself be played, on the contrary, it is necessary to affirm the whole of chance at once (therefore boil and cook it like the player who warms the dice in his hands), in order to reunite all its fragments and to affirm the number which is not probable but fatal and necessary. Only then is chance a friend who visits his friend, a friend who will be asked back, a friend of destiny whose destiny itself assures the eternal return as such.

In a more obscure text loaded with historical significance Nietzsche writes, "Universal chaos which excluded all purposeful activity does not contradict the idea of the cycle; for this idea is only an irrational necessity" (VP II 326). What this means is that chaos and cycle, becoming and eternal return have often been brought together, but as if they were opposites. Thus, for Plato, becoming is itself an unlimited becoming, a becoming insane, a becoming hubric and guilty which, in order to be made circular needs the act of a demiurge who forcibly bends it, who imposes the model of the idea on it. This is how becoming or chaos are transferred to the side of an obscure mechanical causality and the cycle is referred to a kind of finality which is imposed from the outside. There is no chaos in the cycle, the cycle expresses the forced submission of becoming to an external law. Even among the Pre-Socratics perhaps only Heraclitus knew that becoming is not "judged", that it cannot be and has not to be judged, that it does not receive its law from elsewhere, that it is "just" and possesses its own law in itself (PTG). Only Heraclitus foresaw that there is no kind of opposition between chaos and cycle. And, in fact, we only need to affirm chance (chance and not causality) in order to affirm simultaneously the number or the necessity that brings it back (an irrational necessity and not a finality). "There was not first of all chaos, then little by little a regular and circular movement of all the forms: on the contrary, all this is eternal, removed from becoming; if there ever was a chaos of forces the chaos was eternal and has reappeared in every cycle. *Circular movement* has not come into being, it is the original law, in the same way as the *mass of force* is the original law without exception or possible infraction. All becoming happens inside of the cycle and the mass of force" (VP II 325 – circular movement = cycle, mass of force = chaos). We must understand that Nietzsche does not recognise his idea of eternal return in his predecessors of antiquity. They did not see in the eternal return the being of becoming as such, the unity of multiplicity, that is to say the necessary number, the necessary result of all chance. They even saw it as the opposite, a subjugation of becoming, an avowal of its injustice and the expiation of this injustice. With the possible exception of Heraclitus they had not seen "the presence of the law in becoming and of play in necessity" (PTG).

13. Nietzsche's Symbolism

When the dice are thrown on the table of the earth it "trembles and is broken". For the dicethrow is multiple affirmation, the affirmation of the many. But all the parts, all the fragments, are cast in one throw; all of chance, all at once. This power, not of suppression of multiplicity but of affirmation of it all at once, is like fire. Fire is the element which plays, the element of transformations which has no opposite. The earth which is broken under the dice therefore projects "rivers of flame". As Zarathustra says, multiplicity, chance, are only good cooked and boiled. To boil, to put in the fire, does not mean to abolish chance, nor to find the unity behind the multiplicity. On the contrary, boiling in the pot is like the clink of the dice in the hand of the player, the only way of affirming chance or multiplicity. The thrown dice form the number which brings the dicethrow back. Bringing the dicethrow back the number puts chance back into the fire, it maintains the fire which reheats chance. This is because number is being, unity and necessity, but unity affirmed of multiplicity as such, being which is affirmed of becoming as such. Number is present in chance in the same way as being and law are present in becoming. And the number which is present, the number that maintains the fire and which is affirmed of multiplicity when multiplicity is affirmed, is the dancing star or rather the constellation born of the dicethrow. The formula of the game is: give birth to a dancing star with the chaos that one has in oneself (Z Prologue 5 p. 46). And when Nietzsche wonders what led him to choose the character of Zarathustra he finds three very different reasons of unequal value. The first is Zarathustra as prophet of the eternal return (VP IV 155); but Zarathustra is not the only prophet, not even the one who best foresaw the true nature of what he foretold. The second reason is polemical; Zarathustra was the first to introduce morality into metaphysics, the one who made morality a force, a cause and an end *par excellence*; he is therefore the best placed to denounce the mystification, the error of this morality itself (EH IV 3). But an analogous reason would apply to Christ; who is more suitable than Christ to play the role of the antichrist . . . and of Zarathustra himself?[25] The third reason is retrospective but enough on its own, it is the beautiful reason of chance, "Today I learned by chance what Zarathustra means; star of gold. This chance enchants me" (Letter to Gast, 20th May 1883).

This game of images – chaos-fire-constellation – brings together all the elements of the myth of Dionysus. Or rather these images form the truly Dionysian game. The *playthings* of the child Dionysus; multiple affirmation and *the limbs or fragments* of the lacerated Dionysus; the cooking of Dionysus or unity being affirmed of multiplicity; the constellation borne by Dionysus, Ariadne in the sky like a dancing star; the *return* of Dionysus, Dionysus "master of the eternal return". We also have the opportunity to see how Nietzsche understood physical science, the energetics and thermodynamics of his time. It is now clear that he dreamt of a fire machine completely different from the steam engine. Nietzsche had his own conception of physics but no ambition as a physicist. He granted himself the poetic and philosophical right to dream of machines that perhaps one day science will realise by its own means. The machine to affirm chance, to cook chance, to produce the number which brings back the dicethrow, the machine to release these immense forces by small, multiple manipulations, the machine to play with the stars, in short the Heraclitean fire machine.[26]

But a game of images never replaced the deeper game of concepts and philosophical thought for Nietzsche. The poem and the aphorism are Nietzsche's two most vivid means of expression but they have a determinate relation to philosophy. Understood formally, an aphorism is present as a *fragment*; it is the form of pluralist thought; in its content it claims to articulate and formulate a *sense*. The sense of a being, an action, a thing – these are the objects of the aphorism. In spite of his admiration for the authors of maxims Nietzsche sees clearly what the maxim lacks as a genre: it is only suitable for discovering motives, which is why, in general, it only bears on human phenomena. But, for Nietzsche, even the most secret motives are not only an anthropomorphic aspect of things but also a superficial aspect of human activity. Only the aphorism is capable of articulating sense, the aphorism is interpretation and the art of interpreting. In the same way the poem is evaluation and the art of evaluating, it articulates *values*. But because values and sense are such complex notions, the poem itself must be evaluated, the aphorism interpreted. The poem and the aphorism are, themselves, objects of an interpretation, an evaluation. "An aphorism, properly stamped and moulded, has not been 'deciphered' when it has simply been read; rather one has then to begin its exegesis" (GM Preface 8 p. 23). From the pluralist standpoint a sense is referred to the differential element from which its significance is derived, just as values are referred to the differential element from which their value is derived. This element which is always present, but also always implicit and hidden in the poem or aphorism is like the second dimension of sense and values. It is by developing this element and by developing itself in it that philosophy in its essential relation with the poem and the aphorism constitutes complete interpretation and evaluation, that is to say, the art of thinking, faculty of thought or "faculty of rumination" (GM Preface 8 p. 23). Rumination and eternal return: two stomachs are not too many for thinking. There are two dimensions of interpretation and evaluation, the second also being the return of the first, the return of the aphorism or the cycle of the poem. All aphorisms must therefore be read twice. The interpretation of the eternal return begins with the dicethrow but it has only just begun. We must still interpret the dicethrow itself, at the same time as it returns.

14. Nietzsche and Mallermé

There are striking resemblances between Nietzsche and Mallarmé.[27] Four main similarities emerge, bringing the entire array of images into play:

1) To think is to send out a dicethrow. Only a dicethrow, on the basis of chance, could affirm necessity and produce "the unique number which cannot be another". We are dealing with a single dicethrow, not with success in several throws: only the combination which is victorious in one throw can guarantee the return of the throw.[28] The thrown dice are like the sea and the waves (but Nietzsche would say: like earth and fire). The dice which fall are a constellation, their points form the number "born of the stars". The table of the dicethrow is therefore double, sea of chance and sky of necessity, midnight-midday. Midnight, the hour when the dice are thrown . . .

2) Man does not know how to play. Even the higher man is unable to cast the dice. The master is old, he does not know how to cast the dice on the sea and in the sky. The old master is a "bridge", something which must be passed over. A "childish shadow", feather or wing, is fixed on the cap of the adolescent, "of dainty stature, dark and standing in his siren twisting", fit to revive the dicethrow. Is this the equivalent of Dionysus-child or even of the children of the blessed isles, the children of Zarathustra? Mallarmé presents child Igitur invoking his ancestors who are not men but Elohim, a race which was pure, which "raised its purity to the absolute, in order to be it, and only left an idea of it, itself ending in necessity".

3) Not only is the throwing of the dice an unreasonable and irrational, absurd and superhuman act, but it constitutes the tragic attempt and the tragic thought *par excellence*. The Mallarmean idea of the theatre, the celebrated correspondences and equations of "drama", "mystery", "hymn" and "hero" bear witness to a reflection which is comparable, at least apparently, to that of the *Birth of Tragedy*, if only by the powerful shadow of Wagner, as their common predecessor.

4) The number-constellation is, or could be, the book, the work of art as outcome and justification of the world. (Nietzsche wrote, of the aesthetic justification of existence: we see in the artist "how necessity and random play, oppositional tension and harmony, must pair to create a work of art" PTG). Now, the fatal and sidereal number brings back the dicethrow, so that the book is both unique and changing.

The multiplicity of meanings and interpretations is explicitly affirmed by Mallarmé but it is the correlate of another affirmation, that of the unity of the book or of the text which is "as incorruptible as the law". The book is the cycle and the law present in becoming.

Close as they are, these resemblances remain superficial. *For Mallarmé always understood necessity as the abolition of chance*. Mallarmé conceived the dicethrow in such a way that chance and necessity are opposite terms, the second of which must deny the first, and the first of which can only hold the second in check. The dicethrow only succeeds if chance is annulled; it fails because chance continues to exist in a certain way; "By the single fact that it is realised [human action] borrows its means from chance". This is why the number produced by the dicethrow is still chance. It has often been noticed that Mallarmé's poem belongs to the old metaphysical thought of a duality of worlds; chance is like existence which must be denied, necessity like the character of the pure idea or the eternal essence. So that the last hope of the dicethrow is that it will find its intelligible model in the other world, a constellation accepting responsibility for it "on some vacant, higher surface" where chance does not exist. Finally, the constellation is less the product of the dicethrow than of its passing to the limit or into another world. It matters little whether depreciation of life or exaltation of the intelligible prevails in Mallarmé. From a Nietzschean perspective these two aspects are inseparable and constitute "nihilism" itself, that is to say, the way in which life is accused, judged and condemned. Everything else flows from this, the race of Igitur is not the Overman but the emanation of another world. The dainty stature is not that of the children of the isles of the blessed but that of Hamlet, "bitter prince of reefs" of whom Mallarmé says elsewhere, "latent lord who cannot become one". Herodiade is not Ariadne but the frigid creature of *ressentiment* and bad conscience, the spirit which denies life, lost in her bitter reproaches to the Nourrice. The work of art in Mallarmé is "just", but its justice is not that of existence, it is still an accusatory justice which denies life, which presupposes its failure and impotence.[29] Even Mallarmé's atheism is a curious atheism, looking to the Mass for a model of the dreamed-of theatre – the Mass, not the mystery of Dionysus . . . In fact the eternal enterprise of life-depreciation has rarely been pushed so far in all directions. Mallarmé *does* discuss the dicethrow, but the dicethrow revised by nihilism, interpreted in the perspective of bad conscience and *ressentiment*. The dicethrow is nothing when detached from innocence and the affirmation of chance. The dicethrow is nothing if chance and necessity are *opposed* in it.

15. Tragic Thought

Is this difference only psychological? A difference of mood or tone? Nietzsche's philosophy depends, in general, on the principle that *ressentiment*, bad conscience etc. are not psychological determinations. Nietzsche calls the enterprise of denying life and depreciating existence nihilism. He analyses the principal forms of nihilism, *ressentiment*, bad conscience, ascetic ideal; the whole of nihilism and its forms he calls the spirit of revenge. But, the different forms of nihilism are not at all reducible to psychological determinations, historical events or ideological currents, not even to metaphysical structures.[30] The spirit of revenge is undoubtedly expressed biologically, psychologically, historically and metaphysically; the spirit of revenge is a type, it is not separable from a *typology*, the key stone of Nietzschean philosophy. But the problem is: what is the nature of this typology? Far from being a psychological trait the spirit of revenge is the principle on which our whole psychology depends. *Ressentiment* is not part of psychology but the whole of our psychology, without knowing it, is a part of *ressentiment*. In the same way, when Nietzsche shows that Christianity is full of *ressentiment* and bad conscience he does not make nihilism a historical event, it is rather the element of history as such, the motor of universal history, the famous "historical meaning" or "meaning of history" which at one time found its most adequate manifestation in Christianity. And when Nietzsche undertakes the critique of nihilism he makes nihilism the presupposition of all metaphysics rather than the expression of particular metaphysics: there is no *metaphysics* which does not judge and depreciate life in the name of a *supra-sensible* world. We cannot even say that nihilism and its forms are categories of thought, for the categories of thought, of reasonable thought – identity, causality, finality – themselves presuppose an interpretation of force which is that of *ressentiment*. For all these reasons Nietzsche can say: "The instinct of revenge has gained such a hold on humanity over the centuries that the whole of metaphysics, psychology, history and above all morality bear its imprint. As soon as man began thinking he introduced the bacillus of revenge into things" (VP III 458). We must understand this as meaning that the instinct of revenge is the force which constitutes the essence of what we call psychology, history, metaphysics and morality. The spirit of revenge is the genealogical element of *our* thought, the transcendental principle of *our* way of thinking. Nietzsche's struggle against nihilism and the spirit of revenge will therefore mean the reversal of metaphysics, the end of history as history of man and the transformation of the sciences. And we do not really know what a man denuded of *ressentiment* would be like. A man who would not accuse or depreciate existence – would he still be a man, would he think like a man? Would he not already be something other than a man, almost the Overman? To have *ressentiment* or not to have *ressentiment* – there is no greater difference, beyond psychology, beyond history, beyond metaphysics. It is the true difference or transcendental typology – the genealogical and hierarchical difference.

Nietzsche presents the aim of his philosophy as the freeing of thought from nihilism and its various forms. Now, this implies a new way of thinking, an overthrow of the principle on which thought depends, a straightening out of the genealogical principle itself, a "transmutation". For a long time we have only been able to think in terms of *ressentiment* and bad conscience. We have had no other ideal but the ascetic ideal. We have opposed knowledge to life in order to judge life, in order to make it something blameworthy, responsible or erroneous. We turned will into something bad, something stricken by a basic contradiction: we have said that it must be rectified, restrained, limited and even denied and suppressed. It was only any good at this price. There is no philosopher who, discovering the essence of will, has not groaned at his own discovery and, like the timid fortuneteller, has not immediately seen bad omens for the future and the source of all evils of the past. Schopenhauer pushed this old conception to its extreme limit; the penitentiary of the will, he said, and the wheel of Ixion. Nietzsche is the only one who does not groan at the discovery of the will, who does not try to exorcise it, or limit its effect. The phrase "a new way of thinking" means an affirmative thought, a thought which affirms life and the will to life, a thought which finally expels the whole of the negative; to believe in the innocence of the future and the past, to believe in the eternal return. What Nietzsche calls his *glad tidings* is that existence is no longer treated as blameworthy nor does the will feel guilty for existing. "Will, this is what the liberator and the messenger of joy is called" (Z II "Of Redemption").[31] The glad tidings are tragic thought, for tragedy is not found in the recriminations of *ressentiment*, the conflicts of bad conscience or the contradictions of a will which feels guilty and responsible. The tragic does not even fight against *ressentiment*, bad conscience or nihilism. According to Nietzsche it has never been understood that the tragic = the joyful. This is another way of putting the great equation: to will = to create. We have not understood that the tragic is pure and multiple positivity, dynamic gaeity. Affirmation is tragic because it affirms chance and the necessity of chance; because it affirms multiplicity and the unity of multiplicity. The dicethrow is tragic. All the rest is nihilism, Christian and dialectic pathos, carica-ture of the tragic, comedy of bad conscience.

16. The Touchstone

When we want to compare Nietzsche with other authors who called themselves or were called "tragic philosophers" (Pascal, Kierke-gaard, Chestov) we must not take the word *tragedy* at face value. We must take account of Nietzsche's last will and testament. It is not sufficient to ask: "What does the other think, is this comparable to what Nietzsche thinks?" Rather we must ask: "How does this other think? And how much *ressentiment* and bad conscience remains in his thought? The ascetic ideal, the spirit of revenge, do they continue to exist in his way of understanding tragedy?" Pascal, Kierkegaard and Chestov, knew, with genius, how to take criticism further than ever before. They suspended morality, they reversed reason but, ensnared in *ressentiment*, they still drew their strength from the ascetic ideal. They were the poets of this ideal. What they oppose to morality, to reason, is still this ideal in which reason is immersed, this mystical body in which it takes root, *interiority* – the spider. In order to philosophise they need all the resources and the guiding thread of interiority, anguish, wailing, guilt, all the forms of dissatisfaction.[32] They place themselves under the sign of *ressentiment*: Abraham and Job. They lack the sense of affirmation, the sense of exteriority, innocence and the game. "It is not necessary to wait", Nietzsche says, "for unhappiness, as those who make philosophy derive from dissatis-faction think. It is in happiness that one must begin, in full virile maturity, in the fire of this burning joy which is that of the adult and victorious age" (PTG 1). From Pascal to Kierkegaard one bets and then leaps. But these are not the exercises of Dionysus or Zarathustra: leaping is not dancing and betting is not playing. It will be noted how Zarathustra, without preconceptions, opposes *playing* to *betting* and *dancing* to *leaping*: it is the bad player who bets and above all it is the buffoon who leaps, who thinks that leaping means dancing, overcoming, going beyond.[33]

If we mention Pascal's wager it is merely to conclude finally that it has nothing in common with the dicethrow. In the wager it is *not* at all a matter of affirming chance, the whole of chance, but, *on the contrary*, of fragmenting it into probabilities, of minting it into "chances of gain and loss". This is why it is pointless to wonder whether the wager really has a theological sense or whether it is only apologetic. For Pascal's wager is *not* concerned with the existence or non-existence of God. The wager is anthropological, it merely concerns two modes of existence of man, the existence of the man who says that God exists and the existence of the man who says that God does not exist. The existence of God, not being put into play in the wager is, nevertheless, the perspective presupposed by it, the standpoint according to which chance is fragmented into chances of winning and losing. The whole alternative is governed by the ascetic ideal and the depreciation of life. Nietzsche is right to oppose his own game to Pascal's wager. " 'Without the Christian faith, Pascal thought, you, no less than nature and history, will become for yourselves *un monstre et un chaos.*' *This prophecy we have fulfilled*" (VP III 42/WP 83). Nietzsche means that we have managed to discover another game, another way of playing: we have discovered the Overman beyond two human-all-too-human ways of existing; we have managed to make chaos an object of affirmation instead of positing it as something to be denied.[34] And each time we compare Nietzsche and Pascal (or Kierkegaard or Chestov) the same conclusion is forced upon us – the comparison is only valid up to a certain point: abstraction being made from what is essential for Nietzsche, abstraction being made from the way of thinking. Abstraction being made from the little bacillus, the spirit of revenge which Nietzsche diagnoses in the universe. Nietzsche says "Hubris is the touchstone for every Heraclitean. Here he must show whether he has understood or failed to recognise his master" (PTG 7 p. 61). *Ressentiment*, bad conscience, the ascetic ideal, nihilism are the touchstone of every Nietzschean. Here he must show whether he has understood or failed to recognise the true sense of the tragic.

2

Active and Reactive

1. The Body

Spinoza suggested a new direction for the sciences and philosophy. He said that we do not even know what a body *can do*, we talk about consciousness and spirit and chatter on about it all, but we do not know what a body is capable of, what forces belong to it or what they are preparing for.[1] Nietzsche knew that the hour had come, "We are in the phase of modesty of consciousness" (VP II 261/WP 676). To remind consciousness of its necessary modesty is to take it for what it is: a symptom; nothing but the symptom of a deeper transformation and of the activities of entirely non-spiritual forces. "Perhaps the body is the only factor in all spiritual development." What is consciousness? Like Freud, Nietzsche thinks that consciousness is the region of the ego affected by the external world (VP II 253/WP 524, GS 357). However, consciousness is defined less in relation to exteriority (in terms of the real) than in relation to *superiority* (in terms of values). This distinction is essential to a general conception of consciousness and the unconscious. In Nietzsche consciousness is always the consciousness of an inferior in relation to a superior to which he is subordinated or into which he is "incorporated". Consciousness is never self-consciousness, but the consciousness of an ego in relation to a self which is not itself conscious. It is not the master's consciousness but the slave's consciousness in relation to a master who is not himself conscious. "Consciousness usually only appears when a whole wants to subordinate itself to a superior whole . . . Consciousness is born in relation to a being of which we could be a function" (VP II 227). This is the servility of consciousness; it merely testifies to the "formation of a superior body".

What is the body? We do not define it by saying that it is a field of forces, a nutrient medium fought over by a plurality of forces. For in fact there is no "medium", no field of forces or battle. There is no quantity of reality, all reality is already quantity of force. There are nothing but quantities of force in mutual "relations of tension" (VP II 373/WP 635). Every force is related to others and it either obeys or commands. What defines a body is this relation between dominant and dominated forces. Every relationship of forces constitutes a body – whether it is chemical, biological, social or political. Any two forces, being unequal, constitute a body as soon as they enter into a relationship. This is why the body is always the fruit of chance, in the Nietzschean sense, and appears as the most "astonishing" thing, much more astonishing, in fact, than consciousness and spirit.[2] But chance, the relation of force with force, is also the essence of force. The birth of a living body is not therefore surprising since every body is living, being the "arbitrary" product of the forces of which it is composed.[3] Being composed of a plurality of irreducible forces the body is a multiple phenomenon, its unity is that of a multiple phenomenon, a "unity of domination". In a body the superior or dominant forces are known as *active* and the inferior or dominated forces are known as *reactive*. Active and reactive are precisely the original qualities which express the relation of force with force. Because forces which enter into relation do not have quantity without each of them having, at the same time, the quality corresponding to their difference in quantity as such. This difference between forces qualified according to their quantity as active or reactive will be called *hierarchy*.

2. *The Distinction of Forces*

Inferior forces do not, by obeying, cease to be forces distinct from those which command. Obeying is a quality of force as such and relates to power just as much as commanding does: "individual power is by no means surrendered. In the same way, there is in commanding an admission that the absolute power of the opponent has not been vanquished, incorporated, disintegrated. 'Obedience' and 'commanding' are forms of struggle." (VP II 91/WP 642) Inferior forces are defined as reactive; they lose nothing of their force, of their quantity of force, they exercise it by securing mechanical means and final ends, by fulfilling the conditions of life and the functions and tasks of conversation, adaptation and utility. This is the point of departure for a concept whose importance in Nietzsche will be seen below, the concept of reaction: the mechanical and utilitarian accommodations, the *regulations* which express all the power of inferior and dominated forces. Here we must note the immoderate taste of modern thought for this reactive aspect of forces. We always think that we have done enough when we understand an organism in terms of reactive forces. The nature of reactive forces and their quivering fascinates us. This is why we oppose mechanical means to final ends in the theory of life; but these two interpretations are only valid for reactive forces themselves. It is true that we do understand the organism in terms of forces. But it is also true that we can only grasp reactive forces for what they are, that is as forces and not as mechanical means or final ends, if we relate them to what dominates them but is not itself reactive. "One overlooks the essential priority of the spontaneous, aggressive, expansive, form-giving forces that give new interpretations and directions, although "adaptation" follows only after this; the dominant role of the highest functionaries within the organism itself . . . is denied" (GM II 12).

It is no doubt more difficult to characterise these active forces for, by nature, they escape consciousness, "The great activity is unconscious" (VP II 227). Consciousness merely expresses the relation of certain reactive forces to the active forces which dominate them. Consciousness is essentially reactive; this is why we do not know what a body can do, or what activity it is capable of (GS 354). And what is said of consciousness must also be said of memory and habit. Furthermore we must also say it of nutrition, reproduction, conservation and adaptation. These are reactive functions, reactive specialisations, expressions of particular reactive forces (VP II 43, 45, 187, 390/WP 167, 473, 657, 660). It is inevitable that consciousness sees the organism from its own point of view and understands it in its own way; that is to say, reactively. What happens is that science follows the paths of consciousness, relying entirely on *other* reactive forces; the organism is always seen from the petty side, from the side of its reactions. The problem of the organism, according to Nietzsche, is not an issue between mechanism and vitalism. What is the value of vitalism as long as it claims to discover the specificity of life in the same reactive forces that mechanism interprets in another way? The real problem is the discovery of active forces without which the reactions themselves would not be forces.[4] What makes the body superior to all reactions, particularly that reaction of the ego that is called consciousness, is the activity of necessarily unconscious forces: "This entire phenomenon of the body is, from the intellectual point of view, as superior to our consciousness, to our spirit to our conscious ways of thinking, feeling and willing, as algebra is superior to the multiplication table" (VP II 226). The body's active forces make it a self and define the self as superior and astonishing: "A most powerful being, an unknown sage – he is called Self. He inhabits your body, he is your body" (Z I "Of the Despisers of the Body" p. 62*). The only true science is that of activity, but the science of activity is also the science of what is necessarily unconscious. The idea that science must follow in the footsteps of consciousness, in the same directions, is absurd. We can sense the morality in this idea. In fact there can only be science where there is no consciousness, where there can be no consciousness.

"What is active? – reaching out for power" (VP II 43/WP 657). Appropriating, possessing, subjugating, dominating – these are the characteristics of active force. To appropriate means to impose forms, to create forms by exploiting circumstances (BGE 259 and VP II 63/WP 647). Nietzsche criticises Darwin for interpreting evolution and chance within evolution in an entirely reactive way. He admires Lamarck because Lamarck foretold the existence of a truly active *plastic force*, primary in relation to adaptations: a force of metamorphosis. For Nietzsche, as for energetics, energy which is capable of transforming itself is called "noble". The power of transformation, the Dionysian power, is the primary definition of activity. But each time we point out the nobility of action and its superiority to reaction in this way we must not forget that reaction also designates a type of force. It is simply that reactions cannot be grasped or scientifically understood as forces if they are not related to superior forces – forces of *another type*. The reactive is a primordial quality of force but one which can only be interpreted as such in relation to and on the basis of the active.

3. Quantity and Quality

Forces have quantity, but they also have the quality which corresponds to their difference in quantity: the qualities of force are called "active" and "reactive". We can see that the problem of measuring forces will be delicate because it brings the art of qualitative interpretations into play. The problem is as follows:

1) Nietzsche always believed that forces were quantitative and had to be defined quantitatively. "Our knowledge, he says, has become scientific to the extent that it is able to employ number and measurement. The attempt should be made to see whether a scientific order of values could be constructed simply on a numerical and quantitative scale of force. All other 'values' are prejudices, naiveties and misunderstandings. They are everywhere reducible to this numerical and quantitative scale" (VP II 352/WP 710).

2) However Nietzsche was no less certain that a purely quantitative determination of forces remained abstract, incomplete and ambiguous. The art of measuring forces raises the whole question of interpreting and evaluating qualities. " 'Mechanistic interpretation': desires nothing but quantities; but force is to be found in quality. Mechanistic theory can therefore only *describe* processes, not explain them" (VP II 46/WP 660 – for an almost identical text cf. II 187). "Might all quantities not be signs of quality? . . . The reduction of all qualities to quantities is nonsense" (VP II 343/WP 564).

Is there a contradiction between these two kinds of texts? If a force is inseparable from its quantity it is no more separable from the other forces which it relates to. *Quantity itself is therefore inseparable from difference in quantity*. Difference in quantity is the essence of force and of the relation of force to force. To dream of two equal forces, even if they are said to be of opposite senses is a coarse and approximate dream, a statistical dream in which the living is submerged but which chemistry dispels.[5] Each time that Nietzsche criticises the concept of quantity we must take it to mean that quantity as an abstract concept always and essentially tends towards an identification, an equalisation of the unity that forms it and an annulment of difference in this unity. Nietzsche's reproach to every purely quantitative determination of forces is that it annuls, equalises or compensates for differences in quantity. On the other hand, each time he criticises quality we should take it to mean that qualities are nothing but the corresponding difference in quantity between two forces whose relationship is presupposed. In short, Nietzsche is never interested in the irreducibility of quantity to quality; or rather he is only interested in it secondarily and as a symptom. What interests him primarily, from the standpoint of quantity itself, is the fact that differences in quantity cannot be reduced to equality. Quality is distinct from quantity but only because it is that aspect of quantity that cannot be equalised, that cannot be equalised out in the difference between quantities. Difference in quantity is therefore, in one sense, the irreducible element *of* quantity and in another sense the element which is irreducible *to* quantity itself. Quality is nothing but difference in quantity and corresponds to it each time forces enter into relation. "We cannot help feeling that mere quantitative differences are something fundamentally distinct from quantity, namely that they are *qualities* which can no longer be reduced to one another" (VP II 108/WP 565). The remaining anthropomorphism in this text should be corrected by the Nietzschean principle that there is a subjectivity of the universe which is no longer anthropomorphic but cosmic (VP II 15). "To want to reduce all qualities to quantities is madness . . ."

By affirming chance we affirm the relation of *all* forces. And, of course, we affirm all of chance all at once in the thought of the eternal return. But all forces do not enter into relations all at once on their own account. Their respective power is, in fact, fulfilled by relating to a small number of forces. Chance is the opposite of a *continuum* (on the *continuum* cf. VP II 356). The encounters of forces of various quantities are therefore the concrete parts of chance, the affirmative parts of chance and, as such, alien to every law; the limbs of Dionysus. But, in this encounter, each force receives the quality which corresponds to its quantity, that is to say the attachment which actually fulfills its power. Nietzsche can thus say, in an obscure passage, that the universe presupposes "an absolute genesis of arbitrary qualities", but that the genesis of qualities itself presupposes a (relative) genesis of quantities (VP II 334). The fact that the two geneses are inseparable means that we can not abstractly calculate forces. In each case we have to concretely evaluate their respective quality and the nuance of this quality.

4. Nietzsche and Science

The problem of Nietzsche's relations to science has been badly put. It is claimed that these relations depend on the theory of the eternal return – as if Nietzsche was only interested in science insofar as it favoured the eternal return, and then only vaguely, and insofar as it was opposed to the eternal return took no further interest in it. This is not the case and the origin of Nietzsche's critical position in relation to science must be sought in an entirely different direction, although this direction does open up a new viewpoint on the eternal return.

It is true that Nietzsche had little scientific skill or inclination. But what sets him apart from science is a propensity, a way of thinking. Rightly or wrongly Nietzsche believes that science, in the way it handles quantities always tends to equalise them, to make up for inequalities. Nietzsche, as critic of science, never invokes the rights of quality against quantity; he invokes the rights of difference in quantity against equality, of inequality against equalisation of quantities. Nietzsche imagines a "numerical and quantitative scale", but one in which the divisions are not multiples or factors of one another. What he attacks in science is precisely the scientific mania for seeking balances, the *utilitarianism* and *egalitarianism* proper to science.[6] This is why his whole critique operates on three levels; against logical identity, against mathematical equality and against physical equilibrium. *Against the three forms of the undifferentiated* (these three forms have an essential place in VP I and II). According to Nietzsche science will inevitably fall short of and endanger the true theory of force.

What is the significance of this tendency to reduce quantitative differences? In the first place, it expresses the way in which science is part of the *nihilism* of modern thought. The attempt to deny differences is a part of the more general enterprise of denying life, depreciating existence and promising it a death ("heat" or otherwise) where the universe sinks into the undifferentiated. Nietzsche accuses the physical concepts of matter, weight and heat of being, in the final analysis, agents of an equalisation of quantities, principles of an "*adiaphoria*". It is in this sense that Nietzsche shows that science is part of the ascetic ideal and serves it in its own way (GM III 25). But we must also look for the instrument of nihilistic thought in science. The answer is that science, by inclination, understands phenomena in terms of reactive forces and interprets them from this standpoint. Physics is reactive in the same way as biology; things are always seen from the petty side, from the side of reactions. The instrument of nihilistic thought is the triumph of reactive forces.

This is also the principle behind nihilism's manifestations: reactive physics is a physics of *ressentiment*, reactive biology is a biology of *ressentiment*. But we do not yet know why *this* is the only motive of the reactive forces which aim to deny the difference between forces, or how it serves as the principle of *ressentiment*.

Science either affirms or denies the eternal return depending on its standpoint. But the *mechanist* affirmation of the eternal return and its *thermodynamic* negation have something in common: the conservation of energy which is always interpreted so that quantities of energy not only have a constant sum but also cancel out their differences. In both cases we pass from a principle of finitude (the constancy of a sum) to a "nihilistic" principle (the cancelling out of differences in quantities, the sum of which is constant). The mechanist idea affirms the eternal return but only by assuming that differences in quantity balance or cancel each other out between the initial and final states of a reversible system. The final state is identical to the initial state which is itself assumed to be undifferentiated in relation to intermediate states. The thermodynamic idea denies the eternal return but only because it discovers that differences in quantity only cancel each other out in the final state of the system, as a function of the properties of heat. In this way identity is posited in the final undifferentiated state and opposed to the differentiation of the initial state. The two conceptions agree on one hypothesis, that of a final or terminal state, a terminal state of becoming. Being or nothing, being or non-being, are equally undifferentiated: the two conceptions come together in the idea of becoming having a final state, "In metaphysical terms, if becoming could end in being or nothing . . ." (VP II 329). This is why mechanism does not succeed in establishing the existence of the eternal return, any more than thermodynamics succeeds in denying it. Both pass it by and fall into the undifferentiated, fall back into the identical.

According to Nietzsche the eternal return is in no sense a thought of the identical but rather a thought of synthesis, a thought of the absolutely different which calls for a new principle outside science. This principle is that of the reproduction of diversity as such, of the repetition of difference; the opposite of "*adiaphoria*". (VP II 374 "There is no *adiaphoria* although we can imagine it.") And indeed, we fail to understand the eternal return if we make it a consequence or an application of identity. We fail to understand the eternal return if we do not oppose it to identity in a particular way. The eternal return is not the permanence of the same, the equilibrium state or the resting place of the identical. It is not the 'same' or the 'one' which comes back in the eternal return but return is itself the one which ought to belong to diversity and to that which differs.

5. *First Aspect of the Eternal Return: as cosmological and physical doctrine*

Nietzsche's account of the eternal return presupposes a critique of the terminal or equilibrium state. Nietzsche says that if the universe had an equilibrium position, if becoming had an end or final state, it would already have been attained. But the present moment, as the passing moment, proves that it is not attained and therefore that an equilibrium of forces is not possible (VP II 312, 322–4, 329–330). But why would equilibrium, the terminal state, have to have been attained if it were possible? By virtue of what Nietzsche calls the infinity of past time. The infinity of past time means that becoming cannot have started to become, that it is not something that has become. But, not being something that has become it cannot be a becoming something. Not having become, it would already be what it is becoming – if it were becoming something. That is to say, past time being infinite, becoming would have attained its final state if it had one. And, indeed, saying that becoming would have attained its final state if it had one is the same as saying that it would not have left its initial state if it had one. If becoming becomes something why has it not finished becoming long ago? If it is something which has become then how could it have started to become? "If the universe were capable of permanence and fixity, and if there were in its entire course a single moment of being in the strict sense it could no longer have anything to do with becoming, thus one could no longer think or observe any becoming whatever" (VP II 322; see an analogous text, VP II 330/WP 1062). This is the view that Nietzsche claims to have found "in earlier thinkers" (VP II 329/WP 1066). Plato said that if everything that becomes can never avoid the present then, as soon as it is there, it ceases to become and is then what it was in the process of becoming (Plato, *Parmenides*, cf. Second Hypothesis – however Nietzsche is thinking more of Anaximander). "But each time I encountered this thought from antiquity," Nietzsche comments, "it was determined by other, generally theological, ulterior motives." By persisting in demanding how becoming could have started and why it has not yet finished, the philosophers of antiquity are false tragics, invoking hubris, crime and punishment.[7] With the exception of Heraclitus, they did not face up to the thought of pure becoming, nor the opportunity for this thought. That the present moment is not a moment of being or of present "in the strict sense", that it is the passing moment, *forces* us to think of becoming, but to think of it precisely as what could not have started, and cannot finish, becoming.

How does the thought of pure becoming serve as a foundation for the eternal return? All we need to do to think this thought is to stop believing in being as distinct from and opposed to becoming or to believe in the being of becoming itself. What is the being of that which becomes, of that which neither starts nor finishes becoming? *Returning is the being of that which becomes (Revenir, l'être de ce qui devient)*. "That everything recurs is the closest approximation of a world of becoming to a world of being – high point of the meditation" (VP II 170/WP 617). This problem for the meditation must be formulated in yet another way; how can the past be constituted in time? How can the present pass? The passing moment could never pass if it were not already past and yet to come – at the same time as being present. If the present did not pass of its own accord, if it had to wait for a new present in order to become past, the past in general would never be constituted in time, and this particular present would not pass. We cannot wait, the moment must be simultaneously present and past, present and yet to come, in order for it to pass (and to pass for the sake of other moments). The present must coexist with itself as past and yet to come. The synthetic relation of the moment to iself as present, past and future grounds it relation to other moments. The eternal return is thus an answer to the problem of *passage*.[8] And in this sense it must not be interpreted as the return of something that is, that is "one" or the "same". We misinterpret the expression "eternal return" if we understand it as "return of the same". It is not being that returns but rather the returning itself that constitutes being insofar as it is affirmed of becoming and of that which passes. It is not some one thing which returns but rather returning itself is the one thing which is affirmed of diversity or multiplicity. In other words, identity in the eternal return does not describe the nature of that which returns but, on the contrary, the fact of returning for that which differs. This is why the eternal return must be thought of as a synthesis; a synthesis of time and its dimensions, a synthesis of diversity and its reproduction, a synthesis of becoming and the being which is affirmed in becoming, a synthesis of double affirmation. Thus the eternal return itself does not depend on a principle of identity but on one which must, in all respects, fulfill the requirements of a truly sufficient reason.

Why is mechanism such a bad interpretation of the eternal return? Because it does not necessarily or directly imply the eternal return. Because it only entails the false consequence of a final state. This final state is held to be identical to the initial state and, to this extent, it is concluded that the mechanical process passes through the same set of differences again. The cyclical hypothesis, so heavily criticised by Nietzsche (VP II 325 and 334), arises in this way. Because we cannot understand how this process can possibly leave the initial state, re-emerge from the final state, or pass through the same set of differences again and yet not even have the power to pass once through whatever differences there are. The cyclical hypothesis is incapable of accounting for two things – the diversity of co-existing cycles and, above all, the existence of diversity within the cycle.[9] This is why we can only understand the eternal return as the expression of a principle which serves as an explanation of diversity and its reproduction, of difference and its repetition. Nietzsche presents this principle as one of his most important philosophical discoveries. He calls it *will to power*. By will to power "I express the characteristic that cannot be thought out of the mechanistic order without thinking away this order itself" (VP II 374/WP 634*).

6. *What is the Will to Power?*

One of the most important texts which Nietzsche wrote to explain what he understood by will to power is the following: "The *victorious* concept 'force', by means of which our physicists have created God and the world, still needs to be *completed*: an *inner* will must be *ascribed* to it, which I designate as 'will to power' " (VP II 309/WP 619). The will to power is thus ascribed to force, but in a very special way: it is both a complement of force and something internal to it. It is not ascribed to it as a predicate. Indeed, if we pose the question "which one", we cannot say that force is *the one that* wills. The will to power alone is the one that wills, it does not let itself be delegated or alienated to another subject, even to force (VP I 204, II 54; "Who therefore will power? An absurd question, if being is by itself will to power . . .") But how then can it be "ascribed"? We must remember that every force has an essential relation to other forces, that the essence of force is its quantitative difference from other forces and that this difference is expressed as the force's quality. Now, difference in quantity, understood in this way, necessarily reflects a differential element of related forces – which is also the genetic element of the qualities of these forces. This is what the will to power is; the genealogical element of force, both differential and genetic. *The will to power is the element from which derive both the quantitative difference of related forces and the quality that devolves into each force in this relation.* The will to power here reveals its nature as the principle of the synthesis of forces. In this synthesis – which relates to time – forces pass through the same differences again or diversity is reproduced. The synthesis is one of forces, of their difference and their reproduction; the eternal return is the synthesis which has as its principle the will to power. We should not be surprised by the word "will"; *which one* apart from the will is capable of serving as the principle of a synthesis of forces by determining the relation of force with forces? But how should the term "principle" be understood? Nietzsche always attacks principles for being too general in relation to what they condition, for always having too broad a mesh in relation to what they claim to capture or regulate. He likes to oppose the will to power to the Schopenhauerian will to live, if only because of the extreme generality of the latter. If, on the contrary, the will to power is a good principle, if it reconciles empiricism with principles, if it constitutes a superior empiricism, this is because it is an essentially *plastic* principle that is no wider than what it conditions, that changes itself with the conditioned and determines itself in each case along with what it determines. The will to power is, indeed, never separable from particular determined forces, from their quantities, qualities and directions. It is never superior to the ways that it determines a relation between forces, it is always plastic and changing.[10]

Inseparable does not mean identical. The will to power cannot be separated from force without falling into metaphysical abstraction. But to confuse force and will is even more risky. Force is no longer understood as force and one falls back into mechanism – forgetting the difference between forces which constitutes their being and remaining ignorant of the element from which their reciprocal genesis derives. Force is what can, will to power is what wills (*La force est ce qui peut, la volonté de puissance est ce qui veut*). What does this distinction mean? The passage quoted above invites comment on every word. – The concept of force is, by nature, *victorious* because the relation of force to force, understood conceptually, is one of domination: when two forces are related one is dominant and the other is dominated. (Even God and the universe are caught in a relation of domination, however debatable the interpretation of such a relation may be in this case.) Nevertheless, this victorious concept of force needs a *complement* and this complement is *internal*, an internal will. It would not be victorious without such an addition. This is because relations of forces remain indeterminate unless an element which is capable of determining them from a double point of view is added to force itself. Forces in relation reflect a simultaneous double genesis: the reciprocal genesis of their difference in quantity and the absolute genesis of their respective qualities. The will to power is thus added to force, but as the differential and genetic element, as the internal element of its production. It is in no way anthropomorphic. More precisely, it is added to force as the internal principle of the determination of its quality in a relation $(x + dx)$ and as the internal principle of the quantitative determination of this relation itself (dy/dx). The will to power must be described as the genealogical element of force *and* of forces. Thus it is always through the will to power that one force prevails over others and dominates or commands them. Moreover it is also the will to power (dy) which makes a force obey within a relation; it is through will to power that it obeys.[11]

We have already encountered the relationship between the eternal return and the will to power, but we have neither elucidated nor analysed it. The will to power is both the genetic element of force and the principle of synthesis of forces. But we are not yet able to understand how this synthesis forms the eternal return, how the forces in it necessarily reproduce themselves in conformity with its principle. On the other hand, the existence of this problem reveals a historically important aspect of Nietzsche's philosophy; its complex relations with Kantianism. Kantianism centres on the concept of synthesis which it discovered. Now, we know that the post-Kantians reproached Kant, from two points of view, for having endangered this discovery: from the point of view of the principle which governs the synthesis and from the point of view of the reproduction of objects in the synthesis itself. They demanded a principle which was not merely conditioning in relation to objects but which was also truly genetic and productive (a principle of eternal difference or determination). They also condemned the survival, in Kant, of miraculous harmonies between terms that remain external to one another. With regard to such a principle of internal difference or determination they demanded grounds not only for the synthesis but for the reproduction of diversity in the synthesis as such.[12*] If Nietzsche belongs to the history of Kantianism it is because of the original way in which he deals with these post-Kantian demands. He turned synthesis into a synthesis of forces – for, if we fail to see synthesis in this way, we fail to recognise its sense, nature and content. He understood the synthesis of forces as the eternal return and thus found the reproduction of diversity at the heart of synthesis. He established the principle of synthesis, the will to power and determined this as the differential and genetic element of forces which directly confront one another. Although this supposition must be verified later we believe that there is, in Nietzsche, not only a Kantian heritage, but a half-avowed, half-hidden, rivalry. Nietzsche does not have the same position in relation to Kant as Schopenhauer did for, unlike Schopenhauer, he does not attempt an interpretation which would separate Kantianism from its dialectical avatars and present it with new openings. This is because, for Nietzsche, these dialectical avatars do not come from the outside but are primarily caused by the deficiencies of the critical philosophy. Nietzsche seems to have sought (and to have found in the "eternal return" and the "will to power") a radical transformation of Kantianism, a re-invention of the critique which Kant betrayed at the same time as he conceived it, a resumption of the critical project on a new basis and with new concepts.

7. Nietzsche's Terminology

We must now fix certain points in Nietzsche's terminology even if this anticipates analyses which remain to be done. All the rigour of his philosophy, whose systematic precision is wrongly suspected, depends on it. This suspicion is wrong in any case, whether this is cause for rejoicing or regret. In fact Nietzsche uses very precise new terms for very precise new concepts:

1) Nietzsche calls the genealogical element of force the will to power. Genealogcial means differential and genetic. The will to power is the differential element of forces, that is to say the element that produces

the differences in quantity between two or more forces whose relation is presupposed. The will to power is the genetic element of force, that is to say the element that produces the quality due to each force in this relation. The will to power as a principle does not suppress chance but, on the contrary, implies it, because without chance it would be neither plastic nor changing. Chance is the bringing of forces into relation, the will to power is the determining principle of this relation. The will to power is a necessary addition to force but can only be added to forces brought into relation by chance. The will to power has chance at its heart for only the will to power is capable of affirming all chance.

2) The difference in quantity and the respective qualities of forces in relation both derive from the will to power as genealogical element. Forces are said to be dominant or dominated depending on their difference in quantity. Forces are said to be active or reactive depending on their quality. There is will to power in the reactive or dominated force as well as in the active or dominant force. Now, as the difference in quantity is irreducible in every case, it is pointless to want to measure it without interpreting the qualities of the forces which are present. Forces are essentially differentiated and qualified. They express their difference in quantity by the quality which is due to them. This is the problem of interpretation: to estimate the quality of force that gives meaning to a given phenomenon, or event, and from that to measure the relation of the forces which are present. We must not forget that, in every case, interpretation comes up against all kinds of delicate problems and difficulties; and "extremely fine" perception is necessary here, of the kind found in chemistry.

3) The principle of the qualities of force is the will to power. And if we ask: "which one interprets?", we reply *the will to power*; it is the will to power that interprets (VP I 204 and II 130/WP 556 and 643). But, in order to be the source of the qualities of force in this way, the will to power must itself have qualities, particularly fluent ones, even more subtle than those of force. "What rules is the entirely momentary quality of the will to power" (VP II 39). These qualities of the will to power which are immediately related to the genetic or genealogical element, these fluent, primordial and seminal qualitative elements, must not be confused with the qualities of force. It is therefore essential to insist on the terms used by Nietzsche; *active* and *reactive* designate the original qualities of force but *affirmative* and *negative*

designate the primordial qualities of the will to power. Affirming and denying, appreciating and depreciating, express the will to power just as acting and reacting express force. (And just as reactive forces are still forces, the will to deny, nihilism, is still will to power: " . . . a *will to nothingness*, an aversion to life, a rebellion against the most fundamental presuppositions of life; but it is and remains a will!" GM III 28 p. 163) This distinction between two kinds of quality is of the greatest importance and it is always found at the centre of Nietzsche's philosophy. There is a deep affinity, a complicity, but never a confusion, between action and affirmation, between reaction and negation. Moreover, the determination of these affinities brings the whole art of philosophy into play. On the one hand, it is clear that there is affirmation in every action and negation in every reaction. But, on the other hand, action and reaction are more like means, means or instruments of the will to power which affirms and denies, just as reactive forces are instruments of nihilism. And again, action and reaction need affirmation and negation as something which goes beyond them but is necessary for them to achieve their own ends. Finally, and more profoundly, affirmation and negation extend beyond action and reaction because they are the immediate qualities of becoming itself. Affirmation is not action but the power of becoming active, *becoming active* personified. Negation is not simple reaction but a *becoming reactive*. It is as if affirmation and negation were both immanent and transcendent in relation to action and reaction; out of the web of forces they make up the chain of becoming. Affirmation takes us into the glorious world of Dionysus, the being of becoming and negation hurls us down into the disquieting depths from which reactive forces emerge.

4) For all these reasons Nietzsche can say that the will to power is not only the one that interprets but the one that evaluates (VP II 29: "Every will implies an evaluation."). To interpret is to determine the force which gives sense to a thing. To evaluate is to determine the will to power which gives value to a thing. We can no more abstract values from the standpoint from which they draw their value than we can abstract meaning from the standpoint from which it draws its signification. The will to power as genealogical element is that from which senses derive their significance and values their value. It is what we were talking about, without using the name, at the beginning of the preceding chapter. The signification of a sense consists in the quality of

the force which is expressed in a thing: is this force active or reactive and of what nuance? The value of a value consists in the quality of the will to power expressed in the corresponding thing; is the will to power affirmative or negative and of what nuance? The art of philosophy becomes even more complicated as these problems of interpretation and evaluation refer back to and extend one another. What Nietzsche calls *noble*, *high* and *master* is sometimes active force, sometimes affirmative will. What he calls *base*, *vile* and *slave* is sometimes reactive force and sometimes negative will. Later we will understand why he uses these terms. But a value always has a genealogy on which the nobility or baseness of what it invites us to believe, feel and think depends. Only a genealogist is able to discover what sort of baseness can find its expression in one value, what sort of nobility in another, because only he knows how to handle the differential element: he is the master of the critique of values.[13] The notion of value loses all meaning if values are not seen as receptacles to be pierced, statues to be broken open to find what they contain, whether it is the most noble or the most base. Like the scattered limbs of Dionysus only the statues of nobility come back together. Talk of the nobility of values in general shows a type of thought which has too much at stake to hide its own baseness – as if whole domains of values did not derive their sense and their value from serving as refuge and manifestation for all that is vile and slavish. Nietzsche, the creator of the philosophy of values, would have seen, if he had lived longer, his most critical notion serving and turning into the most insipid and base ideological conformism; the hammer strokes of the philosophy of values becoming strokes of flattery; polemic and aggression replaced by *ressentiment*, carping guardian of the established order, watchdog of current values. This is genealogy taken up by slaves – the forgetting of qualities, the forgetting of origins.[14]

8. Origin and Inverted Image

In the beginning, at the origin, there is the difference between active and reactive forces. Action and reaction are not in a relation of succession but in one of coexistence in the origin itself. Moreover, the complicity of active forces and affirmation and that of reactive forces and negation is revealed by the principle that the negative is already wholly on the side of reaction. Conversely, only active force asserts itself, it affirms its difference and makes its difference an object of enjoyment and affirmation. Reactive force, even when it obeys, limits active force, imposes limitations and partial restrictions on it and is already controlled by the spirit of the negative (GM II 11). This is why the origin itself, in one sense, includes an inverted self-image; seen from the side of reactive forces the differential and genealogical element appears upside down, difference has become negation, affirmation has become contradiction. An inverted image of the origin accompanies the origin; "yes" from the point of view of active forces becomes "no" from the point of view of reactive forces and affirmation of the self becomes negation of the other. This is what Nietzsche calls the "inversion of the value-positing eye".[15] Active forces are noble but they find themselves before a plebeian image, reflected in reactive forces. Genealogy is the art of difference or distinction, the art of nobility; but it sees itself upside down in the mirror of reactive forces. Its image then appears as that of an "evolution". – Sometimes this evolution is understood in the German manner, as a dialectical and Hegelian evolution, as the development of contradiction. Sometimes it is understood in the English manner, as a utilitarian derivation, as the development of profit and interest. But true genealogy is always caricatured in the essentially reactive image that evolution presents of it. Whether it is English or German, evolutionism, is the reactive image of genealogy.[16] Thus it is characteristic of reactive forces to deny, from the start, the difference which constitutes them at the start, to invert the differential element from which they derive and to give a deformed image of it. "Difference breeds hatred" (BGE 263). This is why they do not see themselves as forces and prefer to turn against themselves rather than seeing themselves in this way and accepting difference. The "mediocrity" of thought which Nietzsche attacks always reflects a mania for interpreting or evaluating phenomena in terms of reactive forces – every nation chooses its own. But this mania has its origins at the beginning, in the inverted image. Consciousness and consciences are simply enlargements of this reactive image . . .

   Going one step further, let us suppose that, with the help of favourable external or internal circumstances, reactive forces get the better of and neutralise active force. We have now left the origin: it is no longer a question of an inverted image but of a development of this image, an inversion of values themselves (GM I 7) so that the low is placed on high and reactive forces have triumphed. If they do triumph it is through the negative will, through the will to nothingness which develops the image; but their triumph itself is not imaginary. The question is; how do reactive forces triumph? That is to say: when they get the better of active forces do reactive forces themselves also become dominant, aggressive and subjugating? Do they, by getting together, form a greater force that would then be active? Nietzsche's answer is that even by getting together reactive forces do not form a greater force, one that would be active. They proceed in an entirely different way – they decompose; *they separate active force from what it can do*; they take away a part or almost all of its power. In this way reactive forces do not become active but, on the contrary, they make active forces join them and become reactive in a new sense. We can see that, from its beginning and in developing itself, the concept of reaction changes in signification: an active force *becomes reactive* (in a new sense) when reactive forces (in the first sense) separate it from what it can do. Nietzsche will analyse how such a separation is possible in detail. But it is important to notice that, even at this stage, he is careful never to present the triumph of reactive forces as the putting together of a force superior to active force but, rather, as a subtraction or division. Nietzsche devotes a whole book to the analysis of the figures of reactive triumph in the human world – *ressentiment*, bad conscience and the ascetic ideal. In each case he shows that reactive forces do not triumph by forming a superior force but by "separating" active force (cf. the three essays of the GM). In each case this separation rests on a fiction, on a mystification or a falsification. It is the will to nothingness which develops the negative and inverted image and makes the subtraction. Now, there is always something imaginary in the operation of subtraction – as the negative utilisation of number shows. Thus if we want to give a numerical transcription of the victory of reactive forces we must not appeal to an addition by which reactive forces would, by getting together, become stronger than active force, but rather to a subtraction which separates active force from what it can do and denies its difference in order to make it a reactive force. Thus getting the better of action is not enough to stop reaction being reaction; on the contrary. Active force is separated from what it can do by a fiction but is not therefore any less "really" reactive, in fact, this is the way in which it becomes really reactive. This is where Nietzsche's use of the words "vile", "ignoble" and "slave" comes from – these words designate the state of reactive forces that place themselves on high and entice active force into a trap, replacing masters with slaves who do not stop being slaves.

9. The Problem of the Measure of Forces

This is why we cannot measure forces in terms of an abstract unity, or determine their respective quality and quantity by using the real state of forces in a system as a criterion. We have said that active forces are the superior, dominant and strongest forces. But inferior forces can prevail without ceasing to be inferior in quantity and reactive in quality, without ceasing to be slaves in this sense. One of the finest remarks in *The Will to Power* is: "The strong always have to be defended against the weak" (VP I 395). We cannot use the state of a system of forces as it in fact is, or the result of the struggle between forces, in order to decide which are active and which are reactive. Nietzsche remarks, against Darwin and evolutionism, "Supposing, however, that this struggle exists – and it does indeed occur – its outcome is the reverse of that desired by the school of Darwin, of that which one *ought* perhaps to desire with them: namely, the defeat of the stronger, the more privileged, the fortunate exceptions" (TI "Expeditions of an Untimely Man" 14 pp. 75–6). It is primarily in this sense that interpretation is such a difficult art – we must judge whether the forces which prevail are inferior or superior, reactive or active; whether they prevail as *dominated* or *dominant*. In this area there are no facts, only interpretations. The measurement of forces must not be conceived of as a procedure of abstract physics but rather as the fundamental act of a concrete physics, not as an indifferent technique but as the art of interpreting difference and quality independently of fact. (Nietzsche sometimes says; "Outside of the existing social order". VP III 8).

This problem reopens an old argument, a famous debate between Callicles and Socrates (*Gorgias*; discussion on "nature and convention", 481–527). The resemblance is so striking that it seems to us that Nietzsche is close to Callicles and that Callicles is immediately completed by Nietzsche. Callicles strives to distinguish nature and law. Everything that separates a force from what it can do he calls law. Law, in this sense, expresses the triumph of the weak over the strong. Nietzsche adds: the triumph of reaction over action. Indeed, everything which separates a force is reactive as is the state of a force separated from what it can do. Every force which goes to the limit of its power is, on the contrary, active. It is not a law that every force goes to the limit, it is even the opposite of law.[17] – Socrates replies to Callicles that there is no way of distinguishing nature and law; for the weak can only prevail if, by banding together, they can form a stronger force than the strong. Law triumphs from the point of view of nature itself. Callicles does not complain of not having been understood, he begins again. The slave does not stop being a slave by being triumphant; when the weak triumph it is not by forming a greater force but by separating force from what it can do. Forces must not be compared abstractly; from the point of view of nature concrete force is that which goes to its ultimate consequences, to the limit of power or desire. Socrates objects a second time; "what matters for you Callicles is pleasure . . . You define all good in terms of pleasure."

We can see here what happens between the sophist and the dialectician, on which side the good faith and the rigorous reasoning is. Callicles is aggressive but has no *ressentiment*. He prefers to give up talking because it is clear that Socrates does not understand the first time and the second time speaks of something else. How can he explain to Socrates that "desire" is not the association of a pleasure and a pain, the pain of experiencing it and the pleasure of satisfying it? How can he explain that pleasure and pain are reactions, properties of reactive forces, the proof of adaptation or lack of it? And how can Socrates be made to understand that the weak do not form a stronger force? Socrates has partially misunderstood and partially misheard – he is too full of dialectical *ressentiment* and the spirit of revenge. He who is so exacting towards others, so fastidious when they reply to him . . .

10. Hierarchy

Nietzsche also encounters his own Socrates. These are the free thinkers. They say: "What are you complaining about? How could the weak have triumphed if they did not form superior force?" "Let us bow down before accomplished fact" (GM I 9). This is modern positivism. They claim to carry out the critique of values, they claim to refuse all appeals to transcendent values, they declare them unfashionable, but only in order to rediscover them as the forces which run the world of today. The value of Church, morality, State etc. is only discussed so that their human force and content can be admired. The free thinker has the strange craze for recovering every content, everything positive, but without ever questioning the nature of these self-styled positives or the origin or quality of the corresponding human forces. This is what Nietzsche calls "fatalism" (GM III 24). The free thinker wants to recover the content of religion but never considers that religion might in fact contain man's basest forces, forces which we might want to leave behind. This is why we can have no confidence in the free thinker's atheism, even when he's a democrat and a socialist: "It is the church, and not its poison that repels us" (GM I 9 p. 36). The essential characteristics of the free thinker's positivism and humanism are fatalism, interpretative impotence and ignorance of the qualities of force. As soon as something appears as a human force or fact the free thinker applauds it without wondering whether this force is of base extraction, whether this fact is the opposite of a high fact: "Human all-too human". Because it does not take the qualities of forces into account free thought is, by vocation, at the service of reactive forces and expresses their triumph. For the fact is always something used by the weak against the strong; "the fact is always stupid, having at all times resembled a calf rather than a god" (UM II "Use and Abuse of History" 8). Nietzsche opposes the *free spirit* to the free thinker, the spirit of interpretation itself which judges forces from the standpoint of their origin and quality: "There are no facts, nothing but interpretations" (VP II 133). The critique of the free thinker is a fundamental theme in Nietzsche's work – because this critique discloses a perspective from which many different ideologies can be attacked at once; positivism, humanism, the dialectic – positivism's taste for facts, humanism's exaltation of the human fact and the dialectic's mania for recovering human contents.

In Nietzsche the word *hierarchy* has two senses. It signifies, firstly, the difference between active and reactive forces, the superiority of active to reactive forces. Nietzsche can thus speak of an "unalterable and innate order of rank in hierarchy" (BGE 263); and the problem of hierarchy is itself the problem of free spirits (HH Preface 7). But hierarchy also designates the triumph of reactive forces, the contagion of reactive forces and the complex organisation which results – where the weak have conquered, where the strong are contaminated, where the slave who has not stopped being a slave prevails over the master who has stopped being one: the reign of law and of virtue. In this second sense morality and religion are still theories of hierarchy (VP III 385 and 391). If we compare the two senses we see that the second is like the reverse of the first. We make Church, morality and State the masters or keepers of all hierarchy. We have the hierarchy that we deserve, we who are essentially reactive, we who take the triumphs of reaction for a transformation of action and slaves for new masters – we who only recognise hierarchy back to front.

What Nietzsche calls weak or slavish is not the least strong but that which, whatever its strength, is separated from what it can do. The least strong is as strong as the strong if he goes to the limit, because the cunning, the subtelty, the wit and even the charm by which he makes up for his lesser strength are part of this strength so that it is no longer the least. (Zarathustra's two animals are the eagle and the serpent. The eagle is strong and proud but the serpent being crafty and charming is no less strong.) The measure of forces and their qualification does *not* depend on absolute quantity but rather on relative accomplishment. Strength or weakness cannot be judged by taking the result and success of struggle as a criterion. For, once again, it is a fact that the weak triumph: it is even the essence of fact. Forces can only be judged if one takes into account in the first place their active or reactive quality, in the second place the affinity of this quality for the corresponding pole of the will to power (affirmative or negative) and in the third place the nuance of quality that the force presents at a particular moment of its development, in relation to its affinity. Thus reactive force is: 1) utilitarian force of adaptation and partial limitation; 2) force which separates active force from what it can do, which denies active force (triumph of the weak or the slaves); 3) force separated from what it can do, which denies or turns against itself (reign of the weak or of slaves). And, analogously, active force is: 1) plastic, dominant and subjugating force; 2) force which goes to the limit of what it can do; 3) force which affirms its difference, which makes its difference an object of enjoyment and affirmation. Forces are only concretely and completely determined if these three pairs of characteristics are taken into account simultaneously.

11. Will to Power and Feeling of Power

We know that the will to power is the differential element, the genealogical element which determines the relation of force with force and produces their quality. The will to power must therefore *manifest itself* in force as such. The manifestations of the will to power must be studied very carefully because the dynamism of forces is completely dependent on it. But what does "the will to power manifests itself" mean? The relationship between forces in each case is determined to the extent that each force is *affected* by other, inferior or superior, forces. It follows that will to power is manifested as a capacity for being affected. This capacity is not an abstract possibility, it is necessarily fulfilled and actualised at each moment by the other forces to which a given force relates. We should not be surprised by the double aspect of the will to power: from the standpoint of the genesis or production of forces it determines the relation between forces but, from the standpoint of its own manifestations, it is determined by relating forces. This is why the will to power is always determined at the same time as it determines, qualified at the same time as it qualifies. In the first place, therefore, the will to power is manifested as the capacity for being affected, as the determinate capacity of force for being affected. – It is difficult to deny a Spinozist inspiration here. Spinoza, in an extremely profound theory, wanted a capacity for being affected to correspond to every quantity of force. The more ways a body could be affected the more force it had. This capacity measures the force of a body or expresses its power. And, on the one hand, this power is not a simple logical possibility for it is actualised at every moment by the bodies to which a given body is related. On the other hand, this capacity is not a physical passivity, the only passive affects are those not adequately caused by the given body.[18]

Similarly, for Nietzsche, the capacity for being affected is not necessarily a passivity but an *affectivity*, a sensibility, a sensation. It is in this sense that Nietzsche, even before elaborating the concept of the will to power and giving it its full significance, was already speaking of a *feeling of power*. Before treating power as a matter of will he treated it as a matter of feeling and sensibility. But when he had elaborated the full concept of the will to power this first characteristic did not disappear – it became the manifestation of the will to power. This is why Nietzsche always says that the will to power is "the primitive affective form" from which all other feelings derive (VP II 42). Or better still: "The will to power is not a being not a becoming, but a *pathos*" (VP II 311/WP 635). That is to say: the will to power manifests itself as the sensibility of force; the differential element of forces manifests itself as their differential sensibility. "The fact is that the will to power rules even in the inorganic world, or rather that there is no inorganic world. Action at a distance cannot be eliminated, for one thing attracts another and a thing feels itself attracted. This is the fundamental fact . . . *In order for the will to power to be able to manifest itself it needs to perceive the things it sees and feel the approach of what is assimilable to it*" (VP II 89). The effects of force are active insofar as the force appropriates anything that resists it and compels the obedience of inferior forces. When force is affected by superior forces which it obeys its affects are made to submit, or rather, they are acted (*agies*). Again, obeying is a manifestation of the will to power. But an inferior force can bring about the disintegration or splitting of superior forces, the explosion of the energy which they have accumulated. Nietzsche likes to compare the phenomena of atomic disintegration, the division of protoplasm and the reproduction of organic life (VP II 45, 77, 187). And not only do disintegration, division and separation always express will to power but so do being disintegrated, being separated and being divided: "Division appears as the consequence of the will to power" (VP II 73). Given two forces, one superior and the other inferior, we can see how each one's capacity for being affected is fulfilled necessarily. But this capacity for being affected is not fulfilled unless the corresponding force enters into a history or a process of sensible becoming: 1) active force, power of acting or commanding; 2) reactive force, power of obeying or of being acted; 3) developed reactive force, power of splitting up, dividing and separating; 4) active force become reactive, power of being separated, of turning against itself.[19]

All sensibility is only a becoming of forces. There is a cycle of force in the course of which force "becomes" (for example, active force becomes reactive). There are even several becomings of forces that can struggle against one another.[20] Thus it is not sufficient to parallel or oppose the respective characteristics of active and reactive force. The active and the reactive are qualities of force that derive from the will to power. But the will to power itself has qualities, *sensibilia*, which are like the becomings of forces. The will to power manifests itself, in the first place, as the sensibility of forces and, in the second place, as the becoming sensible of forces: pathos is the most elementary fact from which a becoming arises (VP II 311/WP 635). In general, the becoming of forces must not be confused with the qualities of force: it is the becoming of these qualities themselves, the quality of the will to power itself. The qualities of force can no more be abstracted from their becoming than force itself can be abstracted from the will to power. The concrete study of forces necessarily implies a dynamic.

12. The Becoming-Reactive of Forces

But, the dynamic of forces in fact leads us to a distressing conclusion. When reactive force separates active force from what it can do, the latter also becomes reactive. *Active forces become reactive.* And the word 'becoming' must be taken in the strongest sense: the becoming of forces appears as a becoming-reactive. Are there no other ways of becoming? The fact remains that we do not feel, experience or know any becoming but becoming-reactive. We are not merely noting the existence of reactive forces, we are noting the fact that everywhere they are triumphant. How do they triumph? Through the will to nothingness, thanks to the affinity between reaction and negation. What is negation? It is a quality of the will to power, the one which qualifies it as nihilism or will to nothingness, the one which constitutes the becoming-reactive of forces. It must not be said that active force becomes reactive because reactive forces triumph; on the contrary, they triumph because, by separating active force from what it can do, they betray it to the will of nothingness, to a becoming-reactive deeper than themselves. This is why the figures of triumph of reactive forces (*ressentiment*, bad conscience, and the ascetic ideal) are primarily forms of nihilism. The becoming-reactive, the becoming nihilistic, of force seem to be essential components of the relation of force with force. – Is there another becoming? Everything tempts us to think that perhaps there is. But, as Nietzsche often says, we would need another sensibility, another way of feeling. We can not yet reply to this question, we can hardly even contemplate its possibility. But we *can* ask why we only feel and know a becoming-reactive. Is it not because man is essentially reactive? Because becoming-reactive is constitutive of man? *Ressentiment*, bad conscience and nihilism are not psychological traits but the foundation of the humanity in man. They are the principle of human being as such. Man, "skin disease" of the Earth, reaction of the Earth . . . (Z II "Of Great Events"). It is in this sense that Zarathustra speaks of his "great contempt" for man and of his "great disgust". Another sensibility, another becoming – would they still be man's?

This condition of man is of the greatest importance for the eternal return. It seems to compromise or contaminate it so gravely that it becomes an object of anguish, repulsion and disgust. Even if active forces return they will again become reactive, eternally reactive. The eternal return of reactive forces and furthermore the return of the becoming-reactive of forces. Zarathustra not only presents the thought of the eternal return as mysterious and secret but as nauseating and difficult to bear (cf. also VP IV 235, 246). The first exposition of the eternal return is followed by a strange vision of a shepherd "writhing, choking, convulsed, his face distorted", a heavy black snake hanging out of his mouth (Z III "Of the Vision and the Riddle" p. 180). Later, Zarathustra himself explains the vision: "The great disgust at man – *it* choked me and had crept into my throat . . . The man of whom you are weary, the little man recurs eternally . . . Alas man recurs eternally! . . . And eternal return, even for the smallest – that was my disgust at all existence! Ah, disgust! Disgust! Disgust!" (Z III "The Convalescent" pp. 235–6). The eternal return of the mean, small, reactive man not only makes the thought of the eternal return unbearable, it also makes the eternal return itself impossible; it puts contradiction into the eternal return. The snake is an animal of the eternal return; but, insofar as the eternal return is that of reactive forces, the snake uncoils, becomes a "heavy black snake" and hangs out of the mouth which is preparing to speak. For how could the eternal return, the being of becoming, be affirmed of a becoming nihilistic? – In order to affirm the eternal return it is necessary to bite off and spit out the snake's head. Then the shepherd is no longer either man or shepherd, "he was transformed, surrounded with light, he was laughing! Never yet on earth had any man laughed as he laughed" (Z III "Of the Vision and the Riddle" p. 180*). Another becoming, another sensibility: the Overman.

13. Ambivalence of Sense and of Values

A becoming-active of forces, a becoming-active of reactive forces, would be a different becoming from the one that we know now. The evaluation of such a becoming raises several questions and must be the final test of the systematic coherence of Nietzschean concepts in the theory of force. – Let us consider an initial hypothesis. What Nietzsche calls an active force is one which goes to the limit of its consequences. An active force separated from what it can do by reactive force thus becomes reactive. But does not this reactive force, in its own way, go to the limit of what it can do? If active force, being separated, becomes reactive, does not, conversely, reactive force, as that which separates, become active? Is this not its own way of being active? Concretely, is there not a kind of baseness, meanness, stupidity etc. which becomes active through going to the limit of what it can do? "Rigorous and grandoise stupidity . . ." Nietzsche writes (BGE 188). This hypothesis recalls the Socratic objection but is, in fact, distinct from it. One on longer says, like Socrates, that inferior forces only triumph by forming a greater force but rather that reactive forces only triumph by going to the limit of their consequences, that is, by forming an active force.

A reactive force can certainly be considered from different points of view. Illness for example, separates me from what I can do, as reactive force it makes me reactive, it narrows my possibilities and condemns me to a diminished milieu to which I can do no more than adapt myself. But, in another way, it reveals to me a new capacity, it endows me with a new will that I can make my own, going to the limit of a strange power. (This extreme power brings many things into play, for example: "Looking from the perspective of the sick toward *healthier* concepts and values . . ." EH I 1 p. 223). Here we can recognise an ambivalence important to Nietzsche: all the forces whose reactive character he exposes are, a few lines or pages later, admitted to fascinate him, to be sublime because of the perspective they open up for us and because of the disturbing will to power to which they bear witness. They separate us from our power but at the same time they give us another power, "dangerous" and "interesting". They bring us new feelings and teach us new ways of being affected. There is something admirable in the becoming-reactive of forces, admirable and dangerous. Not only the sick man, but even the religious man present this double aspect: reactive on the one hand, possessing a new power on the other.[21] "Human history would be altogether too stupid a thing without the spirit that the impotent have introduced into it" (GM I 7 p. 33). Every time Nietzsche speaks of Socrates, Christ, Judaism, Christianity or any form of decadence or degeneration he discovers this same ambivalence of things, beings and forces.

Is it, however, exactly the same force that both separates me from what I can do and endows me with a new power? Is it the same illness, is it the same invalid who is the slave of his illness and who uses it as a means of exploring, dominating and being powerful. Is the religion of the faithful who are like bleating lambs and that of certain priests who are like new "birds of prey" the same? In fact the reactive forces are not the same and they change nuance depending on the extent to which they develop their affinity for the will to nothingness. One reactive force both obeys and resists, another separates active force from what it can do; a third contaminates active force, carries it along to the limit of becoming-reactive, into the will to nothingness; a fourth type of reactive force was originally active but became reactive and separated from its power, it was then dragged into the abyss and turned against itself – these are the different nuances, affects and types that the genealogist must interpret, that no one else knows how to interpret. "Need I say after all this that in questions of decadence I am *experienced*? I have spelled them forward and backward. That filigree art of grasping and comprehending in general, those fingers for *nuances*, that psychology of 'looking round the corner', and whatever else is characteristic of me . . ." (EH I 1 p. 223). The problem of interpretation is to interpret the state of reactive forces in each case – that is the degree of development that they have reached in relation to negation and the will to nothingness. – The same problem of interpretation would arise on the side of active forces; to interpret their nuance or state in each case, that is, to interpret the degree of development of the relation between action and affirmation. There are reactive forces that become grandiose and fascinating by following the will to nothingness and there are active forces that subside because they do not know how to follow the powers of affirmation (we will see that this is the problem of what Nietzsche calls "culture" or "the higher man"). Finally, evaluation presents ambivalences which are even more profound than those of interpretation. To judge affirmation itself from the standpoint of negation itself and negation from the standpoint of affirmation; to judge affirmative will from the standpoint of nihilistic will and nihilistic will from the standpoint of affirmative will – this is the genealogist's art and the genealogist is a physician. "Looking from the perspective of the sick toward *healthier* concepts and values and, conversely, looking again from the fullness and self-assurance of a *rich* life down into the secret work of the instinct of decadence" (EH I 1 p. 223). But whatever the ambivalence of sense and values we cannot conclude that a reactive force becomes active by going to the limit of what it can do. For, to go "to the limit", "to the ultimate consequences", has two senses depending on whether one affirms or denies, whether one affirms one's own difference or denies that which differs. When a reactive force develops to its ultimate consequences it does this in relation to negation, to the will to nothingness which serves as its motive force. Becoming active, on the contrary, presupposes the affinity of action and affirmation; in order to become active it is not sufficient for a force to go to the limit of what it can do, it must make what it can do an object of affirmation. Becoming-active is affirming and affirmative, just as becoming-reactive is negating and nihilistic.

14. Second Aspect of the Eternal Return: as ethical and selective thought

Because it is neither felt nor known, a becoming-active can only be thought as the product of a *selection*. A simultaneous double selection by the activity of force and the affirmation of the will. But what can perform the selection? What serves as the selective principle? Nietzsche replies: the eternal return. Formerly the object of disgust, the eternal return overcomes disgust and turns Zarathustra into a "convalescent", someone consoled (Z III "The Convalescent"). But in what sense is the eternal return selective? Firstly because, as a thought, it gives the will a practical rule (VP IV 229, 231/WP 1053, 1056 "The great selective *thought*"). The eternal return gives the will a rule as rigorous as the Kantian one. We have noted that the eternal return, as a physical doctrine, was the new formulation of the speculative synthesis. As an ethical thought the eternal return is the new formulation of the practical synthesis: *whatever you will, will it in such a way that you also will its eternal return*. "If, in all that you will you begin by asking yourself: is it certain that I will to do it an infinite number of times? This should be your most solid centre of gravity" (VP IV 242). One thing in the world disheartens Nietzsche: the little compensations, the little pleasures, the little joys and everything that one is granted once, only once. Everything that can be done again the next day only on the condition that it be said the day before: tomorrow I will give it up – the whole ceremonial of the obsessed. And we are like those old women who permit themselves an excess only once, we act and think like them. "Oh, that you would put from you all *half* willing, and decide upon lethargy as you do upon action. Oh that you understood my saying: 'Always do what you will – but first be such as *can* will!' ".[22] Laziness, stupidity, baseness, cowardice or spitefulness that would will its own eternal return would no longer be the same laziness, stupidity etc. How does the eternal return perform the selection here? It is the *thought* of the eternal return that selects. It makes willing something whole. The thought of the eternal return eliminates from willing everything which falls outside the eternal return, it makes willing a creation, it brings about the equation "willing = creating".

It is clear that such a selection falls short of Zarathustra's ambitions. It is content to eliminate certain reactive states, certain states of reactive forces which are among the least developed. But reactive forces which go to the limit of what they can do in their own way, and which find a powerful motor in the nihilistic will, resist the first selection. Far from falling outside the eternal return they enter into it and seem to return with it. We must therefore expect a second selection, very different from the first. But this second selection involves the most obscure parts of Nietzsche's philosophy and forms an almost esoteric element on the doctrine of the eternal return. We can therefore only summarise these Nietzschean themes, leaving a detailed conceptual explanation until later:

1) Why is the eternal return called "the most extreme form of nihilism" (VP III 8/WP 55)? And if the eternal return is the most extreme form of nihilism, nihilism itself (separated or abstracted from the eternal return) is always an "incomplete nihilism" (VP III 7/WP 28): however far it goes, however powerful it is. Only the eternal return makes the nihilistic will whole and complete.

2) The will to nothingness, as we have investigated it up to now, has always appeared in an alliance with reactive forces. Its essence was to deny active force and to lead it to deny and turn against itself. But, at the same time, it laid in this way the foundation for the conservation, triumph and contagion of reactive forces. The will to nothingness was the universal becoming-reactive, the becoming-reactive of forces. This is the sense in which nihilism is always incomplete on its own. Even the ascetic ideal is the opposite of what we might think, "it is an expedient of the art of conserving life". Nihilism is the principle of conservation of a weak, diminished, reactive life. The depreciation

and negation of life form the principle in whose shadow the reactive life conserves itself, survives, triumphs and becomes contagious (GM III 13).

3) What happens when the will to nothingness is related to the eternal return? This is the only place where it breaks its alliance with reactive forces. Only the eternal return can complete nihilism *because it makes negation a negation of reactive forces themselves*. By and in the eternal return nihilism no longer expresses itself as the conservation and victory of the weak but as their destruction, their *self-destruction*. "This perishing takes the form of a self-destruction – the instinctive selection of that which must destroy . . . The will to destruction as the will of a still deeper instinct, the instinct of self-destruction, the will for nothingness" (VP III 8/WP 55). This is why Zarathustra, as early as the Prologue, sings of the "one who wills his own downfall", "for he does not want to preserve himself", "for he will cross the bridge without hesitation" (Z Prologue 4). The Prologue to *Zarathustra* contains the premature secret of the eternal return.

4) Turning against oneself should not be confused with this destruction of self, this self-destruction. in the reactive process of turning against oneself active force becomes reactive. In self-destruction reactive forces are themselves denied and led to nothingness. This is why self-destruction is said to be an active operation an *"active destruction"* (VP III 8, EH III 1). It and it alone expresses the becoming-active of forces: forces become active insofar as reactive forces deny and suppress themselves in the name of a principle which, a short time ago, was still assuring their conservation and triumph. Active negation or active destruction is the state of strong spirits which destroy the reactive in themselves, submitting it to the test of the eternal return and submitting themselves to this test even if it entails willing their own decline; "it is the condition of strong spirits and wills, and these do not find it possible to stop with the negative of 'judgement'; their nature demands *active negation*" (VP III 102/WP 24). This is the only way in which reactive forces *become active*. Furthermore this is why negation, by making itself the negation of reactive forces themselves, is not only active but is, as it were, *transmuted*. It expresses affirmation and becoming-active as the power of affirming. Nietzsche then speaks of the "eternal joy of becoming . . . that joy which includes even joy in destroying", "The affirmation of passing away and *destroying*, which is the decisive feature of a Dionysian philosophy" (EH III "The Birth

of Tragedy" 3 p. 273);

5) The second selection in the eternal return is thus the following: the eternal return produces becoming-active. It is sufficient to relate the will to nothingness to the eternal return in order to realise that reactive forces do not return. However far they go, however deep the becoming-reactive of forces, reactive forces will not return. The small, petty, reactive man will not return. In and through the eternal return negation as a quality of the will to power transmutes itself into affirmation, it becomes an affirmation of negation itself, it becomes a power of affirming, an affirmative power. This is what Nietzsche presents as Zarathustra's cure and Dionysus' secret. "Nihilism vanquished by itself" thanks to the eternal return (VP III). This second selection is very different from the first. It is no longer a question of the simple thought of the eternal return eliminating from willing everything that falls outside this thought but rather, of the eternal return making something come into being which cannot do so without changing nature. It is no longer a question of selective thought but of selective being; for the eternal return is being and being is selection. (Selection = hierarchy)

15. The Problem of the Eternal Return

All this must be taken as a simple summary of texts. These texts will only be elucidated in terms of the following points: the relation of the two qualities of the will to power (negation and affirmation), the relation of the will to power itself with the eternal return, and the possibility of transmutation as a new way of feeling, thinking and above all being (the Overman). In Nietzsche's terminology the reversal of values means the active in place of the reactive (strictly speaking it is the reversal of a reversal, since the reactive began by taking the place of action). But *transmutation* of values, or *transvaluation*, means affirmation instead of negation – negation transformed into a power of affirmation, the supreme Dionysian metamorphosis. All these as yet unanalysed points form the summit of the doctrine of the eternal return.

From afar we can hardly see this summit. The eternal return is the being of becoming. But becoming is double: becoming-active and becoming-reactive, becoming-active of reactive forces and becoming reactive of active forces. But only becoming-active has being; it would be contradictory for the being of becoming to be affirmed of a becoming-reactive, of a becoming that is itself nihilistic. The eternal return would become contradictory if it were the return of reactive forces. The eternal return teaches us that becoming-reactive has no being. Indeed, it also teaches us of the existence of a becoming-active. It necessarily produces becoming-active by reproducing becoming. This is why affirmation is twofold: the being of becoming cannot be fully affirmed without also affirming the existence of becoming-active. The eternal return thus has a double aspect: it is the universal being of becoming, but the universal being of becoming ought to belong to a single becoming. Only becoming-active has a being which is the being of the whole of becoming. Returning is everything but everything is affirmed in a single moment. Insofar as the eternal return is affirmed as the universal being of becoming, insofar as becoming-active is also affirmed as the symptom and product of the universal eternal return, affirmation changes nuance and becomes more and more profound. Eternal return, as a physical doctrine, affirms the being of becoming. But, as selective ontology, it affirms this being of becoming as the "self-affirming" of becoming-active. We see that, at the heart of the complicity which joins Zarathustra and his animals, a misunderstanding arises, a problem the animals neither understand nor recognise, the problem of Zarathustra's disgust and cure. "O you buffoons and barrel organs! answered Zarathustra and smiled again . . . you – have already made an old song of it" (Z III "The Convalescent" pp. 234-5). The old song is the cycle and the whole, universal being. But the complete formula of affirmation is: the whole, yes, universal being, yes, but universal being ought to belong to a single becoming, the whole ought to belong to a single moment.

3

Critique

In Nietzsche's view the balance sheet of the sciences is a depressing one: *passive*, *reactive* and *negative* concepts predominate everywhere. They always try to interpret phenomena in terms of reactive forces. We have already seen this in the case of physics and biology. But when we look seriously at the sciences of man we see the development of the reactive and negative interpretation of phenomena: "utility", "adaptation", "regulation" and even "forgetting" serve as explanatory concepts (GM I 2). Ignorance of origins and of the genealogy of forces is obvious everywhere – in the sciences of man and even in those of nature. It could be said that the scientist sets up the triumph of reactive forces as his model and wants to chain thought to it. He makes much of his respect for facts and his love of truth. But the "fact" is an interpretation: what type of interpretation? Truth expresses a will: who wills truth? And what does he who says "I am seeking the truth" will? Science today is taking the exploration of nature and man further than ever in a particular direction, but it is also taking submission to the ideal and the established order further than ever. Scholars, even democratic and socialist ones, do not lack piety, they have merely invented a theology which no longer depends on the heart.[1] "Observe the ages in the history of peoples when the scholar steps into the foreground: they are ages of exhaustion, often of evening and decline" (GM III 25 p. 154).

The misrecognition of action, of all that is active, is obvious in the sciences of man: for example, action is judged in terms of its *utility*. It would be precipitate to say that utilitarianism is today an outdated doctrine. In the first place, if this is so it is partly thanks to Nietzsche. Furthermore, a doctrine only lets itself become outdated when it has spread its principles and hidden its postulates in the doctrines which succeed it. Nietzsche asks; what does the concept of utility refer to?

That is: to whom is an action useful or harmful? *Who* considers action from the standpoint of its utility or harmfulness, its motives and consequences? Not the one who acts: he does not "consider" action. It is rather the third party, the sufferer or the spectator. He is the person who considers the action that he does not perform – precisely because he does not perform it – as something to evaluate from the standpoint of the advantage which he draws or can draw from it. The person who does not act considers that he possesses a natural light over action, that he deserves to derive advantage or profit from it (GM I 2 and 10, BGE 260). We can guess the source of "utility": it is the source of all passive concepts in general, *ressentiment*, nothing but the requirements of *ressentiment*. Utility serves us as an example here. But, in any case, the taste for replacing real relations between forces by an abstract relation which is supposed to express them all, as a measure, seems to be an integral part of science and also of philosophy. In this respect Hegel's objective spirit is no more valid than the no less "objective" concept of utility. Now, in this abstract relation, whatever it is, we always end up replacing real activities (creating, speaking, loving etc.) by the third party's perspective on these activities: the essence of the activity is confused with the gains of a third party, which he claims that he ought to profit from, whose benefits he claims the right to reap (whether he is God, objective spirit, humanity, culture or even the proletariat . . .).

Take another example, that of linguistics. Language is usually judged from the standpoint of the hearer. Nietzsche dreams of another philology, an active philology. The secret of the word is no more on the side of the one who hears than the secret of the will is on the side of the one who obeys or the secret of force on the side of the one who reacts. Nietzsche's active philology has only one principle: a word only means[2]* something insofar as the speaker *wills* something by saying it; and one rule: treating speech as a real activity, placing oneself at the point of view of the speaker. "The lordly right of giving names extends so far that one should allow oneself to conceive the origin of language itself as an expression of power on the part of rulers: they say 'this *is* this and this', they seal every thing and event with a sound and, as it were, take possession of it" (GM 1 2 p. 26). Active linguistics looks to discover who it is that speaks and names. "Who uses a particular word, what does he apply it to first of all; himself, someone else who listens, something else, and with what intention?

What does he will by uttering a particular word?" The transformation of the sense of a word means that someone else (another force and another will) has taken possession of it and is applying it to another thing because he wants something else. The whole Nietzschean conception of etymology and philology, which is often misunderstood, depends on this principle and this rule. – Nietzsche applies it brilliantly in the *Genealogy of Morals* where he considers the word "good", its etymology, its sense and the transformation of this sense: he shows how the word "good" was originally created by the masters who applied it to themselves, then taken from their mouths by the slaves, who were then able to call the masters "the evil ones" (GM I 4, 5, 10, 11).

What would a truly active science be like, one permeated by active concepts like this new philology? Only an active science is capable of discovering active forces and also of recognising reactive forces for what they are – forces. Only an active science is capable of interpreting real activities and real relations between forces. It therefore appears in three forms. A *symptomatology*, since it interprets phenomena, treating them as symptoms whose sense must be sought in the forces that produce them. A *typology*, since it interprets forces from the standpoint of their quality, be it active or reactive. A *genealogy*, since it evaluates the origin of forces from the point of view of their nobility or baseness, since it discovers their ancestry in the will to power and the quality of this will. All the sciences, including the sciences of nature, are brought together in such a conception, as are science and philosophy (GM I Final Note). When science stops using passive concepts it stops being a positivism and philosophy ceases to be a utopia, a reverie on activity which makes up for this positivism. The philosopher as such is a symptomatologist, a typologist and a genealogist. We can recognise the Nietzschean trinity of the "philosopher of the future": the *philosopher-physician* (the physician interprets symptoms), the *philosopher-artist* (the artist moulds types), the *philosopher-legislator* (the legislator determines rank, genealogy) (cf. PTG, VP IV).

2. The Form of the Question in Nietzsche

Metaphysics formulated the question of essence in the form: "what is . . .?" We have perhaps picked up the habit of considering that this question is obvious; in fact we owe it to Socrates and Plato. We must go back to Plato to see just how far the question "what is . . .?" presupposes a particular way of thinking. Plato asks: "what is beauty? what is justice?" etc. He wants to oppose this form of the question to all other forms. He sometimes sets Socrates against very young men, sometimes against stubborn old men, sometimes against famous sophists. They all seem to produce the same form of reply, citing *the one that* is just, *the one that* is beautiful: a young virgin, a mare, a cooking pot . . .³* Socrates triumphs: one does not reply to the question "what is beauty?" by citing *the one that* is beautiful. So we get the distinction, dear to Plato, between beautiful things – which are only beautiful, for example, accidentally and according to becoming – and Beauty – which is nothing but beautiful, necessarily beautiful, *the one that is beautiful* in its being and essence. This is why, in Plato, the opposition of essence and appearance, of being and becoming, depends primarily on a mode of questioning, a form of question. Nevertheless, we should ask ourselves whether Socrates' triumph is deserved. For this Soctratic method does not seem to be fruitful: it dominates the so-called "aporetic" dialogues, where nihilism is king. It is undoubtedly a blunder to cite something beautiful when you are asked "what is beauty?" But it is less certain that the question: "what is beauty?" is not itself a blunder. It is by no means certain that it is legitimate and well put, even and above all as a way of discovering essence. Sometimes a brief flash of light in the dialogues gives us a momentary indication of what the sophist idea was. Mixing the sophists up with old men and youngsters is a procedure of amalgamation. The sophist Hippias was not a child who was content to answer the question "which one?" when asked the question "what is?" He thought that the question "which one?" was the best kind of question, the most suitable one for determining essence. For it does not refer, as Socrates believed, to discrete examples, but to the continuity of concrete objects taken in their becoming, to the becoming-beautiful of all the objects citable or cited as examples. Asking which one is beautiful, which one is just and not what beauty is, what justice is, was therefore the result of a worked-out method, implying an original conception of essence and a whole sophistic art which was opposed to the dialectic. An empirical and pluralist art.

"What is it? I cried out with curiosity – *which one is it?* you ought to ask! Thus spoke Dionysus, then kept quiet in his own special way, that is to say, in an enticing way."⁴ According to Nietzsche the

question "which one?" (*qui*) means this: what are the forces which
take hold of a given thing, what is the will that possesses it? Which one
is expressed, manifested and even hidden in it? We are led to essence
only by the question: which one? For *essence is merely the sense and
value of the thing*; essence is determined by the forces with affinity for
the thing and by the will with affinity for these forces. Moreover,
when we ask the question "what is it?" (*qu'est-ce que*) we not only fall
into the worst metaphysics but in fact we merely ask the question
"which one?" in a blind, unconscious and confused way. The question "what is it?" is a way of establishing a sense seen from another
point of view. Essence, being, is a perspectival reality and presupposes a plurality. Fundamentally it is always the question "What is it
for me?" (for us, for everyone that sees etc.) (VP I 204). What we ask
what beauty is we ask from what standpoint things appear beautiful:
and something which does not appear beautiful to us, from what
standpoint would it become so? And for a particular thing, what are
the forces which make or would make it beautiful by appropriating it,
what are the other factors which yield to these or, on the contrary,
resist them. The pluralist art does not deny essence: it makes it
depend, in each case, on an affinity of phenomena and forces, on a
coordination of force and will. The essence of a thing is discovered in
the force which possesses it and which is expressed in it, it is
developed in the forces with affinity for this first one, endangered or
destroyed by the forces which are opposed to it and which can take
hold of it. Essence is always sense and value. And so the question
"which one?" reverberates in and for all things: which forces, which
will? This is the *tragic* question. At the deepest level the whole of it is
held out to Dionysus. For Dionysus is the god who hides and reveals
himself, Dionysus is will, Dionysus is the one that . . . The question
"which one?" finds its supreme instance[5*] in Dionysus or in the will
to power; Dionysus, the will to power, is the one that answers it each
time it is put. We should not ask "which one wills?", "which one
interprets?", "which one evaluates?" for everywhere and always the
will to power is *the one that* (VP I 204). Dionysus is the god of
transformations, the unity of multiplicity, the unity that affirms
multiplicity and is affirmed of it. "Which one is it?" – it is always him.
This is why Dionysus keeps tantalisingly quiet: to gain time to hide
himself, to take another form and to change forces. In Nietzsche's
work the admirable poem "Ariadne's Complaint" expresses this fun-

damental relation between a way of questioning and the divinity hidden behind every question – between the pluralist question and Dionysian or tragic affirmation (DD "Ariadne's Complaint").

3. Nietzsche's Method

From this form of question there derives a method. Any given concept, feeling or belief will be treated as symptoms of a will that wills something. What does *the one that* says this, that thinks or feels that, will? It is a matter of showing that he could not say, think or feel this particular thing if he did not have a particular will, particular forces, a particular way of being. What does he will the one who speaks, loves or creates? And conversely what does the one who profits from an action that he does not do, the one who appeals to "disinterestedness", what does he will? And what about the ascetic, and the utilitarians with their concept of utility? And Schopenhauer when he creates the strange concept of a *negation of the will*? Was this true? But what do they ultimately want, the truth-seekers, those who say: I'm looking for the truth.[6] – Willing is not an act like any other. Willing is the critical and genetic instance of all our actions, feelings and thoughts. The method is as follows: relating a concept to the will to power in order to make it the symptom of a will without which it could not even be thought (nor the feeling experienced, nor the action undertaken). This method corresponds to the tragic question. It is itself the *tragic method*. Or, more precisely, if we remove from the word "drama" all the Christian and dialectical pathos which taints it, it is the method of *dramatisation*. "What do you will?" Ariadne asks Dionysus. What a will wants – this is the latent content of the corresponding thing.

We must not be deceived by the expression: *what* the will wants. What a will wants is not an object, an objective or an end. Ends and objects, even motives, are still symptoms. What a will wants, depending on its quality, is to affirm its difference or to deny what differs. Only qualities are ever willed: the heavy, the light . . . What a will wants is always its own quality and the quality of the corresponding forces. As Nietzsche says of the noble, affirmative and light soul, it has "some fundamental certainty . . . in regard to itself, something which may not be sought or found and perhaps may not be lost either" (BGE 287 p. 196). Thus, when we ask: "what does the one who thinks this want?" we do not abandon the fundamental question "which one?" we merely give it a rule and a methodical development. We are demanding that the question be answered not by *examples* but by the determination of a *type*. And, a type is in fact constituted by the quality of the will to power, the nuance of this quality and the corresponding relation of forces: everything else is symptom. What a will wants is not an object but a type, the type of the one that speaks, of the one that thinks, that acts, that does not act, that reacts etc. A type can only be defined by determining what the will wants in the examplars of this type. What does the one that seeks truth want? This is the only way of knowing which one seeks truth. The method of dramatisation is thus presented as the only method adequate to Nietzsche's project and to the form of the questions that he puts: a differential, typological and genealogical method.

There is, however, a second objection to such a method: its anthropological character. But all we need to consider is the *type* of man himself. If it is true that the triumph of reactive forces constitutes man, then the whole method of dramatisation aims to discover other types expressing other relations of forces, to discover another quality of the will to power capable of transmuting its too-human nuances. According to Nietzsche the inhuman and the superhuman – a thing, an animal or a god – are no less capable of dramatisation than a man or his determinations. They too are transformations of Dionysus, symptoms of a will which wants something. They too express a type, a type of forces unknown to man. The method of dramatisation surpasses man on every side. A will of the Earth, what would a will capable of affirming the Earth be like? What does it want, this will without which the Earth itself remains meaningless? What is its quality, a quality which also becomes the quality of the Earth? Nietzsche replies: "The weightless . . ."[7]

4. *Against his Predecessors*

What does "will to power" mean? Not, primarily, that the will wants power, that it desires or seeks out power as an end, nor that power is the motive of the will. The expression "desiring power" is no less absurd than "willing to live". He who shot the doctrine of "will to life" at truth certainly did not hit the truth: this will does not exist! "For what does not exist cannot will; but that which is alive, how could it still will to live?" (Z II "Of Self-Overcoming" p. 138 and Z III "Of Three Evil Things"). This is why, in spite of appearances, Nietzsche is of the opinion that the will to power is an entirely new concept that he has created himself and introduced into philosophy. He says, with appropriate modesty; "To conceive psychology as I have done, as morphology and the development-theory of the will to power – has never yet so much entered the mind of anyone else: insofar as it is permissible to see in what has hitherto been written a symptom of what has hitherto been kept silent" (BGE 23 p. 38). But more than one writer before Nietzsche had spoken of a will to power or something analogous; more than one after Nietzsche spoke of it again. But the latter were no more disciples of Nietzsche than the former were his masters. They always spoke of it in the sense expressly condemned by Nietzsche: as if power were the ultimate aim of the will and also its essential motive. *As if power were what the will wanted*. But, such a conception implies at least three misunderstandings which threaten the whole philosophy of the will:

1) Power is interpreted as the object of a *representation*. In the expression "the will wants power or desires domination", the relation of representation and power is so close that all power is represented and every representation is of power. The aim of the will is also the object of representation and vice versa. In Hobbes, man in the state of nature wants to see his superiority represented and recognised by others. In Hegel, consciousness wants to be recognised by another and represented as self-consciousness. Even in Adler it is still a matter of the representation of a superiority which, when necessary, compensates for the existence of an organic inferiority. In all these cases power is always the object of a representation, of a *recognition* which materially presupposes a comparison of consciousnesses. It is therefore necessary for the will to power to have a corresponding motive which would also serve as the motor of comparison: vanity, pride, self-love, display or even a feeling of inferiority. Nietzsche asks: *who* conceives of the will to power as a will to get oneself recognised? Who conceives of power itself as the object of a recognition? Who essentially wants to be represented as superior and even wants his inferiority to be represented as superiority? It is the sick who want "to represent superiority under any form whatsoever" (GM III 14). "It is the slave who seeks to persuade us to have a good opinion of him; it is also the slave who then bends his knee before these opinions as if it wasn't him

who produced them. And I repeat: vanity is an atavism."[8] What we present to ourselves as power itself is merely the representation of power formed by the slave. What we present to ourselves as the master is the idea of him formed by the slave, the idea formed by the slave when he imagines himself in the master's place, it is the slave as he is when he actually triumphs, "this need *for* the noble is fundamentally different from the needs of the noble soul itself, and in fact an eloquent and dangerous sign of its lack" (BGE 287 p. 196). Why have philosophers accepted this false image of the master which resembles only the triumphant slave? Everything is ready for an eminently dialectical sleight of hand: having put the slave into the master, they realise that the truth of the master is in the slave. In fact everything has happened between slaves, conquering or conquered. The mania for representing, for being represented, for getting oneself represented; for having representatives and representeds: this is the mania that is common to all slaves, the only relation between themselves they can conceive of, the relation that they impose with their triumph. The notion of representation poisons philosophy: it is the direct product of the slave and of the relations between slaves, it constitutes the worst, most mediocre and most base interpretation of power (VP III 254).

2) What is the nature of this first error of the philosophy of the will? When we make power an object of representation we necessarily make it dependent upon the factor according to which a thing is represented or not, recognised or not. Now, only values which are already current, only accepted values, give criteria of recognition in this way. The will to power, understood as the will to get oneself recognised, is necessarily the will to have the values current in a given society attributed to oneself (power, money, honours, reputation).[9] But here again, who conceives of power as the acquisition of assignable values? "The common man never had any value but that which was attributed to him; in no way accustomed to positing values himself, he attributed to himself no other value than that which was recognised in him" (BGE 261), or even that which he got them to recognise. Rousseau reproached Hobbes for having produced a portrait of man in the state of nature which presupposed society. In a very different spirit an analogous reproach is found in Nietzsche: the whole conception of the will to power, from Hobbes to Hegel, presupposes the existence of established values that wills seek only to have attributed to themselves. What seems symptomatic in this philosophy of the will is

conformism, absolute misrecognition of the will to power as *creation* of new values.

3) We must still ask: how are established values attributed? It is always as the result of a combat, a struggle, whatever form this takes – whether secret or open, honest or underhand. From Hobbes to Hegel the will to power is engaged in combat, precisely because the combat determines those who will profit from current values. It is characteristic of established values to be brought into play in a struggle, but it is characteristic of the struggle to be always referred to established values: whether it is struggle for power, struggle for recognition or struggle for life – the schema is always the same. One cannot over-emphasise *the extent to which the notions of struggle, war, rivalry or even comparison are foreign to Nietzsche and to his conception of the will to power.* It is not that he denies the existence of struggle: but he does not see it as in any way creative of values. At least, the only values that it creates are those of the triumphant slave. Struggle is not the principle or the motor of hierarchy but the means by which the slave reverses hierarchy. Struggle is never the active expression of forces, nor the manifestation of a will to power that affirms – any more than its result expresses the triumph of the master or the strong. Struggle, on the contrary, is the means by which the weak prevail over the strong because they are the greatest number. This is why Nietzsche is opposed to Darwin: Darwin confused struggle and selection. He failed to see that the result of struggle was the opposite of what he thought; that it does select, but it selects only the weak and assures their triumph (VP I 395, TI). Nietzsche says of himself that he is much too well bred to struggle.[10] He also says of the will to power "Abstraction being made from struggle" (VP II 72).

5. *Against Pessimism and against Schopenhauer*

These three misundestandings would be unimportant if they did not introduce an extremely unfortunate "tone" or emotional tonality into the philosophy of the will. The essence of the will is always discovered with grief and dejection. All those who discover the essence of the will in a will to power or something analogous never stop complaining about their discovery, as if they ought to draw from it the strange resolve to flee from it or to ward off its effects. It is as if the essence of the will puts us into an unlivable, untenable and deceptive situation

And this is easily explained: making the will a will to power in the sense of a "desire to dominate", philosophers see this desire as infinite; making power an object of representation they see the unreal character of a thing represented in this way; engaging the will to power in combat they see the contradiction in the will itself. According to Hobbes the will to power is as if in a dream from which only the fear of death will rescue it. Hegel insists on the unreality of the situation of the master, for the master depends on the slave for recognition. Everyone puts contradiction into the will and also the will into contradiction. Represented power is only appearance; the essence of the will does not establish itself in what is willed without losing itself in appearance. Thus philosophers promise the will a *limitation*, a rational or contractual limitation which is the only thing which will be able to make it livable and resolve contradiction. Schopenhauer does not inaugurate a new philosophy of the will in any of these respects. On the contrary, his genius consists in drawing out the extreme consequences of the old philosophy, in pushing the old philosophy as far as it can go. Schopenhauer is not content with an essence of the will, he makes the will the essence of things, "the world seen from the inside". The will has become essence in general and in itself. But, on this basis, what it wants (its objectification) has become representation, appearance in general. Its contradiction become the basic contradiction: as essence it wills the appearance in which it is reflected. "The fate which awaits the will in the world in which it is reflected" is just the suffering of this contradiction. This is the formula of the will to live; the world as will *and* representation. We recognise here the development of a mystification which began with Kant. By making will the essence of things or the world seen from the inside, the distinction between two worlds is denied in principle: the same world is both sensible and super-sensible. But while denying this distinction between worlds one merely replaces it with the distinction between interior and exterior – which is just like that between essence and appearance, that is to say like the two worlds themselves. By making will the essence of the world Schopenhauer continues to understand the world as an illusion, an appearance, a representation (BGE 36, VP I 216 and III 325). – Limiting the will is therefore not going to be enough for Schopenhauer. The will must be denied, it must deny itself. The Schopenhauerian choice: "We are stupid beings or, at best, beings who suppress themselves" (VP III 40). Schopenhauer teaches us that a rational or contractual limitation of the will is not enough, that we must go all the way to mystical suppression. This was the aspect of Schopenhauer that was influential, that influenced Wagner, for example: not his critique of metaphysics, not his "cruel sense of reality", not his anti-Christianity, nor his profound analysis of human mediocrity, not the way in which he showed that phenomena are symptoms of a will, but the complete opposite, the way in which he made the will less and less bearable, less and less livable, at the same time as he was christening it will to live . . . (GS 99).

6. *Principles for the Philosophy of the Will*

According to Nietzsche the philosophy of the will must replace the old metaphysics: it destroys and supersedes it. Nietzsche thinks that he produced the first philosophy of the will, that all the others were the final avatars of metaphysics. The philosophy of the will as he conceives it has two principles which together form the glad tidings: "willing = creating" and "will = joy", "my *willing* always comes to me as my liberator and bringer of joy. Willing liberates: that is the true doctrine of will and freedom – thus Zarathustra teaches you" (Z II "On the Blissful Isles" p. 111). "Will – that is what the liberator and bringer of joy is called: thus I have taught you my friends! But now learn this as well; The will itself is still a prisoner. Willing liberates . . ." (Z II "Of Redemption" p. 161). "That willing becomes not-willing – how you, my brothers, know this fable-song of madness! I have led you away from these fable-songs when I taught you: " 'The will is a creator' " (ibid. p. 162)." "It is the intrinsic *right of masters* to create values" (BGE 261 p. 179). Why does Nietzsche present these two principles, creation and joy, as the main point of Zarathustra's teaching, as the two ends of a hammer head which must drive in and pull out? Although these principles may appear vague or undetermined they take on an extremely precise meaning if one understands their critical aspect, that is to say, the way in which they are opposed to previous conceptions of the will. Nietzsche says: the will to power has been conceived as if the will wanted power, as if the power were what the will wanted. Consequently power has turned into something represented, an idea of power of the slave and the impotent was formed, power was judged according to the attribution of ready-made established values; the will to power was not conceived of independently of a combat in which the prize was these established values; consequently the will to power was identified with contradiction and the suffering of contradiction. Against this *fettering* of the will Nietzsche announces that willing *liberates*; against the *suffering* of the will Nietzsche announces that the will is *joyful*. Against the image of a will which dreams of having *established* values attributed to it Nietzsche announces that to will is *to create* new values.

Will to power does not mean that the will wants power. Will to power does not imply any anthropomorphism in its origin, signification or essence. Will to power must be interpreted in a completely different way: power is *the one that* wills in the will. Power is the genetic and differential element in the will. This is why the will is essentially creative. This is also why power is never measured against representation: it is never represented, it is not even interpreted or evaluated, it is "the one that" interprets, "the one that" evaluates, "the one that" wills. But what does it will? It wills precisely that which derives from the genetic element. The genetic element (power) determines the relation of force with force and qualifies related forces. As plastic element it simultaneously determines and is determined, simultaneously qualifies and is qualified. What the will to power wills is a particular relation of forces, a particular quality of forces. And also a particular quality of power: affirming or denying. This complex, which varies in every case, forms a type to which given phenomena correspond. All phenomena express relations of forces, qualities of forces and of power, nuances of these qualities, in short, a type of force and will. In Nietzsche's terms, we must say that every phenomenon not only reflects a type which constitutes its sense and value, but also the will to power as the element from which the signification of its sense and the value of its value derive. *In this way the will to power is essentially creative and giving*: it does not aspire, it does not seek, it does not desire, above all it does not desire power. It *gives*: power is something inexpressible in the will (something mobile, variable, plastic); power is in the will as "the bestowing virtue", through power the will itself bestows sense and value.[11] We should not ask whether, in the final analysis, the will to power is unitary or multiple – this would show a general misunderstanding of Nietzsche's philosophy. The will to power is plastic, inseparable from each case in which it is determined; just as the eternal return is being, but being which is affirmed of becoming, the will to power is unitary, but unity which is affirmed of multiplicity. The monism of the will to power is inseparable from a pluralist typology.

The element which creates sense and values must also be defined as the *critical* element. A type of forces not only signifies a quality of forces but a relation between qualified forces. The active type not only designates active forces but a hierarchical whole in which active forces prevail over the reactive forces and where reactive forces are acted; conversely the reactive type designates a whole in which reactive forces triumph and separate active forces from what they can do. It is in this sense that the type implies the quality of power by which certain forces prevail over others. *High* and *noble* designate, for Nietzsche, the superiority of active forces, their affinity with affirmation, their tendency to ascend, their lightness. *Low* and *base* designate the triumph of reactive forces, their affinity with the negative, their heaviness or clumsiness. Many phenomena can only be interpreted as expressing this heavy triumph of reactive forces. Is the whole human phenomenon not an example of this? There are things which are only able to exist through reactive forces and their victory. There are things which can only be said, thought or felt, values which can only be believed, if one is animated by reactive forces. Nietzsche makes this more specific; if one has a heavy and base soul. There is a certain baseness of the soul which is more than error, more than stupidity itself.[12] Thus the typology of forces and the doctrine of the will to power are inseparable, in turn, from a critique which can be used to determine the genealogy of values, their nobility and baseness. – Of course one may ask in what sense and why noble is "worth more" than base or high "worth more" than low. By what right? There is no possible reply to this question if as we consider the will to power in itself or abstractly, as merely endowed with two opposite qualities, affirmation and negation. Why should affirmation be better than negation?[13] We will see that the solution can only be given by the test of the eternal return: what is better and better absolutely is that which returns, that which can bear returning, that which wills its return. The test of the eternal return will not let reactive forces subsist, any more than it will let the power of denying subsist. The eternal return transmutes the negative: it turns the heavy into something light, it makes the negative cross over to affirmation, it makes negation a power of affirming. But negation in this new form has become critique: destruction becomes active, aggression profoundly linked to affirmation. Critique is destruction as joy, the aggression of the creator. The creator of values cannot be distinguished from a destroyer, from a criminal or from a critic: a critic of established values, reactive values and baseness.[14]

7. *Plan of* The Genealogy of Morals

The Genealogy of Morals is Nietzsche's most systematic book. Its interest is twofold: in the first place it is presented neither as a collection of aphorisms nor as a poem, but as a key for the interpretation of aphorisms and the evaluation of poems (GM Preface 8). In the second place it gives a detailed analysis of the reactive type, of the mode and principle of the triumph of reactive forces. The first essay deals with *ressentiment*, the second with bad conscience and the third with the ascetic ideal: *ressentiment*, bad conscience and the ascetic ideal are the figures of the triumph of reactive forces and also the forms of nihilism. – This double aspect of *The Genealogy of Morals* – its presentation as key for interpretation in general and as analysis of the reactive type in particular – is not accidental. Indeed, is it not the pressure of reactive forces themselves that puts obstacles in the way of the arts of interpretation and evaluation, that perverts genealogy and reverses hierarchy? The two aspects of *The Genealogy of Morals* thus form a *critique*. But what critique is and in what sense philosophy is a critique – all this remains to be analysed.

We know that reactive forces triumph by relying on a fiction. Their victory always rests on the negative as something imaginary: they separate active force from what it can do. Active force thus becomes reactive in reality, but as a result of a mystification.

1) From the first essay Nietzsche presents *ressentiment* as "an imaginary revenge", "an essentially spiritual vindication" (GM I 7 and 10). Moreover, the constitution of *ressentiment* implies a *paralogism* that Nietzsche analyses in detail: the paralogism of force separated from what it can do (GM I 13).

2) The second essay underlines the fact that bad conscience is inseparable from "spiritual and imaginary events" (GM II 18). Bad conscience is by nature *antinomic*, expressing a force which is turned against itself.[15] In this sense it is the basis of what Nietzsche calls "the inverted world" (GM III 14 p. 124). We may note, in general, how much Nietzsche enjoys underlining the insufficiency of the Kantian

conception of antimony: Kant did not understand their source or their true extention.[16]

3) Finally, the ascetic ideal refers to the deepest mystification – that of the *Ideal*, which includes all the others, all the fictions of morality and knowledge. *Elegantia syllogismi*, Nietzsche says. Here we are dealing with a will that wants nothingness, "but it is at least, and always remains, a will" (GM III 28).

We are merely trying to bring out the formal structure of the *Genealogy of Morals*. If we stop thinking that the organisation of the three essays is fortuitous we must conclude that Nietzsche, in the *Genealogy of Morals*, wanted to rewrite the *Critique of Pure Reason*. Paralogism of the soul, antimony of the world, mystification of the ideal: Nietzsche thinks that the idea of critique is identical to that of philosophy but that this is precisely the idea that Kant has missed, that he has compromised and spoilt, not only in its application but in principle. Chestov takes pleasure in finding the true *Critique of Pure Reason* in Dostoyevsky, in the *Notes From the Underground*. It is, in fact, primarily a Nietzschean idea to say that Kant's critique failed. But Nietzsche does not rely on anyone but himself to conceive and accomplish the true critique. This project is of great importance for the history of philosophy; for it runs counter not only to Kantianism, with which it competes, but to the whole Kantian inheritance, to which it is violently opposed. What became of critique after Kant, from Hegel to Feuerbach via the famous "critical critique"? – It became an art by which mind, self-consciousness, the critic himself, adapted themselves to things and ideas; or an art by which man reappropriated determinations which he claimed to have been deprived of: in short, the dialectic. But this dialectic, this new critique, carefully avoids asking the preliminary question: "*Who* must undertake critique, who is fit to undertake it?" They talk of reason, spirit, self-consciousness and man; but *to whom* do all these concepts refer? They do not tell us who man or spirit is. Spirit seems to hide forces which are ready to be reconciled with any kind of power, with Church or State. When the little man reappropriates little things, when the reactive man reappropriates reactive determinations, is it thought that critique has made great progress, that it has thereby proved its activity? If man is a reactive being what right has he to undertake a critique? Does the recuperation of religion stop us being religious? By turning theology into anthropology, by putting man in God's place, do we abolish the essential, that is to say, the place? All these ambiguities begin with the Kantian critique.[17] In Kant, critique was not able to discover the truly active instance which would have been capable of carrying it through. It is exhausted by compromise: it never makes us overcome the reactive forces which are expressed in man, self-consciousness, reason, morality and religion. It even has the opposite effect – it turns these forces into something a little more "our own". Finally, Nietzsche's relation to Kant is like Marx's to Hegel: Nietzsche stands critique on its feet, just as Marx does with the dialectic. But this analogy, far from reconciling Marx and Nietzsche, separates them still further. For the dialectic comes from the original Kantian form of critique. There would have been no need to put the dialectic back on its feet, nor "to do" any form of dialectics if critique itself had not been standing on its head from the start.

8. Nietzsche and Kant from the Point of View of Principles

Kant is the first philosopher who understood critique as having to be total and positive *as* critique. Total because "nothing must escape it"; positive, affirmative, because it can not restrict the power of knowing without releasing other previously neglected powers. But what are the results of such a vast project? Can the reader seriously believe that, in the *Critique of Pure Reason*, "Kant's *victory* over the dogmatic concepts of theology ('God', 'soul', 'freedom', 'immorality') damaged that ideal" (GM III 25 p. 156) and can we really believe that Kant "ever had any intention of doing such a thing"? As for the *Critique of Practical Reason* does not Kant admit, from its opening pages, that it is not really a critique at all? He seems to have confused the positivity of critique with a humble recognition of the rights of the criticised. There has never been a more conciliatory or respectful total critique. This opposition between project and results (moreover between the general project and the particular intentions) is easily explained. Kant merely pushed a very old conception of critique to the limit, a conception which saw critique as a force which should be brought to bear on all claims to knowledge and truth, but not on knowledge and truth themselves; a force which should be brought to bear on all claims to morality, but not on morality itself. Thus total critique turns into the politics of compromise: even before the battle the spheres of influence have already been shared out. Three ideals are distinguished: what can I know? what should I do? what can I hope for? Limits are drawn to each one, misuses and trespasses are denounced, but the uncritical character of each ideal remains at the heart of Kantianism like the worm in the fruit: true knowledge, true morality and true religion. What Kant still calls – in his own terms – a fact: the fact of morality, the fact of knowledge . . . The Kantian taste for the demarcation of domains was finally freed, allowed to play its own game, in the *Critique of Judgment*; we learn here what we had known from the start, that the only object of Kant's critique is justification, it begins by believing in what it criticises.

Is this the announcement of the great politics? Nietzsche notes that there has not yet been a "great politics". Critique is nothing and says nothing insofar as it is content to say that true morality makes fun of morality. Critique has done nothing insofar as it has not been brought to bear on truth itself, on true knowledge, on true morality, on true religion.[18] Every time that Nietzsche denounces virtue he is not denouncing false virtues, nor those which make use of virtue as a mask. It is virtue itself in itself, that is to say the pettiness of true virtue, the unbelievable mediocrity of true morality, the baseness of its authentic values that he attacks. "Zarathustra leaves no doubt at this point: he says that it was insight precisely into the good, the 'best', that made him shudder at man in general; that it was from this aversion that he grew wings" (EH IV pp. 330–31). However much we criticise false morality or false religion we remain poor critics, "her majesty's opposition", sad apologists. It is a "justice of the peace's" critique. We may criticise pretenders, we may condemn those who trespass on domains, but we regard the domains themselves as sacred. Similarly for knowledge: a critique worthy of the name must not bear on the pseudo-knowledge of the unknowable, but primarily on the true knowledge of what can be known (VP I 189). This is why Nietzsche, in this domain as in others, thinks that he has found the only possible principle of a total critique in what he calls his "perspectivism": there are no moral facts or phenomena, but only a moral interpretation of phenomena (VP II 550); there are no illusions of knowledge, but knowledge itself is an illusion; knowledge is an error, or worse, a falsification.[19] (Nietzsche owes this final proposition to Schopenhauer. This was the way in which Schopenhauer interpreted Kantianism, radically transforming it in an opposite direction to the dialecticians. Schopenhauer was thus able to prepare the principle of critique: he had stumbled across its weak point, morality.)

9. *Realisation of Critique*

Kant's genius, in the *Critique of Pure Reason*, was to conceive of an immanent critique. Critique must not be a critique of reason by feeling, by experiencing or by any kind of external instance. And what is criticised is no longer external to reason: we should not seek, in reason, errors which have come from elsewhere – from body, senses or passions – but illusions coming from reason as such. Now, caught between these two demands, Kant concludes that critique must be a critique *of* reason *by* reason itself. Is this not the Kantian contradiction, making reason both the tribunal and the accused; constituting it as judge and plaintiff, judging and judged? (VP I 185). – Kant lacked a method which permitted reason to be judged from the inside without giving it the task of being its own judge. And, in fact, Kant does not realise his project of immanent critique. Transcendental philosophy discovers conditions which still remain external to the conditioned. Trascendental principles are principles of conditioning and not of internal genesis. We require a genesis of reason itself, and also a genesis of the understanding and its categories: what are the forces of reason and of the understanding? What is the will which hides and expresses itself in reason? What stands behind reason, in reason itself? In the will to power and the method which derives from it Nietzsche has at his disposal a principle of internal genesis. When we compared the will to power with a transcendental principle, when we compared nihilism in the will to power with an *a priori* structure, our main aim was to indicate how they differed from psychological determinations. Nevertheless, in Nietzsche, principles are never transcendental; it is these very principles which are replaced by genealogy. Only the will to power as genetic and genealogical principle, as legislative principle, is capable of realising internal critique. Only the will to power makes a transmutation possible.

In Nietzsche the *philosopher-legislator* appears as the philosopher of the future; to legislate means to create values. "*Actual philosophers . . . are commanders and law givers*" (BGE 211 p. 123). This is the Nietzschean inspiration behind Chestov's fine writings: "For us all truths derive from the *parere* – even metaphysical ones. And nevertheless, the only source of metaphysical truths is the *jubere*, insofar as men will not participate in the *jubere*, it will seem to them that metaphysics is impossible." "The Greeks felt that submission, the obedient acceptance of all that presents itself, hides true being from man. In order to reach true reality one must consider oneself as the master of the world, one must learn to command and create . . . Here, where sufficient reason is lacking and where, according to us, all possibility of thinking ceases, they saw the beginning of metaphysical truth."[26] It is not that the philosopher must add the activity of the legislator to his other activities because he is in the best position to do this – as if his own subjection to wisdom qualified him to discover the best possible laws to which men in their turn ought to be subjected. The point is a completely different one: that the philosopher, as philosopher, *is not* a sage, that the philosopher, as philosopher, ceases to obey, that he replaces the old wisdom by command, that he destroys the old values and creates new ones, that the whole of his science is legislative in this sense. "Their 'knowing' is creating, their *creating* is a law-giving, their will to truth is – *will to power*" (BGE 211 p. 123). While it is true that this idea of the philosopher has pre-socratic roots it seems that its reappearance in the modern world is Kantian and critical. *Jubere* instead of *parere*: is this not the essence of the Copernican revolution and the way in which critique is opposed to the old wisdom, to dogmatic or theological subjection? The idea that *philosophy legislates* as *philosophy* makes the idea that critique *as* critique is internal complete: together they form Kantianism's principal achievement, its liberating achievement.

But in what way did Kant understand his idea of philosophy-legislation? Why does Nietzsche, at the very moment when he seems to revive and develop the Kantian idea, rank Kant among the "philosophical labourers", those who are content to make inventories of current values, the opposite of the philosophers of the future? (BGE 211 p. 123). For Kant, what legislates (in a domain) is always one of our faculties: understanding, reason. We are legislators ourselves only insofar as we make proper use of this faculty and allot our other faculties tasks which conform to it. We are legislators only insofar as we submit to one of our faculties, as it were the whole of ourselves. But to what do we submit in such a faculty, to what forces? Understanding and reason have a long history: they are instances which still make us obey when we no longer want to obey anyone. When we stop obeying God, the State, our parents, reason appears and persuades us to continue being docile because it says to us: it is you who are giving the orders. Reason represents our slavery and our subjection as something superior which make us reasonable beings. Under the name of practical reason, "Kant invented a reason expressly for those cases in which one has no need to bother about reason: namely, when the needs of the heart, when morality, when 'duty' speaks".[21] And, finally, what is concealed in the famous Kantian unity of legislator and subject? Nothing but a renovated theology, theology with a protestant flavour: we are burdened with the double task of priest and believer, legislator and subject. Kant's dream was not to abolish the distinction between two worlds (sensible and super-sensible) but to secure *the unity of the personal* in the two worlds. The same person as legislator and subject, as subject and object, as noumenon and phenomenon, as priest and believer. This arrangement succeeds as theology: "Kant's success is only a theologian's success" (AC 10). Can we really believe that by installing the priest and the legislator *in us* we stop being primarily believers and subjects? The legislators and the priest practise the ministry, the legislation and the representation of established values; all they do is internalise current values. Kant's "proper usage of the faculties" mysteriously coincides with these established values: true knowledge, true morality, true religion . . .

10. Nietzsche and Kant from the Point of View of Consequences

The Nietzschean and the Kantian conceptions of critique are opposed on five main points.

1) Genetic and plastic principles that give an account of the sense and value of beliefs, interpretations and evaluations rather than transcedental principles which are simple conditions for so-called facts.

2) A thought which thinks *against* reason rather than a thought that believes itself to be legislative because it is subject to reason alone – "That which will always be impossible, a reasonable being" (Z). It is a serious mistake to think that irrationalism opposes anything but thought to reason – whether it be the rights of the given, of the heart, of feeling, caprice or passion. In irrationalism we are concerned only with thought, only with thinking. What is opposed to reason is thought itself; what is opposed to the reasonable being is the thinker himself.[22] Because it is reason which receives and expresses the rights of that which dominates thought, thought reconquers its rights and becomes a legislator against reason: *the dicethrow*, this was the sense of the dicethrow.

3) The genealogist rather than the Kantian legislator. Kant's legislator is an arbitrator, a justice of the peace who supervises the distribution of domains and the allocation of established values. The genealogical inspiration is the opposite of the judicial inspiration. The genealogist is the true legislator. The genealogist is something of a fortuneteller, the philosopher of the future. He does not foretell a critical peace but wars such as we have never known (EH IV 1). He also sees thinking as judging, but judging is evaluating and interpreting, it is creating values. The problem of judgment becomes that of justice and hierarchy.

4) The reactive man serving himself rather than the reasonable being, functionary of current values, both priest and believer, legislator and subject, conquering and conquered slave. But, in that case, which one undertakes critique? What is the critical standpoint? The critical instance is not the realised man, nor any sublimated form of man, spirit, reason or self-consciousness. It is neither God nor man – for there is still not enough difference between man and God, they can replace each other too easily. The critical instance is the will to power, the critical perspective is that of the will to power. But in what form? Not that of the Overman who is the positive product of critique itself. But there is a "relatively superhuman type" (EH IV 5): the critical type, man *insofar as he wants to be gone beyond, overcome* . . . "But you could transform yourselves into forefathers and ancestors of the Overman: and let this be your finest creation!" (Z II "On the Blissful Isles" p. 110).

5) The aim of critique is not the ends of man or of reason but in the end the Overman, the overcome, overtaken man. The point of critique is not justification but a different way of feeling: another sensibility.

11. *The Concept of Truth*

"Truth was posited as being, as God, as the highest court of appeal . . . The will to truth requires a critique – let us thus define our own task – the value of truth must for once be experimentally *called into question*" (GM III 24 p. 152 and 153). It is at this point that Kant is the last of the classical philosophers: he never questions the value of truth or the reasons for our subjection to it. In this respect he is as dogmatic as anyone else. None of them ask: who is seeking truth? In other words: what does the one who seeks the truth want? What is his type, his will to power? Let us try and understand the nature of this deficiency in philosophy. It is well known that in fact man rarely seeks after truth: our interests and also our stupidity separate us from truth even more than our errors do. But philosophers claim that thought seeks truth, that it loves and wills truth "by right". By establishing a bond of right between thought and truth, by relating the will of a pure thinker to truth in this way, philosophy avoids relating truth to a concrete will of its own, to a type of forces, to a quality of the will to power. Nietzsche accepts the problem on its own terms, he does not call the will to truth into doubt, he does not remind us once again that men *in fact* do not love truth. He asks what truth means as a concept, what forces and what will, qualified in that way, this concept presupposes *by right*. Nietzsche does not criticise false claims to truth but truth in itself and as an ideal. According to Nietzsche's method the concept of truth must be dramatised. "The will to truth, which is still going to tempt us to many a hazardous enterprise; that celebrated veracity of which all philosophers have hitherto spoken with reverence: what questions this will to truth has already set before us! . . . *What* really is it in us that wants 'the truth'? – We did indeed pause for a long time before the question of the origin of this will – until finally we came to a complete halt before an even more fundamental question. We asked after the value of this will. Granted we want truth: *why not rather* untruth? And uncertainty? Even ignorance? . . . And, would you believe it, it has finally almost come to seem to us that this problem has never before been posed – that we have been the first to see it, to fix our eye on it, to *hazard* it?" (BGE I p. 15).

The concept of truth describes a "truthful" world. Even in science the truth of phenomena forms a "world" distinct from that of phenomena themselves. But a truthful world presupposes a truthful man as its centre.[23] – Who is this truthful man, what does he want? First hypothesis: He wants not to be deceived, not to let himself be deceived, because it is "harmful, dangerous and inauspicious to be deceived". But this hypothesis presupposes the truthfulness of the world itself. For, in a radically false world it is the will to not let oneself be deceived that becomes inauspicious, dangerous and harmful. In fact, the will to truth had to be formed "in spite of the danger and the uselessness of the truth at any price". There remains another hypothesis: *I want the truth* means *I do not want to deceive*, and "I do not want to be deceived comprises, as a special case, I do not want to deceive myself" (GS 344). – If someone wills the truth it is not in the name of what the world is but in the name of what the world *is not*. It is understood that "life aims to mislead, to dupe, to dissimilate, to dazzle, to blind". But he who wills the truth always wants to depreciate this high power of the false: he makes life an "error" and this world an "appearance". He therefore opposes knowledge to life and to the world he opposes another world, a world-beyond, the truthful world. The truthful world is inseparable from this will, the will to treat *this world* as appearance. Thus the opposition of knowledge and life, the distinction between worlds, reveals its true character: it is a distinction of moral origin, an *opposition of moral origin*. The man who does not want to deceive wants a better world and a better life; all his reasons for not deceiving are moral ones. And we always come up against the *virtuism* of the one who wills the truth: one of his favourite occupations is the distribution of wrongs, he renders responsible, he denies innocence, he accuses and judges life, he denounces appearance. "It has gradually become clear to me . . . that the moral (or immoral) intentions in every philosophy have every time constituted the real germ of life out of which the entire plant has grown . . . I accordingly do not believe a "drive to knowledge" to be the father of philosophy" (BGE 6 p. 19). – However, this moral opposition is itself only a symptom. The one who wants another world, another life, wants something more profound: "Life against life" (GM III 13 p. 120). He wants life to become virtuous, to correct itself and to correct appearance, for it to serve as the way to the other world. He wants life to repudiate itself and to turn against itself: "An attempt to use force to taint force" (GM III 11). Thus behind the moral opposition there stands another kind of contradiction, the religious or ascetic contradiction.

From the speculative position to the moral opposition, from the moral opposition to the ascetic contradiction . . . But the ascetic contradiction is, in turn, a symptom which must be interpreted. What does the man of the ascetic ideal want? The one who repudiates life is also the one who wants a diminished life, the conservation of *his* type and moreover its power and triumph, the triumph and contagion of reactive forces. At this point reactive forces discover the disturbing ally that leads them to victory: nihilism, the will to nothingness (GM III 13). The will to nothingness which can only bear life in its reactive form. The will to nothingness is the one that used reactive forces as a way of ensuring that life *must* contradict, deny and annihilate itself. The will to nothingness from the beginning, inspires all the values that are called "superior" to life. This is Schopenhauer's greatest error: he believed that the will is denied in all values superior to life. In fact, it is not the will which is denied in superior values, it is the superior values that are related to a will to deny, to annihilate life. This will to deny defines "the value" of superior values. Its weapon is to hand life over to the domination of reactive forces in such a way that the whole of life slips further and further away, separated from what it can do, getting smaller and smaller, towards nothingness, towards the poignant feeling of his nothingness" (GM III 25). The will to nothingness *and* reactive forces, these are the two constituent elements of the ascetic ideal.

Thus interpretation makes its discoveries by excavating three layers: knowledge, morality and religion; the true, the good and the divine as values superior to life. All three are connected: the ascetic ideal is the third moment, but also the sense and value of the other two moments. We can therefore quite easily divide the spheres of influence, we can even oppose each moment to the others, we always come across the ascetic ideal, occupying all the spheres in a more or less condensed state – it is a refinement which endangers no one. Do we really believe that knowledge, science and even the science of the free thinker, "truth at any price", endanger the ascetic ideal? "Everywhere else that the spirit is strong, mighty and at work without counterfeit today, it does without ideals of any kind . . . *except for its will to truth*. But this, this *remnant* of an ideal is, if you will believe me, this ideal itself in its strictest, most spiritual formulation, esoteric through and through, with all external additions abolished" (GM III 27 p. 160).

12. Knowledge, Morality and Religion

Nevertheless, there is perhaps one reason why we might like to distinguish and even oppose knowledge, morality and religion. We ascended from truth to the ascetic ideal in order to discover the source of the concept of truth. Let us for a moment turn our attention to evolution instead of genealogy: let us descend again from the ascetic or religious ideal to the will to truth. We must then acknowledge that morality has replaced religion as a dogma and that science is increasingly replacing morality. "Christianity as dogma has been ruined by its own morality" (GM III 27); "what has triumphed of the Christian God is Christian morality itself", or "the instinct for truth in the end forbids itself the lie of faith in God" (GS 356). There are things today that a believer or even a priest can no longer say or think. They are reserved for a few bishops or popes: providence and divine goodness, divine reason, divine finality, "these are ways of thinking that now belong to the past, that have the voice of our conscience against them" (GM III 27), they are *immoral*. Religion often needs free thinkers to survive and adapt. Morality is the continuation of religion but by other means; knowledge is the continuation of morality and religion but by other means. The ascetic ideal is everywhere, but its means change, they are no longer the same reactive forces. This is why critique is so easily confused with a settling of accounts between different reactive forces.

"Christianity as dogma was ruined by its own morality . . ." But Nietzsche adds. "Therefore Christianity as morality must also be on the road to ruin". Does he mean that the will to truth must be the ruin of morality in the same way that morality is the ruin of religion? The gain would be slight, the will to truth is still part of the ascetic ideal, the mode of approach is always Christian. Nietzsche requires something else; a change of ideal, another ideal, "a different way of feeling". But how is this change possible in the modern world? As soon as we ask what the ascetic and religious ideal is, as soon as we put this question to the ideal itself, morality or virtue come forward to answer in its stead. Virtue says: "What you are attacking is myself, I answer for the ascetic ideal; in religion there is bad but there is also good; I have collected this good together, it is I who wills this good." And when we ask: "but what is this virtue, what does it want?" the same story begins again. Truth itself comes forward saying: "It is I who wills virtue, I answer for virtue. It is my mother and my goal. I am nothing if I do not lead to virtue. And who will deny that I am something?" – We are made to go back through the genealogical stages that we have covered (from truth to morality, from morality to religion) at a brisk and determined pace, under the pretext of evolution. Virtue answers for religion, truth for virtue. It is then enough to extend this movement. We cannot be made to go through these steps again without rediscovering our point of departure which is also our springboard: truth itself is not beyond criticism or in possession of a divine right. Critique must be a critique of truth itself. "After Christian truthfulness has drawn one inference after another, it must end by drawing its *most striking inference*, its inference against itself; this will happen, however, when it poses the question *'what is the meaning of all will to truth?'* And here again I touch on my problem, on our problem, my *unknown* friends (for I as yet *know* of no friend): what meaning would *our* whole being possess if it were not this, that in us the will to truth becomes conscious of itself as a *problem*? As the will to truth thus gains self-consciousness – there can be no doubt of that – morality will gradually *perish* now: this is the great spectacle in a hundred acts reserved for the next two centuries in Europe – the most terrible, most questionable and perhaps also the most hopeful of all spectacles" (GM III 27 p. 161). In this extremely rigorous text every term is carefully considered. "One inference after another" means descending steps: from the ascetic ideal to its moral form, from moral consciousness to its speculative form. But "the most striking inference" "its inference against itself" means this: the ascetic ideal no longer has any hiding place beyond the will to truth, no longer has anyone to answer for it. It is enough for us to continue the deduction, to descend even further than they want. Then the ascetic ideal is flushed out, unmasked. It no longer has any characters at its disposal to take on its role; no more moral or scholarly characters. We have returned to our problem, but we are also at the moment which will govern the reascent: the moment of feeling differently, of changing ideals. Thus Nietzsche is not arguing that the ideal of truth must replace the ascetic or even the moral ideal; he says, on the contrary, that calling the will to truth into question (its interpretation and evaluation) must prevent the ascetic ideal from replacing itself by other ideals which continue it in other forms. When we denounce the permanence of the ascetic ideal in the will to truth we deprive this ideal of the condition of its permanence or its final disguise. In this sense we too are "truthfull" or "seekers after knowledge".[24] But we do not replace the ascetic ideal, we let nothing of the place itself remain, we want to destroy the place, we want another ideal in another place, another way of knowing, another concept of truth, that is to say a truth which is not presupposed in a will to truth but which presupposes a *completely different will*.

13. Thought and Life

Nietzsche often takes knowledge to task for its claim to be opposed to life, to measure and judge life, for seeing itself as an end. The Socratic reversal already appeared in this form in the *Birth of Tragedy*. And Nietzsche never stops saying that, although it is a simple means subordinated to life, knowledge sets itself up as end, as judge, as supreme instance. But we must assess the importance of these texts: the opposition between knowledge and life and the operation by which knowledge makes itself judge of life are symptoms, only symptoms. Knowledge *is* opposed to life, but because it expresses a life which contradicts life, a reactive life which finds in knowledge a means of preserving and glorifying its type. (Thus knowledge gives life laws that separate it from what it can do, that keep it from acting, that forbid it to act, maintaining it in the narrow framework of scientifically observable reaction: almost like an animal in a zoo. But this knowledge that measures, limits and moulds life is itself entirely modelled on reactive life, within the limits of reactive life.) – It is not therefore surprising that other Nietzschean texts are more complex, not confining themselves to symptoms but penetrating into interpretation. In these texts Nietzsche takes knowledge to task, not for seeing itself as an end, but for making thought a simple means of serving life. Nietzsche no longer reproaches Socrates for having put life at the service of knowledge but, on the contrary, for having put thought at the service of life. "In Socrates thought serves life, whereas in all previous philosophers life served thought" (PTG). There is no contradiction between these two kinds of texts, if we are first of all sensitive to the different nuances of the word "life". When Socrates makes life the servant of knowledge this must be understood as the whole of life which, in this way, becomes reactive. But when he makes thought the servant of life this life must be understood as a particular type of life, the reactive life, which then becomes the model for the whole of life and for thought itself. And the conflict between the two kinds of texts will be further reduced if we are sensitive to the difference between "knowledge" and "thought". (Here again, is this not here a Kantian theme profoundly transformed and turned back against Kant?).

When knowledge becomes a legislator, the most important thing to be subjected is thought. Knowledge is thought itself, but thought subject to reason and to all that is expressed in reason. The instinct for knowledge is therefore thought, but thought in its relation to the reactive forces which seize and conquer it. For rational knowledge sets the same limits to life as reasonable life sets to thought; life is subject to knowledge and at the same time thought is subject to life. Reason sometimes dissuades and sometimes forbids us to cross certain limits: because it is useless (knowledge is there to predict) because it would be evil (life is there to be virtuous), because it is impossible (there is nothing to see or think behind the truth).[25] – But does not critique, understood as critique of knowledge itself, express new forces capable of giving thought another sense? A thought that would go to the limit of what life can do, a thought that would lead life to the limit of what it can do? A thought that would *affirm* life instead of a knowledge that is opposed to life. Life would be the active force of thought, but thought would be the affirmative power of life. Both would go in the same direction, carrying each other along, smashing restrictions, matching each other step for step, in a burst of unparalleled creativity. Thinking would then mean *discovering, inventing, new possibilities of life*. "There are lives with prodigious difficulties; these are the lives of the thinkers. And we must lend an ear to what we are told about them, for here we discover possibilities of life the mere story of which gives us joy and strength and sheds light on the lives of their successors. There is as much invention, reflection, boldness, despair and hope here as in the voyages of the great navigators; and to tell the truth, these are also voyages of exploration in the most distant and perilous domains of life. What is surprising in these lives is that two opposed instincts, which pull in opposite directions, seem to be forced to walk under the same yoke: the instinct that leads to knowledge is constantly constrained to abandon the ground where man habitually lives and to throw itself into the uncertain, and the instinct that wills life is forced to grope ceaselessly in the dark for a new place to establish itself" (PTG). In other words, life goes beyond the limits that knowledge fixes for it, but thought goes beyond the limits that life fixes for it. Thought ceases to be a *ratio*,[26*] life ceases to be a reaction. The thinker thus expresses the noble affinity of thought and life: life making thought active, thought making life affirmative. In Nietzsche this general affinity is not only the pre-Socratic secret *par excellence*, but also the essence of art.

14. Art

Nietzsche has a tragic conception of art. It rests on two principles which must be understood as ancient ones, but also as principles of the future. Firstly, art is the opposite of a "disinterested" operation: it does not heal, calm, sublimate or pay off, it does not "suspend" desire, instinct or will. On the contrary, art is a "stimulant of the will to power", "something that excites willing". The critical sense of this principle is obvious: it exposes every reactive conception of art. When Aristotle understood tragedy as medical purging or moral sublimation he gave it an interest, but an interest that was identical with that of reactive forces. When Kant distinguished beauty from all interests, even moral ones, he was still putting himself in the position of the spectator, but of a less and less gifted spectator who now has only a disinterested regard for beauty. When Schopenhauer elaborated his theory of disinterestedness he was, on his own admission, generalising a personal experience, the experience of the young man on whom art has the effect of a sexual sedative (like sport has for others) (GM III 6). Nietzsche's question is more insistent than ever: "Who looks at beauty in a disinterested way?" Art is always judged from the point of view of the spectator and a less and less artistic spectator at that. Nietzsche demands an aesthetics of creation, the aesthetics of Pygmalion. But why, from this new standpoint, does art emerge as a stimulant of the will to power? Why does the will to power need something to excite it when it needs no motive, goal or representation? This is because it can only be set up as affirmative in relation to active forces, to an active life. Affirmation is the product of a way of thinking which presupposes an active life as its condition and concomitant. According to Nietzsche we have not yet understood what the life of an artist means: the activity of this life serves as a stimulant to the affirmation contained in the work of art itself, to the will to power of the artist as artist.

The second principle of art is as follows: art is the highest power of falsehood, it magnifies the "world as error", it sanctifies the lie; the will to deception is turned into a superior ideal.[27] This second principle is, in a way, the converse of the first; what is active in life can only be brought into effect in relation to a deeper affirmation. The activity of life is like a power of falsehood, of duping, dissimulating, dazzling and seducing. But, in order to be brought into effect, this power of falsehood must be selected, redoubled or repeated and thus elevated to a higher power. The power of falsehood must be taken as far as a *will* to deceive, an artistic will which alone is capable of competing with the ascetic ideal and successfully opposing it (GM III 25). It is *art* which invents the lies that raise falsehood to this highest affirmative power, that turns the will to deceive into something which is affirmed in the power of falsehood. For the artist, *appearance* no longer means the negation of the real in this world but this kind of selection, correction, redoubling and affirmation.[28] Then truth perhaps takes on a new sense. Truth is appearance. Truth means bringing of power into effect, raising to the highest power. In Nietzsche, "we the artists" = "we the seekers after knowledge or truth" = "we the inventors of new possibilities of life".

15. New Image of Thought

The dogmatic image of thought can be summarised in three essential theses:

1) We are told that the thinker *as* thinker wants and loves *truth* (truthfulness of the thinker); that thought as thought possesses or formally contains truth (innateness of the idea, *a priori* nature of concepts); that thinking is the natural exercise of a faculty, that it is therefore sufficient to think "truly" or "really" in order to think with truth (sincere nature of the truth, universally shared good sense).

2) We are also told that we are "diverted" from the truth but by forces which are foreign to it (body, passions, sensuous interests). We fall into error, we take falsehood to be truth, because we are not merely thinking beings. *Error*: this would be merely the effect, in thought as such, of external forces which are opposed to thought.

3) We are told, finally, that all we need to think well, to think truthfully, is a *method*. Method is an artifice but one through which we are brought back to the nature of thought, through which we adhere to this nature and ward off the effect of the alien forces which alter it and distract us. Through method we ward off error. Time and place matter little if we apply method: it enables us to enter the domain of "that which is valid for all times and places".

The most curious thing about this image of thought is the way in which it conceives of truth as an abstract universal. We are never referred to the real forces that *form* thought, thought itself is never related to the real forces that it presupposes *as thought*. Truth is never related to what it presupposes. But there is no truth that, before being a truth, is not the bringing into effect of a sense or the realisation of a value. Truth, as a concept, is entirely undetermined. Everything depends on the value and sense of what we think. We always have the truths we deserve as a function of the sense of what we conceive, of the value of what we believe. Any thinkable or thought sense is only brought into effect insofar as the forces that correspond to it in thought also take hold of something, appropriate something, outside thought. Clearly thought cannot think by itself, any more than it can find truth by itself. The truth of a thought must be interpreted and evaluated according to the forces or power that determine it to think and to think this rather than that. When we speak of "plain truth", of truth "in itself", "for itself" or even "for us", we must ask what forces are hiding themselves in the thought of *this* truth, and therefore what its sense and value is. It is disturbing that truth conceived as an abstract universal, thought conceived as *pure science*, has never hurt anyone. In fact the established order and current values constantly find their best support in truth conceived in this way. "The 'truth' . . . is an easy-going and pleasant creature, who is continually assuring the powers that be that no one need fear any trouble from its quarter: for, after all, it is only pure science" (UM III "Schopenhauer Educator", 3*). This is what the dogmatic image of thought conceals: the work of established forces that determine thought as pure science, the work of established powers that are ideally expressed in truth in itself. Leibniz's strange statement still burdens philosophy: produce new truths, but above all "without overthrowing established feelings". And from Kant to Hegel we see the philosopher remaining, in the last resort, a thoroughly civil and pious character, loving to blend the aims of culture with the good of religion, morality or the State. Science christened itself critique because it made the powers of the world appear before it to be judged, but only in order to give them back what it owed them, the sanction of truth as it is in itself, for itself or for us (UM III "Schopenhauer Educator" 3, 4, 8).

A new image of thought means primarily that truth is not the element of thought. The element of thought is sense and value. The categories of thought are not truth and falsity but the *noble* and the *base*, the *high* and the *low*, depending on the nature of the forces that take hold of thought itself. We always have the share of truth and falsity that we deserve: there are truths of baseness, truths that are those of the slave. Conversely, our highest thoughts take falsehood into account; moreover, they never stop turning falsehood into a higher power, an affirmative and artistic power that is brought into effect, verified and becomes-true in the work of art.[29] A second consequence follows from this: the negative state of thought is not error. The inflation of the concept of error in philosophy shows the persistence of the dogmatic image of thought. According to this image everything in fact opposed to thought has only one effect on thought as such: leading it into error. The concept of error would therefore express, by right, the worst that can happen to thought, that is to say the state of thought separated from truth. Here again Nietzsche accepts the problem as it is posed *by right*. But, in reality, the almost laughable character of the examples usually invoked by philosophers in order to illustrate error (saying "Hello Thaetetus . . ." when one meets Theodore . . . saying "3 + 2 = 6") is enough to show that this concept of error is merely the extrapolation of puerile, artificial or grotesque factual situations. Who says "3 + 2 = 6" apart from the small child at school? Who says "Hello Thaetetus . . ." apart from the short-sighted or the absent-minded? Mature, considered thought has other enemies; negative states which are profound in entirely different ways. Stupidity is a structure of thought as such: it is not a means of self-deception, it expresses the non-sense in thought by right. Stupidity is not error or a tissue of errors. There are imbecile thoughts, imbecile discourses, that are made up entirely of truths; but these truths are base, they are those of a base, heavy and leaden soul. The state of mind dominated by reactive forces, *by right*, expresses *stupidity and, more profoundly, that which it is a symptom of: a base way of thinking*. In truth, as in error, stupid thought only discovers the most base – base errors and base truths that translate the triumph of the slave, the reign of petty values or the power of an established order. As he battles against his time Nietzsche's denunciations are constant; what baseness is necessary to be able to say this, to be able to think that!

The concept of truth can only be determined on the basis of a pluralist typology. And typology begins with a topology. It is a matter of knowing what *region* such errors and such truths belong to, what their *type* is, *which one* formulates and conceives them. Subjecting truth to the test of the base, but also subjecting falsity to the test of the high: this is the really critical task and the only way of knowing where one is in relation to "truth". When someone asks "what's the use of philosophy?" the reply must be aggressive, since the question tries to be ironic and caustic. Philosophy does not serve the State or the Church, who have other concerns. It serves no established power. The use of philosophy is to *sadden*. A philosophy that saddens no one, that annoys no one, is not a philosophy. It is useful for harming stupidity, for turning stupidity into something shameful.[30] Its only use is the exposure of all forms of baseness of thought. Is there any discipline apart from philosophy that sets out to criticise all mystifications, whatever their source and aim, to expose all the fictions without which reactive forces would not prevail? Exposing as a mystification the mixture of baseness and stupidity that creates the astonishing complicity of both victims and perpetrators. Finally, turning thought into something aggressive, active and affirmative. Creating free men, that is to say men who do not confuse the aims of culture with the benefit of the State, morality or religion. Fighting the *ressentiment* and bad conscience which have replaced thought for us. Conquering the negative and its false glamour. Who has an interest in all this but philosophy? Philosophy is at its most positive as critique, as an enterprise of demystification. And we should not be too hasty in proclaiming philosophy's failure in this respect. Great as they are, stupidity and baseness would be still greater if there did not remain some philosophy which always prevents them from going as far as they would wish, which forbids them – if only by yea-saying – from being as stupid and base as they would wish. They are forbidden certain excesses, but only by philosophy.

There exists, of course, a properly philosophical mystification; the dogmatic image of thought and the caricature of critique illustrate this. Philosophy's mystification begins, however, from the moment it renounces its role as demystifier and takes the established powers into consideration: when it gives up the harming of stupidity and the denunciation of baseness. It is true, Nietzsche says, that philosophers today have become *comets*.[31] But, from Lucretius to the philosophers of the eighteenth century we must observe these comets, follow them if possible, rediscover their fantastic paths. The philosopher-comets knew how to make pluralism an art of thinking, a critical art. They knew how to tell men what their bad conscience and the *ressentiment* concealed. They knew how to oppose established powers and values, though with only the image of the free man. After Lucretius how is it still possible to ask: what use is philosophy?

It is possible to ask this because the image of the philosopher is constantly obscured. He is turned into a sage, he who is only the friend of wisdom, friend in an ambiguous sense, that is to say, an anti-sage, he who must be masked with wisdom in order to survive. He is turned into a friend of truth he who makes truth submit to its hardest test, from which it emerges as dismembered as Dionysus: the test of sense and value. The image of the philosopher is obscured by all his necessary disguises, but also by all the betrayals that turn him into the philosopher of religion, the philosopher of the State, the collector of current values and the functionary of history. The authentic image of the philosopher does not survive the one who can embody it for a time, for his epoch. It must be taken up again, reanimated, it must find a new field of activity in the following epoch. If philosophy's critical task is not actively taken up in every epoch philosophy dies and with it die the images of the philosopher and the free man. Stupidity and baseness are always those of our own time, of our contemporaries, our stupidity and baseness. [32] Unlike the atemporal concept of error, baseness is inseparable from time, that is from this rapture of the present, from this present condition in which it is incarnated and in which it moves. This is why philosophy has an essential relation to time: it is always against its time, critique of the present world. The philosopher creates concepts that are neither eternal nor historical but untimely and not of the present. The opposition in terms of which philosophy is realised is that of present and non-present, of our time and the untimely (UM II "Use and Abuse of History" Preface). And in the untimely there are truths that are more durable than all historical and eternal truths put together: truths of times to come. Thinking actively is "acting in a non-present fashion, therefore against time and even on time, in favour (I hope) of a time to come" (UM III "Schopenhauer Educator", 3–4). The succession of philosophers is not an eternal sequence of sages, still less a historical sequence, but a broken succession, a succession of comets. Their discontinuity and repetition do not amount to the eternity of the sky which they cross, nor the historicity of the earth which they fly over. There is no eternal or historical philosophy. Eternity, like the historicity of philosophy amounts to this: philosophy always untimely, untimely at every epoch.

By placing thought in the element of sense and value, by making thought an active critique of stupidity and baseness, Nietzsche proposes a new image of thought. Thinking is never the natural exercise of a faculty. Thought never thinks alone and by itself; moreover it is never simply disturbed by forces which remain external to it. Thinking depends on forces which take hold of thought. Insofar as our thinking is controlled by reactive forces, insofar as it finds its sense in reactive forces, we must admit that we are not yet thinking. Thinking means the activity of thought; but thought has its own ways of being inactive which can occupy it and all its forces entirely. The fictions through which reactive forces triumph form the most base element in thought, the way in which it remains inactive and busies itself with not thinking. When Heidegger declares: "we are not yet thinking", one origin of this theme is in Nietzsche. We are awaiting the forces capable of making thought something active, absolutely active, the power capable of making it an affirmation. Thinking, like activity, is always a second power of thought, not the natural exercise of a faculty, but an extraordinary event *in* thought itself, *for* thought itself. Thinking is the n-th power of thought. It is still necessary for it to become "light", "affirmative", "dancing". But it will never attain this power if forces do not do violence to it. Violence must be done to it *as* thought, a power, *the force of thinking*, must throw it into a becoming-active. A constraint a training of this kind is what Nietzsche calls "Culture". Culture, according to Nietzsche, is essentially training and selection (UM III "Schopenhauer Educator" 6). It expresses the violence of the forces which seize thought in order to make it something affirmative and active. – We will only understand the concept of culture if we grasp all the ways in which it is opposed to method. Method always presupposes the good will of the thinker, "a premeditated decision". Culture, on the contrary, is a violence undergone by thought, a process of formation of thought through the action of selective forces, a training which brings the whole unconscious of the thinker into play. The Greeks did not speak of method but of *paideia*; they knew that thought does not think on the basis of a good will, but by virtue of the forces that are exercised on it in order to constrain it to think. Even Plato still distinguished what forces us to think and what leaves thought inactive; and in the myth of the cave he subordinated the *paideia* to the violence undergone by a prisoner, either in order to leave the cave or in order to return to it.[33] It is this Greek idea of a selective violence of culture that Nietzsche hits on in some famous passages. "One has only to look at our former codes of punishments to understand what effort it costs on this earth to breed a 'nation of thinkers' ", even tortures are necessary. "Learning to *think*: our schools no longer have any idea what this means", "the strange fact is that all there is or has been on earth of freedom, subtlety, boldness, dance and masterly certainty . . . has evolved only by virtue of the "tyranny of such arbitrary laws".[34]

These texts are undoubtedly ironical: the "people of thinkers" of which Nietzsche speaks is not the Greek people, but turns out to be the German people. Nevertheless, where is the irony? *Not* in the idea that thought only attains thinking through the action of forces that do it violence. The irony appears rather in a doubt about cultural development. Starting like the Greeks one ends up like the Germans. In several strange passages Nietzsche makes the most of this disappointment of Dionysus or Ariadne: coming across a German when one wanted a Greek.[35] – The species activity of culture has a final aim: to form the artist, the philosopher (UM III "Schopenhauer Educator" 8). All its selective violence serves this end, "I have to do with a class of men whose teleological conceptions extend further than the well-being of a State" (UM III "Schopenhauer Educator" 4). The principal cultural activities of Churches and States form in fact the long martyrology of culture itself. When a State encourages culture "it only encourages it in order to be encouraged itself, and it never conceives that there is an aim superior to its own good and existence". But, on the other hand, the confusion of cultural activity with the good of the State is based on something real. The cultural work of active forces constantly risks being diverted from its course and sometimes it does benefit reactive forces. The Church or the State take on this violence of culture in order to realise their own ends. Reactive forces divert this violence from culture, turning it into a reactive force itself, a means of making even more stupid, of lowering thought. They confuse the violence of culture with their own violence, their own force (UM III 6). Nietzsche calls this process "cultural degeneration". How far it is unavoidable, how far avoidable, for what reasons and by what means we will see below. Be that as it may, Nietzsche underlines the ambivalence of culture in this way; from being Greek it becomes German . . .

This is a way of re-emphasising the extent to which the new image of thought implies extremely complex relations of forces. The theory of forces depends on a typology of forces. And once again a typology begins with a topology. Thinking depends on certain coordinates. We have the truths that we deserve depending on the place we are carrying our existence to, the hour we watch over and the element that we frequent. There is nothing more false than the idea of "founts" of truth. We only find truths where they are, at their time and in their element. Every truth is truth of an element, of a time and a place: the minotaur does not leave the labyrinth (VP III 408). We are not going to think unless as we are forced to go where the forces which give food for thought are, where the forces that make thought something active and affirmative are made use of. Thought does not need a method but a paideia, a formation, a culture. Method in general is a means by which we avoid going to a particular place, or by which we maintain the option of escaping from it (the thread of the labyrinth). "And we, we beg you earnestly, hang yourselves with this thread!" Nietzsche says that three anecdotes are sufficient to define the life of a thinker (PTG) – one for the place, one for the time and one for the element. The anecdote is to life what the aphorism is to thought: something to interpret. Empedocles and his volcano – this is an anecdote of a thinker. The height of summits and caves, the labyrinths; midday-midnight; the halcyon aerial element and also the element of the subterranean. It is up to us to go to extreme places, to extreme times, where the highest and the deepest truths live and rise up. The places of thought are the tropical zones frequented by the tropical man, not temperate zones or the moral, methodical or moderate man.

4

From *Ressentiment* to the Bad Conscience

1. Reaction and Ressentiment

In the normal or healthy state the role of reactive forces is always to limit action. They divide, delay or hinder it by means of another action whose effects we feel. But, conversely, active forces produce a burst of creativity: they set it off at a chosen instant, at a favourable moment, in a given direction, in order to carry out a quick and precise piece of adjustment. In this way a *riposte* is formed. This is why Nietzsche can say: "The true reaction is that of action" (GM I 10). The active type, in this sense, is not a type that only contains active forces, it expresses the "normal" relation between a reaction that delays action and an action that precipitates reaction. The master is said to react precisely because he acts[1]* his reactions. The active type therefore includes reactive forces but ones that are defined by a capacity for obeying or being acted. The active type expresses a relation between active and reactive forces such that the latter are themselves acted.

We can see, therefore, that a reaction alone cannot constitute *ressentiment*. *Ressentiment* designates a type in which reactive forces prevail over active forces. But they can only prevail in one way: by ceasing to be acted. Above all we must not define *ressentiment* in terms of the strength of a reaction. If we ask what the man of *ressentiment* is, we must not forget this principle: he does not re-act. And the word *ressentiment* gives a definite clue: *reaction ceases to be acted in order to become something felt (senti)*. Reactive forces prevail over active forces because they escape their action. But at this point two questions arise: 1) How do they prevail, how do they escape? What is the mechanism of this "sickness"? 2) And, conversely, how are reactive forces normally acted? "Normal" here does not mean "frequent" but on the contrary, "normative" and "rare". What is the definition of this norm, of this "health"?

2. *Principle of* Ressentiment

Freud often expounds a schema of life that he calls the "topical hypothesis". The system which receives an excitation is not the system which retains a lasting trace of it: the same system could not at one and the same time faithfully record the transformations which it undergoes and offer an ever fresh receptivity. "We will therefore suppose that an external system of the apparatus receives the perceptible excitations but retains nothing of them, and thus has no memory; and that, lying behind this system there is another which transforms the momentary excitation of the first into lasting traces." These two systems or recordings correspond to the distinction between the conscious and the unconscious. "Our memories are by nature unconscious"; and conversely, "Consciousness is born at the point where the mnemonic trace stops". We must therefore see the formation of the conscious system as the result of a process of evolution: at the boundary between the outside and the inside, between the internal world and the external world, we could say that "a skin has been formed which has been made so supple by the excitations it constantly receives, that it has acquired properties making it uniquely suited to receive new excitations", retaining only a direct and changeable image of objects completely distinct from the lasting or even changeless trace in the unconscious system.[2]

Freud is far from accepting this topical hypothesis without reservations. The fact is that we find all the elements of this hypothesis in Nietzsche. Nietzsche distinguishes two systems within the reactive apparatus: the conscious and the unconscious.[3] The reactive unconscious is defined by mnemonic traces, by lasting imprints. It is a digestive, vegetative and ruminative system, which expresses "the purely passive impossibility of escaping from the impression once it is received". Of course, even in this endless digestion, reactive forces have a job to do, attaching themselves to the indelible imprint, investing the trace. But the inadequacy of this first kind of reactive force is obvious. Adaptation would never be possible if the reactive apparatus did not have another system of forces at its disposal. Another system is necessary, a system in which reaction is not a reaction to traces but becomes a reaction to the present excitation or to the direct image of the object. This second kind of reactive forces is inseparable from consciousness: that constantly renewed skin surrounding an ever fresh receptivity, a milieu "where there is always room for new things". It will be remembered that Nietzsche wished to remind consciousness of its need for modesty: its origin, nature and function are wholly reactive. But consciousness can nevertheless claim a relative nobility. The second kind of reactive forces show us in what form and under what conditions reaction can be acted: when reactive forces take conscious excitation as their object, then the corresponding reaction is itself acted.

But the two systems or the two kinds of reactive forces must still be separated. The traces must not invade consciousness. A specific active force must be given the job of supporting consciousness and renewing its freshness, fluidity and mobile, agile chemistry at every moment. This active super-conscious faculty is the faculty of forgetting. Psychology's mistake was to treat forgetting as a negative determination, not to discover its active and positive character. Nietzsche defines the faculty of forgetting as "no mere *vis inertiae* as the superficial imagine; it is rather an active and in the strictest sense positive faculty of repression", "an apparatus of absorption", "a plastic, regenerative and curative force."[4] *Thus, there are two simultaneous processes: reaction becomes something acted because it takes conscious excitation as its object and reaction to traces remains in the unconscious, imperceptible.* "What we experience and absorb enters our consciousness as little while we are digesting it . . . as does the thousandfold process involved in physical nourishment . . . so that it will be immediately obvious how there could be no happiness, no cheerfulness, no hope, no pride, no *present*, without forgetfulness" (GM II 1 pp. 57–58). But this faculty is in a very special situation: although it is an active force it is delegated by activity to work with reactive forces. It serves as "guard" or "supervisor", preventing the two systems of the reactive apparatus from becoming confused. Although it is an active force its only activity is functional. It comes from activity but is abstracted from it. And in order to renew consciousness it constantly has to borrow the energy of the second kind of reactive forces, making this energy its own in order to give it to consciousness.

This is why it is more prone than any other active force to variations, failures and functional disturbances. "The man in whom this apparatus of repression is damaged and ceases to function properly, may be compared (and more than merely compared) with a dyspeptic – he cannot 'have done' with anything" (GM II 1 p. 58). Let us suppose that there is a lapse in the faculty of forgetting: it is as if the wax of consciousness were hardened, excitation tends to get confused with its trace in the unconscious and conversely, reaction to traces rises into consciousness and overruns it. *Thus at the same time as reaction to traces becomes perceptible, reaction ceases to be acted.* The consequences of this are immense: no longer being able to act a reaction, active force are deprived of the material conditions of their functioning, they no longer have the opportunity to do their job, *they are separated from what they can do*. We can thus finally see in what way reactive forces prevail over active forces: when the trace takes the place of the excitation in the reactive apparatus, reaction itself takes the place of action, reaction prevails over action. Now it is striking that, when victory is won in this way, the real struggles are only between reactive forces; reactive forces do not triumph by forming a force greater than that of active forces. Even the functional decay of the faculty of forgetting derives from the fact that it no longer finds in one kind of reactive forces the energy necessary to repress the other kind and to renew consciousness. *Everything takes place between reactive forces*: some prevent others from being acted, some destroy others. This is a strange subterranean struggle which takes place entirely inside the reactive apparatus, but which nevertheless has consequences for the whole of activity. We rediscover the definition of *ressentiment*: *ressentiment* is a reaction which simultaneously becomes perceptible and ceases to be acted: a formula which defines sickness in general. Nietzsche is not simply saying that *ressentiment* is a sickness, but rather that sickness as such is a form of *ressentiment* (EH I 6).

3. *Typology of* Ressentiment[5]

The first aspect of *ressentiment* is therfore topological. There is a topology of reactive forces: it is their change of place, their displacement which constitutes *ressentiment*. The man of *ressentiment* is characterised by the invasion of consciousness by mnemonic traces, the ascent of memory into consciousness itself. Of course, this is not all there is to say about memory: we will have to ask how consciousness is capable of constructing a memory suitable for itself, an acted and almost active memory that no longer rests on traces. In Nietzsche, as in Freud, the theory of the memory becomes a theory of two memories.[6] But insofar as we remain at the level of the first memory we remain within the limits of the pure principle of *ressentiment*; the man of *ressentiment* is like a dog, a kind of dog which only reacts to traces (a bloodhound). He only invests traces: for him excitation is locally confused with the trace, the man of *ressentiment* can no longer act his reaction. – But this topological definition must introduce us to a "typology" of *ressentiment*. For, when reactive forces prevail over active forces in this way they themselves form a type. We can see that the principal symptom of this type is a prodigious memory. Nietzsche stresses this incapacity to forget anything, this faculty of forgetting nothing and its profoundly reactive nature – which must be considered from all points of view (GM I 10 and II 1). A type is a reality which is simultaneously biological, psychical, historical, social and political.

Why is *ressentiment* the *spirit of revenge*? It might be thought that the man of *ressentiment* comes into being by accident: having experienced too strong an excitation (a pain), he would have had to abandon the attempt to react, not being strong enough to form a riposte. He would therefore experience a desire for revenge and, by a process of generalisation, would want to take this out on the whole world. Such an interpretation is mistaken; it only takes quantities into account, the quantity of excitation received, "objectively" compared to the quantity of force of a receptive subject. But, for Nietzsche, what counts is not the quantity of force considered abstractly but a determinate relation in the subject itself between the different forces of which it is made up this is what he means by a type. Whatever the force of the excitation which is received, whatever the total force of the subject itself, the man of *ressentiment* only uses the latter to invest the trace of the former, so that he is incapable of acting and even of reacting to the excitation. There is therefore no need for him to have experienced an excessive excitation. This may happen, but it is not necessary. He does not need to generalise in order to see the whole world as the object of his *ressentiment*. As a result of his type the man of *ressentiment* does not "react": his reaction is endless, it is felt instead of being acted. This reaction therefore blames its object, whatever it is, as an object on which revenge must be taken, which must be made to pay for this infinite delay. *Excitation can be beautiful and good and the man of* ressentiment *can experience it as such*; it *can* be less than the force of the man of *ressentiment* and he can possess an abstract quantity of force as great as that of anyone else. He will none the less feel the corresponding object as a personal offence and affront because he makes the object responsible for his own powerlessness to invest anything but the trace – a qualitative or typical powerlessness. The man of *ressentiment* experiences every being and object as an offence in exact proportion to its effect on him. Beauty and goodness are, for him, necessarily as outrageous as any pain or misfortune that he experiences. "One cannot get rid of anything, one cannot get over anything, one cannot repel anything – everything hurts. Men and things obtrude too closely; experiences strike one too deeply; memory becomes a festering wound" (EH I 6 p. 320). The man of *ressentiment* in himself is a being full of pain: the sclerosis or hardening of his consciousness, the rapidity with which every excitation sets and freezes within him, the weight of the traces that invade him are so many cruel sufferings. And, more deeply, *the memory of traces is full of hatred in itself and by itself*. It is venomous and depreciative because it blames the object in order to compensate for its own inability to escape from the traces of the corresponding excitation. This is why *ressentiment's* revenge, even when it is realised, remains "spiritual", imaginary and symbolic in principle. This essential link between revenge and memory resembles the Freudian anal-sadistic complex. Nietzsche himself presents memeory as an unfinished digestion and the type of *ressentiment* as an anal type.[7] This intestinal and venomous memory is what Nietzsche calls the spider, the tarantula, the spirit of revenge . . . We can see what Nietzsche's intention is: to produce a psychology that is really a typology, to put psychology "on the plane of the subject".[8] Even the possibilities of a cure will be subordinated to the transformation of types (reversal and transmutation).

4. *Characteristics of* Ressentiment

We must not be deceived by the expression "spirit of revenge". *Spirit* does not make revenge an intention, an unrealised end but, on the contrary, gives revenge a means. We have not understood *ressentiment* if we only see it as a *desire* for revenge, a desire to rebel and triumph. The topological principle of *ressentiment* entails a state of real forces: the state of reactive forces that no longer let themselves act, that evade the action of active forces. It gives revenge a means: a means of reversing the normal relation of active and reactive forces. This is why *ressentiment* itself is always a revolt and always the triumph of this revolt. *Ressentiment* is the triumph of the weak *as* weak, the revolt of the slaves and their victory *as* slaves. It is in their victory that the slaves form a type. The type of the master (the active type) is defined in terms of the faculty of forgetting and the power of acting reactions. The type of slave (the reactive type) is defined by a prodigious memory, by the power of *ressentiment*; several characteristics which determine this second type follow from this.

Inability to admire, respect or love (BGE 260, GM I 10). The memory of traces is itself full of hatred. Hatred or revenge is hidden even in the most tender and most loving memories. The ruminants of memory disguise this hatred by a subtle operation which consists in reproaching themselves with everything with which, in fact, they reproach the being whose memory they pretend to cherish. For this reason we must beware of those who condemn themselves before that which is good or beautiful, claiming not to understand, not to be worthy: their modesty is frightening. What hatred of beauty is hidden in their declarations of inferiority. Hating all that is experienced as lovable or admirable, diminishing by buffoonery or base interpretations, seeing traps to be avoided in all things: always saying, "please don't engage me in a battle of wits". What is most striking in the man of *ressentiment* is not his nastiness but his disgusting malevolence, his capacity for disparagement. Nothing can resist it. He does not even respect his friends or even his enemies. He does not even respect misfortune or its causes.[9] Think of the Trojans who, in Helen, respected and admired the cause of their own misfortune. But the man of *ressentiment* must turn misfortune into something mediocre, he must recriminate and distribute blame: look at his inclination to play down the value of causes, to make misfortune "someone's fault". By contrast, the aristocrat's respect for the causes of misfortune goes together with an ability to take his own misfortunes seriously. The way in which the slave takes *his* misfortunes seriously shows a difficult digestion and a base way of thinking which is incapable of feeling respect.

"Passivity". In *ressentiment* happiness "appears essentially as a narcotic drug, rest, peace, 'sabbath', slackening of tension and relaxing of

limbs, in short *passively*" (GM I 10 p. 38). In Nietzsche "passive" does not mean "non-active"; "non-active" means "reactive"; but "passive" means "non-acted". The only thing that is passive is reaction insofar as it is not acted. The term "passive" stands for the triumph of reaction, the moment when, ceasing to be acted, it becomes a *ressentiment*. The man of *ressentiment* does not know how to and does not want to love, but wants to be loved. He wants to be loved, fed, watered, caressed and put to sleep. He is the impotent, the dyspeptic, the frigid, the insomniac, the slave. Furthermore the man of *ressentiment* is extremely touchy: faced with all the activities he cannot undertake he considers that, at the very least, he ought to be compensated by benefiting from them. He therefore considers it a proof of obvious malice that he is not loved, that he is not fed. The man of *ressentiment* is the man of profit and gain. Moreover, *ressentiment* could only be imposed on the world through the triumph of the principle of gain, by making profit not only a desire and a way of thinking but an economic, social and theological system, a complete system, a divine mechanism. A failure to recognise profit – this is *the* theological crime and the only crime against the spirit. It is in this sense that slaves have a *morality*, and that this morality is that of *utility* (BGE 260). We asked: who considers action from the standpoint of its utility or harmfulness? And even: who considers action from the standpoint of good and evil, of praiseworthiness and blameworthiness? If we review all the qualities that morality calls "praiseworthy" or "good" in themselves, for example, the incredible notion of disinterestedness, we realise that they conceal the demands and recriminations of a passive third party: it is he who claims an interest in actions that he does not perform; he praises the disinterested character of precisely the actions from which he benefits.[10] Morality in itself conceals the utilitarian standpoint; but utilitarianism conceals the standpoint of the passive third party, the triumphant standpoint of a slave who intervenes between masters.

The imputation of wrongs, the distribution of responsibilities, perpetual accusation. All this replaces aggression. "The *aggressive* pathos belongs just as necessarily to strength as vengefulness and rancour belong to weakness" (EH I 7 p. 232). Considering gain as a right, considering it a right to profit from actions that he does not perform, the man of *ressentiment* breaks out in bitter reproaches as soon as his expectations are disappointed. And how could they not be disappointed, since frustration and revenge are the *a prioris* of *ressentiment*? "It is your fault if no one loves me, it is your fault if I've failed in life and also your fault if you fail in yours, your misfortunes and mine are equally your fault." Here we rediscover the dreadful feminine power of *ressentiment*: it is not content to denounce crimes and criminals, it wants sinners, people who are responsible. We can guess what the creature of *ressentiment* wants: he wants others to be evil, he needs others to be evil in order to be able to consider himself good. *You are evil, therefore I am good*; this is the slave's fundamental formula, it expresses the main point of *ressentiment* from the typological point of view, it summarises and brings together all the preceding characteristics. This formula must be compared with that of the master: *I am good, therefore you are evil*. The difference between the two measures the revolt of the slave and his triumph: "This inversion of the value-positing eye . . . is of the essence of *ressentiment*: in order to exist, slave morality always first needs a hostile world" (GM I 10 pp. 36–37). The slave needs, to set the other up as evil *from the outset*.

5. Is he Good? Is he Evil?

Here are the two formulae: "I am good, therefore you are evil" – "You are evil therefore I am good". We can use the method of dramatisation. Who utters the first of these formulae, who utters the second? And what does each one want? The same person cannot utter both *because the good of the one is precisely the evil of the other*. "There is no single concept of good" (GM I 11); the words "good", "evil" and even "therefore" have several senses. We find, once again, that the method of dramatisation, which is essentially pluralist and immanent, governs the inquiry. Nowhere else can this investigation find the scientific rule that constitutes it as a semeiology and an axiology, enabling it to determine the sense and value of a word. We ask: who is it that *begins* by saying: "I am good"? It is certainly not the one who compares himself to others, nor the one who compares his actions and his works to superior and transcendent values: such a one would not begin . . . The one who says: "I am good", does not wait to be called good. He refers to himself in this way, he names himself and decribes himself thus to the extent that he acts, affirms and enjoys. "Good" qualifies activity, affirmation and the enjoyment which is experienced in their exercise: a certain quality of the soul, "some fundamental certainty which a noble soul possesses in regard to itself, something which may not be sought or found and perhaps may not be lost either" (BGE 287 p. 196). What Nietzsche often calls *distinction* is the eternal character of what is affirmed (it does not have to be looked for), of what is put into action (it is not found), of what is enjoyed (it cannot be lost). He who affirms and acts is at the same time the one who *is*: "The root of the word coined for this, *esthlos* signifies one who is, who possesses reality, who is actual, who is true" (GM I 5 p. 29). "He knows himself to be that which in general first accords honour to things, he creates values. Everything he knows to be part of himself, he honours: such a morality is self-glorification. In the foreground stands the feeling of plenitude, of power which seeks to overflow, the happiness of high tension, the consciousness of a wealth which would like to give away and bestow".[11] " 'The good' themselves, that is to say, the noble, powerful, high-stationed and high-minded, who felt and established themselves and their actions as good, that is, of the first rank, in contradistinction to all the low, low-minded, common and plebeian" (GM I 2 pp 25–6). But no comparison interferes with the principle. It is only a secondary consequence, a negative conclusion that others are evil insofar as they do not affirm, do not act, do not enjoy. "Good" primarily designates the master. "Evil" means the consequence and designates the slave. What is "evil" is negative, passive, bad, unhappy. Nietzsche outlines a commentary on Theognis' admirable poem based entirely on the fundamental lyrical affirmation: we are good, they are evil, bad. We search in vain for the least nuance of morality in this aristocratic appreciation: it is a question of an ethic and a typology – a typology of forces, an ethic of the corresponding ways of being.

"I am good, therefore you are evil": in the mouths of the masters the word *therefore* merely introduces a negative conclusion. And this latter is merely advanced as the consequence of a full affirmation: "we the aristocrats, the beautiful, the happy" (GM I 10). In the master everything positive is in the premises. He must have premises of action and affirmation, and the enjoyment of these premises in order to conclude with something negative which is not the main point and has scarcely any importance. It is only an "accessory, a complementary nuance" (GM I 11). Its only importance is to augment the tenor of the action and the affirmation, to content their alliance and to redouble the corresponding enjoyment: the good "only looks for its antithesis in order to affirm itself with more joy" (GM I 10). This is the status of *aggression*: it is the negative, but the negative as the conclusion of positive premises, the negative as the product of activity, the negative as the consequence of the power of affirming. The master acknowledges himself in a syllogism where two positive propositions are necessary to make a negation, the final negation being only a means of reinforcing the premises – "You are evil therefore I am good." Everything has changed: the negative passes into the premises, the positive is conceived as a conclusion, a conclusion from negative premises. The negative contains the essential and the positive only exists through negation. The negative becomes "the original idea, the beginning, the act *par excellence*" (GM I 11). The slave must have premises of reaction and negation, of *ressentiment* and nihilism, in order to obtain an apparently positive conclusion. Even so, it only appears to be positive. This is why Nietzsche insists on distinguishing *ressentiment* and aggression: they differ in nature. The man of *ressentiment* needs to conceive of a non-ego, then to oppose himself to this non-ego in order finally to posit himself as self. This is the strange syllogism of the slave: he needs two negations in order to produce an appearance of affirmation. We already sense the form in which the syllogism of the slave has been so successful in philosophy: *the dialectic*. The dialectic, as the ideology of *ressentiment*.

"You are evil, therefore I am good." In this formula it is the slave who speaks. It cannot be denied that values are still being created. But what bizarre values! They begin by positing the other as evil. He who called himself good is the one who is now called evil. This evil one is the one who acts, who does not hold himself back from acting, who does not therefore consider action from the point of view of the consequences that it will have for third parties. And the one who is good is now the one who holds himself back from acting: he is good just because he refers all actions to the standpoint of the one who does not act, to the standpoint of the one who experiences the consequences, or better still to the more subtle standpoint of a divine third party who scrutinises the *intentions* of the one who acts. "And he is good who does not outrage, who harms nobody, who does not attack, who does not requite, who leaves revenge to God, who keeps himself hidden as we do, who avoids evil and desires little from life, like us, the patient, humble and just" (GM I 13 p. 46). This is how good and evil are born: ethical determination, that of good and bad, gives way to moral judgment. The good of ethics has become the evil of morality, the bad has become the good of morality. Good and evil are not the good and the bad but, on the contrary, the exchange, the inversion, the *reversal* of their determination. Nietzsche stresses the following point: "Beyond good and evil" does not mean: "Beyond the good and the bad", on the contrary . . . (GM I 17). Good and evil are new values, but how strangely these values are created! They are created by reversing good and bad. They are not created by acting but by holding back from acting, not by affirming, but by beginning with denial. This is why they are called un-created, divine, transcendent, superior to life. But think of what these values hide, of their mode of creation. They hide an extraordinary hatred, a hatred for life, a hatred for all that is active and affirmative in life. No moral values would survive for a single instant if they were separated from the premises on which they are the conclusion. And, more profoundly, no religious values are separable from this hatred and revenge from which they draw the consequences. The positivity of religion is only apparent: they conclude that the wretched, the poor, the weak, the slaves, are the good since the strong are "evil" and "damned". They have invented the good wretch, the good weakling: there is no better revenge against the strong and happy. What would Christian love be without the Judaic power of *ressentiment* which inspires and directs it? Christian love is not the opposite of Judaic *ressentiment* but its consequence, its conclusion and its crowning glory (GM I 8). Religion conceals the principles from which it is directly descended to a greater or lesser extent (and often, in periods of crisis, it no longer conceals anything at all); the weight of negative premises, the spirit of revenge, the power of *ressentiment*.

6. The Paralogism

"You are evil; I am the opposite of what you are; therefore I am good." – Where does the paralogism lie? Let us suppose that we have a lamb who is a logician. The syllogism of the bleating lamb is formulated as follows: birds of prey are evil (that is, the birds of prey are all the evil ones, the evil ones are birds of prey); but I am the opposite of a bird of prey; therefore I am good.[12] It is clear that in the minor premise the bird of prey is taken for what it is: a force which does not separate itself from its effects or its manifestations. But it is assumed in the major premise that the bird of prey is able to not manifest its force, that it can hold back from its effects and separate itself from what it can do: it is evil because it does not hold itself back. It is therefore assumed that one and the same force is effectively held back in the virtuous lamb but given free rein in the evil bird of prey. Since the strong could prevent themselves from acting, the weak could act if they did not prevent themselves.

Here we have the foundation of the paralogism of *ressentiment*: *the fiction of a force separated from what it can do*. It is thanks to this fiction that reactive forces triumph. It is not sufficient for them to hold back from activity: they must also reverse the relation of forces, they must oppose themselves to active forces and represent themselves as superior. The process of accusation in *ressentiment* fulfills this task: reactive forces "project" an abstract and neutralised image of force; such a force separated from its effects will be *blameworthy* if it acts, *deserving*, on the contrary, if it does not. Moreover it is thought that more (abstract) force is needed to hold back than is needed to act. It is all the more important to analyse this fiction in detail since by means of it, as we shall see, reactive forces acquire a contagious power, while active forces become *really* reactive.

1) Moment of causality: force is split in two. Although force is not separated from its manifestation, the manifestation is turned into an effect which is referred to the force as if it were a distinct and separated cause. "The same event is posited first as cause and then a second time as its effect. Scientists do no better when they say 'force moves', 'force causes' and the like" (GM I 13 p. 45*). A "simple sign to aid the memory, an abridged formula" is taken to be a cause: when, for example, one says that the light shines (VP I 100). An imaginary relation of causality is substituted for a real relation of significance.[13] Force is first repressed into itself, then its manifestation is made into a different thing which finds its distinct, efficient cause in the force.

2) Moment of substance: force, which has been divided in this way, is projected into a substrate, into a subject which is free to manifest it or not. Force is neutralised, it is made the act of a subject which could just as easily not act. Nietzsche constantly exposes "the subject" as a fiction or a grammatical funtion. All subjects – the Epicureans' atom, Descartes' substance or Kant's thing-in-itself – are the projection of "little imaginery incubuses" (GM I 13 p. 141).

3) Moment of reciprocal determination: the force thus neutralised is moralised. For, if it is assumed that a force *is* able to not manifest the force that it "has", it is no more absurd to assume, conversely, that a force could manifest the force that it "has not". As soon as forces are projected into a fictitious subject this subject proves to be blameworthy or deserving – blameworthy if active force performs the activity which is its own, deserving if reactive force does not perform the activity which it . . . does not have. "Just as if the weakness of the weak – that is to say their *essence*, their effects, their sole ineluctable, irremovable reality – were a voluntary achievement, willed, chosen, a *deed*, a *meritorious act*" (GM I 13 p. 46). For the concrete distinction between forces, for the original difference between qualified forces (the good and the bad), is substituted the moral opposition between substantialised forces (good and evil).

7. *Development of* Ressentiment: *the Judaic priest*

The analysis has led us from a first to a second aspect of *ressentiment*. When Nietzsche speaks of bad conscience he explicitly distinguishes two aspects: a first in which bad conscience is in a "raw state", pure matter or a "question of animal psychology, no more"; a second, without which bad conscience would not be what it is, a moment which takes advantage of this previous content and makes it take form (GM III 20). This distinction corresponds to that between topology and typology. All the indications are that this is also valid for *ressentiment*. *Ressentiment* also has two aspects or moments. The one, topological, a question of animal psychology, constitutes *ressentiment* as raw content: it expresses the way in which reactive forces escape the action of active forces (*displacement* of reactive forces, invasion of consciousness by the memory of traces). The second, typological, expresses the way in which *ressentiment* takes on form: the memory of traces becomes a typical character because it embodies the spirit of revenge and engages in an enterprise of perpetual accusation; reactive forces are then opposed to active forces and separate them from what they can do (*reversal* of the relation of forces, *projection* of a reactive image). It should be noted that the revolt of reactive forces would still not be a complete triumph without this second aspect of *ressentiment*. It should also be noted that in neither of the two cases do reactive forces triumph by forming a greater force than active forces: in the first case everything takes place between reactive forces (*displacement*); in the second reactive forces separate active forces from what they can do, but by means of a fiction, by means of a mystification (*reversal by projection*). Consequently two problems remain to be resolved in order for us to understand the whole of *ressentiment*: 1) How do reactive forces produce this fiction? 2) Under what influence do they produce it? That is, what makes reactive forces move from the first to the second stage? Who elaborates the content of *ressentiment*? Who gives form to *ressentiment*, who is the "artist" of *ressentiment*?

Forces are inseparable from the differential element from which their quality derives. But reactive forces give an inverted image of this element: the difference between forces seen from the side of reaction becomes the opposition of reactive to active forces. It will therefore be enough for reactive forces to have the opportunity to develop or project this image in order for the relation of forces, and the values that correspond to it, to be inverted in their turn. They discover this opportunity at the same time as they find the means of escaping from activity. Ceasing to be acted, reactive forces *project* the inverted image. It is this reactive projection that Nietzsche calls a fiction; the fiction of a super-sensible world in opposition to this world, the fiction of a God in contradiction to life. Nietzsche distinguishes this projection from the active power of the dream and even from the positive image of gods who affirm and glorify life: "Whereas the world of dreams reflects reality, the world of fictions falsifies, depreciates and denies it" (AC 15, also 16 and 18). It presides over the whole evolution of *ressentiment*, that is to say, over the operations by which active force is, simultaneously, separated from what it can do (falsification), accused and treated as blameworthy (depreciation), and the corresponding values are reversed (negation). In and through this fiction reactive forces *represent themselves as superior*. "To be able to reject all that represents the ascending movement of life, well-constitutedness, power, beauty, self-affirmation on earth, the instinct of *ressentiment* here become genius had to invent another world from which that life-affirmation would appear evil, reprehensible as such" (AC 24 p. 135).

Ressentiment still had to become "genius". It was still necessary to have an artist in fiction, capable of profiting from the opportunity and of directing the projection, conducting the prosecution and carrying out the reversal. We must not think that the transition from one

moment of *ressentiment* to the other – however swift and smooth – can
be reduced to a simple mechanical sequence. It needs the intervention
of an artist of genius. The Nietzschean question "Which one?"
resounds more loudly than ever. *"The Genealogy of Morals contains the
first psychology of the priest"* (EH III "Genealogy of Morals"). The one
who gives *ressentiment* form, the one who conducts the prosecution
and pursues the enterprise of revenge even further, the one who dares
to reverse values, is the priest. And, more especially, the Jewish
priest, the priest in his Judiac form.[14] It is he, the master of dialectics,
who gives the slave the idea of the reactive syllogism. It is he who
forges the negative premises. It is he who conceives of love, a new love
that the Christians take up, as the conclusion, the crowning glory, the
venomous flower of an unbelievable hatred. It is he who begins by
saying "the wretched alone are the good; the poor, impotent, lowly
alone are the good; the suffering, deprived, sick, ugly alone are pious,
alone are blessed by God, blessedness is for them alone – and you, the
powerful and the noble are on the contrary the evil, the cruel, the
lustful, the insatiable, the godless to all eternity; and you shall be in all
eternity the unblessed, accursed and damned!" (GM I 7 p. 34).
Without him the slave would never have known how to raise himself
above the brute state of *ressentiment*. Consequently, in order to
appreciate correctly the intervention of the priest we must see in what
way he is the accomplice of reactive forces, but only their accomplice
and not part of them. He ensures the triumph of reactive forces, he
needs this triumph, but he pursues an aim that is not identical to
theirs. His will is will to power, his will to power is nihilism.[15] We
rediscover the fundamental proposition that nihilism, the power of
denial, needs reactive forces, but also its opposite: it is nihilism, the
power of denial, that leads reactive forces to triumph. This double
game gives the Jewish priest an unequalled depth and ambivalence: he
"took the side of all *decadence* instincts – *not* as being dominated by
them because he . . . divined in them a power by means of which one
can prevail against 'the world' ".[16]

We will have to return to those famous passages where Nietzsche
considers the Judaism of the Jewish priest. They have often produced
the most dubious interpretations. We know that the Nazis had
ambiguous relations with Nietzsche's work: ambiguous because they
liked to appeal to it but could not do so without mutilating quotations,
falsifying editions and banning important texts. On the other hand,

Nietzsche himself did not have ambiguous relations with the Bismarckian regime, still less with Pan-Germanism and anti-semitism. He despised and hated them: "Do not associate with anyone who is implicated in this shameless racial hoax."[17] And the *cri de coeur*, "But, finally, what do you think I feel when the name of Zarathustra comes from the mouths of anti-semites!"[18] In order to understand the sense of Nietzschean reflections on Judaism it must be recalled that the "Jewish question" had become, in the Hegelian school, a dialectical theme *par excellence*. Nietzsche takes up the question once again but according to his own method. He asks: how is the priest constituted in the history of the Jewish people? Under what conditions is he constituted – conditions which will prove *decisive for the whole of European history*? Nothing is more striking than Nietzsche's admiration for the Kings of Israel and the Old Testament.[19] The Jewish problem is the same as the problem of the constitution of the priest in this world of Israel: this is the true typological problem. This is why Nietzsche is so insistent on the following point: I am the inventor of the psychology of the priest (EH III GM). It is true that there are racial considerations in Nietzsche. But race only ever intervenes as an element in a *crossbreeding*, as a factor in a *complex* which is physiological but also psychological, political, historical and social. Such a complex is exactly what Nietzsche calls a type. The type of the priest – there is no other problem for Nietzsche. And this same Jewish people which, at one moment in its history found its conditions of existence in the priest, is today the people to save Europe, to protect it from itself by inventing new conditions.[20] What Nietzsche wrote about Judaism cannot be read without recalling what he wrote to Fritsch, an anti-semitic and racist writer: "I beg you to stop sending me your publications if you please: I fear for my patience."

. Bad Conscience and Interiority

The objective of both forms of *ressentiment* is to deprive active force of its material conditions of operation, to keep it strictly separate from what it can do. But while it is true that active force is fictitiously separated from what it can do, it is also true that something real happens to it as a result of this fiction. In this respect our question continues to resound: what does active force really become? Nietzsche's answer is extremely precise: whatever the reason that an active force is falsified, deprived of its conditions of operation and separated from what it can do, *it is turned back inside, turned back against itself*. Being interiorised, being turned back against itself – this is the way in which active force becomes truly reactive. "All instincts that do not discharge themselves outwardly *turn inward* – that is what I call the *internalisation* of man . . . *that* is the origin of the 'bad conscience' " (GM II 16 pp. 84–5). It is in this sense that bad conscience takes over the job of *ressentiment*. As it has appeared to us *ressentiment* is inseparable from a ghastly invitation, from a temptation and from a will to spread an infection. It hides its hatred under a tempting love: I who accuse you, it is for your own good; I love you in order that you will join me, until you are joined with me, until you yourself become a painful, sick, reactive being, a good being . . . "When would men of *ressentiment* achieve the ultimate, subtlest, sublimest triumph of revenge? Undoubtedly if they succeeded in poisoning the consciences of the fortunate with their own misery, with all misery, so that one day the fortunate began to be ashamed of their own good fortune and perhaps said to one another: 'it is disgraceful to be fortunate: *there is too much misery!*' " (GM III 14 p. 124). In *ressentiment* reactive force accuses and projects itself. But *ressentiment* would be nothing if it did not lead the accused himself to admit his wrongs, to "turn back to himself": the *introjection* of active forces is not the opposite of *projection* but the consequence and the continuation of reactive projection. We should not see bad conscience as a new type: at best we will find the reactive type, the slave type, to be concrete varieties in which *ressentiment* is in almost the pure state; we will find others where bad conscience, reaching its full development, covers *ressentiment* up. Reactive forces continue to pass through the successive stages of their triumph: bad conscience extends *ressentiment*, leads us further into a domain where the contagion has spread. Active force becomes reactive, the master becomes slave.

Separated from what it can do, active force does not evaporate. Turning back against itself *it produces pain*. No longer rejoicing in itself but producing pain: "this uncanny, dreadfully joyous labour of a soul voluntarily at odds with itself that makes itself suffer out of joy in making suffer" (GM II 18 p. 87), "while pleasure is felt and *sought* in ill constitutedness, decay, pain, mischance, ugliness, voluntary deprivation, self-mortification, self-flagellation, self-sacrifice" (GM III p. 118). Rather than being regulated by reactive forces pain is produced by the former active force. This results in a curious, unfathomable phenomenon: a multiplication, a self-impregnation, a hyper-production of pain. Bad conscience is the conscience that multiplies its pain, which has found a technique for manufacturing pain by turning active force back against itself: the squalid workshop. *The multiplication of pain by the interiorisation or introjection of force* – this is the first definition of bad conscience.

9. The Problem of Pain

Such, at least, is the definition of the first aspect of bad conscience, of the topological aspect, its raw or material state. Interiority is a complex notion. What is interiorised is primarily active force; but interiorised force becomes manufacturer of pain; and as pain is produced more abundantly, interiority gains "in depth, width and height", an ever more voracious abyss. This means, secondly, that pain in its turn is *interiorised*, sensualised, spiritualised. What do these expressions mean? *A new sense is invented for pain, an internal sense, an inward sense*: pain is made the consequence of a sin, a fault. You have produced your pain because you have sinned, you will save yourself by manufacturing your pain. Pain conceived as the consequence of an inward fault and the interior mechanism of salvation, pain being interiorised as fast as it is produced, "pain transformed into feelings of guilt, fear and punishment": (GM III 20) this is the second aspect of bad conscience, its typological moment, bad conscience as feeling of guilt.

In order to understand the nature of this invention we must assess the importance of a more general problem: what is the meaning of pain? The meaning of existence is completely dependent on it: existence is meaningful only to the extent that the pain of existence has a meaning (UM III, 5). Now, pain is a reaction. Thus it appears that its only meaning consists in the possibility of acting this reaction or at least of localising it, isolating its trace, in order to avoid all propagation until one can re-act once more. The active meaning of pain therefore appears as an external meaning. In order for pain to be judged from an active point of view it must be kept in the element of its exteriority. There is a whole art in this, an art which is that of the masters. The masters have a secret. They know that pain has only one meaning: giving pleasure to someone, giving pleasure to someone who inflicts or contemplates pain. If the active man is able not to take his own pain seriously it is because he always imagines someone to whom it gives pleasure. It is not for nothing that such an imagination is found in the belief in the active gods which peopled the Greek world " 'Every evil the sight of which edifies a god is justified' . . . what was at bottom the ultimate meaning of Trojan Wars and other such tragic terrors? There can be no doubt whatever: they were intended as *festival plays* for the gods" (GM II 7 p. 69). There is a tendency to invoke pain as an argument against existence; this way of arguing testifies to a way of thinking which is dear to us, a reactive way. We not only put ourselves in the position of the one who suffers, but in the position of the man of *ressentiment* who no longer acts his reactions. It must be understood that the active meaning of pain appears in other perspectives: pain is not an argument against life, but, on the contrary, a stimulant to life, "a bait for life", an argument in its favour. Seeing or even inflicting suffering is a structure of life as active life, an active manifestation of life. Pain has an immediate meaning in favour of life: its external meaning. "Our delicacy and even more our tartuffery . . . resist a really vivid comprehension of the degree to which *cruelty* constituted the great festival pleasure of more primitive men and was indeed an ingredient of almost every one of their pleasures . . . Without cruelty there is no festival: thus the longest and most ancient part of human history teaches – and in punishment there is so much that is festive!" (GM II 6 p. 66 and p. 67*). This is Nietzsche's contribution to a peculiarly spiritual problem: what is the meaning of pain and suffering?

We must admire the astonishing invention of the bad conscience all the more: a new meaning for suffering, *an internal meaning*. It is no longer a question of acting one's pain, nor of judging it from an active standpoint. On the contrary, one is numbed against pain by passion. "The passion of the most savage": pain is made the consequence of fault and the means of a salvation; pain is healed by manufacturing yet more pain, by internalising it still further; one tries to forget, that is to say, one cures oneself of pain by infecting the wound (GM III 15). Nietzsche had already pointed out an essential thesis in the *Birth of Tragedy*: tragedy dies at the same time as drama becomes an inward conflict and suffering is internalised. But who invents and wills the internal meaning of pain?

10. Development of Bad Conscience: the Christian priest

Internalisation of force, then internalisation of pain itself: the passage
from the first to the second moment of bad conscience is no more
axiomatic than the linkage of the two aspects of *ressentiment* was. The
intervention of the priest is again necessary. This second incarnation
of the priest is the Christian one: "It was only in the hands of the
priest, that artist in guilt feelings, that it achieved form" (GM III 20 p.
140).

The Christian-priest brings bad conscience out of its raw animal
state, he presides over the internalisation of pain. The doctor-priest
heals pain by infecting the wound. The artist-priest raises bad conscience to its superior form: pain, the consequence of a sin. – But how
does he go about it? "If one wanted to express the value of the priestly
existence in the briefest formula it would be: the priest *alters the
direction of ressentiment*" (GM III 15 p. 127). It will be recalled that the
man of *ressentiment*, who is by nature full of pain, is looking for a cause
for his suffering. He accuses, he accuses everything that is active in
life. The priest appears in an initial form here: he presides over the
accusation, he organises it. "Look at these men who call themselves
good, I tell you: these are the evil ones." The power of *ressentiment* is
therefore completely directed towards the other, against others. But
ressentiment is an explosive substance: it makes active forces become
reactive. *Ressentiment* must then adapt itself to these new conditions;
it must change direction. The reactive man must now find the cause of
his suffering *in himself*. Bad conscience suggests to him that he must
look for this cause "in himself, in some *guilt*, in a piece of the past, he
must understand his suffering as a *punishment*" (GM III 20 p. 140).
And the priest appears a second time in order to preside over this
change of direction: "Quite so, my sheep! someone must be to blame
for it – *you alone are to blame for yourself!*" (GM III 15 p. 128). The
priest invents the notion of *sin*. " 'Sin' . . . has been the greatest event
so far in the history of the sick soul: we possess in it the most
dangerous and fateful artifice of religious interpretation" (GM III 20
p. 140). The word "fault" now refers to the fault which I have
committed, to my own fault, to my guilt. This is how pain is internalised: as the consequence of a sin it now has only an inward meaning.

The relationship between Judaism and Christianity must be evaluated from two standpoints. On the one hand, Christianity is the end

result of Judaism. It follows on from it, it completes its project. The whole power of *ressentiment* ends with the God of the poor, the sick and the sinners. In some well-known passages Nietzsche insists on the spiteful character of St Paul, on the baseness of the New Testament (AC 42–43, 46). Even the death of Christ is a detour which leads back to Judaic values: by means of this death a pseudo-opposition between love and hate is set up, this love is made more seductive, as if it were independent of this hate (GM I 8). The truth that Pontius Pilate discovered remains hidden: Christianity is the consequence of Judaism, all its premises are found there, it is merely the conclusion from *these* premises. – But, from another standpoint, Christianity does sound a new note. It is not content to complete *ressentiment*, it changes its direction. It imposes the new invention, bad conscience. But, once again, it should not be thought that the new direction of *ressentiment* in bad conscience is opposed to the first direction. Once again, we are merely concerned with an additional temptation, an additional seduction. *Ressentiment* said "it is your fault", bad conscience says "it is my fault". But *ressentiment* is really only appeased when its contagion is spread. Its aim is for the whole of life to become reactive, for those in good health to become sick. It is not enough for it to accuse, the accused must feel guilty. It is in bad conscience that *ressentiment* comes into its own and reaches the summit of its contagious power: by changing direction. It cries "It is my fault, it is my fault" until the whole world takes up this dreary refrain, until everything active in life develops this same feeling of guilt. And these are the only preconditions for the priest's power: by nature the priest is the one who makes himself master of those who suffer (GM III 15).

In all this we discover Nietzsche's ambition; wherever dialecticians see antitheses or oppositions to show that there are finer differences to be discovered, deeper coordinations and correlations to be evaluated. Bad conscience instead of the Hegelian unhappy consciousness which is a mere symptom! The definition of the first aspect of the bad conscience was: *the multiplication of pain by the internalisation of force*. The definition of the second aspect is: *the internalisation of pain by the change of direction of ressentiment*. We have stressed the way in which bad conscience takes over the job of *ressentiment*. We must also insist on the parallels between bad conscience and *ressentiment*. Not only does each of these varieties have two moments, topological and typological, but the passage from one moment to the other brings in the priest in both cases. And the priest always acts through fiction. We have analysed the fiction on which the reversal of values in *ressentiment* rests. But one problem remains to be resolved: on what fiction does the internalisation of pain, the change of direction of *ressentiment* in bad conscience, rest? This problem is all the more complicated since, according to Nietzsche, it brings into play the whole phenomenon called *culture*.

11. *Culture Considered from the Prehistoric Point of View*

Culture means training and selection. Nietzsche calls the movement of culture the "morality of customs" (D9); this latter is inseparable from iron collars, from torture, from the atrocious means which are used to train man. But the genealogist's eye distinguishes two elements in this violent training (BGE 188): 1) That which is obeyed, in a people, race or class, is always historical, arbitrary, grotesque, stupid and limited; this usually represents the worst *reactive* forces. 2) But in the fact that something, no matter what it is, is obeyed, appears a principle which goes beyond peoples, races and classes. To obey the law because it is the law: the form of the law means that a certain *activity*, a certain active force, is exercised on man and is given the task of training him. *Even if they are historically inseparable* these two aspects must not be confused: on the one hand, the historical pressure of a State, a Church etc., on the individuals that it aims to assimilate; on the other hand, the activity of man as generic being, the activity of the human species as such. Hence Nietzsche's use of the words "primitive", "prehistoric": the morality of customs *precedes* universal history (D 18); culture is generic activity; "the labour performed by man upon himself during the greater part of the existence of the human race, his entire *prehistoric* labour . . . notwithstanding the severity, tyranny, stupidity and idiocy involved in it" (GM II 2 p. 59). Every historical law is arbitrary, but what is not arbitrary, what is prehistoric and generic, is the law of obeying laws. (Bergson will rediscover this thesis when he shows, in *Les Deux Sources*, that all habits are arbitrary but that the habit of taking on habits is natural.)

Prehistoric means generic. Culture is man's prehistoric activity. But what does this activity consist in? It is always a matter of giving man habits, of making him obey laws, of training him. Training man means forming him in such a way that he can act his reactive forces.

The activity of culture is, in principle, exercised on reactive forces, it gives them habits and imposes models on them in order to make them suitable for being acted. Culture as such is exercised in many directions. It even attacks the reactive forces of the unconscious and the most subterranean digestive and intestinal forces (the diet and something analogous to what Freud will call the education of the sphincters – EH II "Why I am so Clever"). But its principal object is to reinforce consciousness. This consciousness which is defined by the fugitive character of excitations, this consciousness which is itself based on the faculty of forgetting must be given a consistency and a firmness which it does not have on its own. Culture endows consciousness with a new faculty which is apparently opposed to the faculty of forgetting: memory.[22] But the memory with which we are concerned here is not the memory of traces. This original memory is no longer a function of the past, but a function of the future. It is not the memory of the sensibility but of the will. It is not the memory of traces but of words.[22] It is the faculty of promising, commitment to the future, memory of the future itself. Remembering the promise that has been made is not recalling that it was made at a particular past moment, but that one must hold to it at a future moment. This is precisely the selective object of culture: forming a man capable of promising and thus of making use of the future, a free and powerful man. Only such a man is active; he acts his reactions, everything in him is active or acted. The faculty of promising is the effect of culture as the activity of man on man; the man who can promise is the product of culture as species activity.

We understand why culture does not, in principle, recoil from any kind of violence: "perhaps indeed there was nothing more fearful and uncanny in the whole prehistory of man than mnemotechnics . . . Man could never do without blood, torture and sacrifices when he felt the need to create a memory for himself" (GM II 3 p. 61). How many tortures are necesary in order to train reactive forces, to constrain them to be acted, before culture reaches its goal (the free, active and powerful man). Culture has always used the following means: it made pain a medium of exchange, a currency, an equivalent; precisely the exact equivalent of a forgetting, of an inquiry caused, a promise not kept (GM II 4). Culture, when related to this means, is called *justice*; the means itself is called *punishment*. "Injury caused = pain undergone" – this is the equation of punishment that determines a relationship of man to man. This relationship between men is determined, following the equation, as a *relationship of a creditor and a debtor*: justice makes man *responsible for a debt*. The debtor-creditor relationship expresses the activity of culture during the process of training or formation. Corresponding to prehistoric activity this relationship itself is the relationship of man to man, "the most primitive of individuals" preceding even "the origins of any social organisation".[23] It also serves as a model "for the crudest and most primitive social constitutions". Nietzsche sees the archetype of social organisation in credit rather than exchange. The man who pays for the injury he causes by his pain, the man held responsible for a debt, the man treated as responsible for his reactive forces: these are the means used by culture to reach its goal. – Nietzsche therefore offers us the following genetic lineage: 1) Culture as prehistoric or generic activity, an enterprise of training and selection; 2) The means used by this activity, the equation of punishment, the relationship of debt, the responsible man; 3) The product of this activity: the active man, free and powerful, the man who can promise.

12. Culture Considered from the Post-Historic Point of View

We have posed the problem of bad conscience. The genetic lineage of culture does not seem to get us any nearer a solution. On the contrary: the most obvious conclusion is that neither bad conscience nor *ressentiment* intervene in the process of culture and justice. "The 'bad conscience', this most uncanny and most interesting plant of all our earthly vegetation, did *not* grow on this soil" (GM II 14 p. 82). On the one hand, revenge and *ressentiment* are not the origin of justice. Moralists, even socialist ones, make justice derive from a reactive feeling, from deeply felt offence, a spirit of revenge or justiciary reaction. But such a derivation explains nothing it would have to show how the pain of others can be a satisfaction of revenge, a reparation for revenge. We will never understand the cruel equation "injury caused = pain undergone" if a third term is not introduced – the pleasure which is felt in inflicting pain or in contemplating it.[24] But this third term, the external meaning of pain, has an origin which is completely different from revenge or reaction: it reflects an active standpoint, active forces, which are given the training of reactive forces as their task and for their pleasure. Justice is the generic activity that trains man's reactive forces, that makes them suitable for being acted and holds man responsible for this suitability itself. To justice we can oppose the way in which *ressentiment* and then bad conscience are formed: by the triumph of reactive forces, through their unsuitability for being acted, through their hatred for everything that is active, through their resistance, through their fundamental injustice. Thus *ressentiment*, far from being at the origin of justice, is "the last sphere to be conquered by the spirit of justice . . . The active, aggressive, arrogant man is still a hundred steps closer to justice than the reactive man."[25]

Just as *ressentiment* is not the origin of justice so bad conscience is not the product of punishment. However many meanings punishment can have there is always one meaning which it *does not have*. Punishment cannot awaken a feeling of guilt in the culprit. "It is precisely among criminals and convicts that the sting of conscience is extremely rare; prisons and penitentiaries are *not* the kind of hotbed in which this species of gnawing worm is likely to flourish . . . Generally speaking, punishment makes men hard and cold; it concentrates; it sharpens the feeling of alienation; it strengthens the power of resistance. If it happens that punishment destroys the vital energy and brings about a miserable prostration and self-abasement, such a result is certainly even less pleasant than the usual effects of punishment – characterised by dry and gloomy seriousness. If we consider those millenia *before* the history of man, we may unhesitatingly assert that it was precisely through punishment that the development of the feeling of guilt was most powerfully *hindered* – at least in the victims upon whom the punitive force was vented" (GM II 14 pp. 81–82). We can oppose point by point the state of culture in which man, at the cost of his pain, feels himself responsible for his reactive forces and the state of bad conscience where man, on the contrary, feels himself to blame for his active forces and experiences them as culpable. However we consider culture or justice we always see in them the exercise of a formative activity, the opposite of *ressentiment* and bad conscience.

This impression is further reinforced if we consider the product of cultural activity: the free and active man, the man who can promise. Just as culture is the prehistoric element of man the product of culture is his post-historic element. "If we place ourselves at the end of this tremendous process, where the tree at last brings forth fruit, where society and the morality of customs at last reveal *what* they have simply been the means to: then we discover that the ripest fruit is the *sovereign individual*, like only to himself, liberated again from morality of customs, autonomous and supramoral (for 'autonomous' and 'moral' are mutually exclusive), in short, the man who has his own independent, protracted will and the *right to make promises*" (GM II 2 p. 59). Nietzsche's point is that we must not confuse the product of culture with its means. Man's species activity constitutes him as responsible for his reactive forces: *responsibility-debt*. But this responsibility is only a means of training and selection: it progressively measures the suitability of reactive forces for being acted. The finished product of species activity is *not* the responsible man himself or the moral man, but the autonomous and supramoral man, that is to say the one who actually acts his reactive forces and in whom all reactive forces are acted. He alone "is able to" promise, precisely because he is no longer responsible to any tribunal. The product of culture is not the man who obeys the law, but the sovereign and legislative individual who defines himself by power over himself, over destiny, over the law: the free, the light, the *irresponsible*. In Nietzsche the notion of responsibility, even in its higher form, has the limited value of a simple means: the autonomous individual is no longer responsible to justice for his reactive forces, he is its master, the sovereign, the legislator, the author and the actor. It is he who speaks, he no longer has to *answer*. The only active sense of responsibility-debt is its disappearing in the movement by which man is liberated: the creditor is liberated because he participates in the right of the masters, the debtor liberates himself, even at the price of his flesh and his pain: both of them liberate themselves from the process which trained them (GM II 5, 13, 21). This is the general movement of culture: the means disappearing in the product. Responsibility as responsibility before the law, law as the law of justice, justice as the means of culture – all this disappears in the product of culture itself. The morality of customs, the spirit of the laws, produces the man emancipated from the law. This is why Nietzsche speaks of a self destruction of justice.[26] Culture is man's species activity; but, since this activity is selective, it produces the individual as its final goal, where species is itself suppressed.

13. Culture Considered from the Historical Point of View

We have proceeded as if culture goes straight from pre-history to post-history. We have seen it as a species activity which, through the long labour of pre-history, arrives at the individual as its post-historic product. And indeed, this is its essence, in conformity to the superiority of active forces over reactive forces. But we have neglected an important point: the triumph, in fact, of inferior and reactive forces. We have neglected *history*. We must say of culture both that it diappeared long ago and that it has not yet begun. Species activity disappears into the night of the past as its product does into the night of the future. In history culture takes on a sense which is very different from its own essence, having been seized by strange forces of a completely different nature. Species activity in history is inseparable from a movement which perverts it and its product. Furthermore, history is this very perversion, it is identical to the "degeneration of culture". – Instead of species activity, history presents us with races, peoples, classes, Churches and States. Onto species activity are grafted social organisations, associations, communities of a *reactive* character, parasites which cover it over and absorb it. By means of species activity – the movement of which they falsify – reactive forces form collectivities, what Nietzsche calls "herds" (GM III 18). – Instead of justice and its process of self-destruction, history presents us with societies which have no wish to perish and which cannot imagine anything superior to their own laws. What state would listen to Zarathustra's advice: "Let yourself, therefore be overthrown" (Z II "Of Great Events"). In history the law becomes confused with the content which determines it, reactive content which provides its ballast and prevents it from disappearing, unless this is to benefit other, even heavier and more stupid, contents. – Instead of the sovereign individual as the product of culture, history presents us with its own product, the domesticated man in whom it finds the famous meaning of history: "the sublime abortion", "the gregarious animal, docile, sickly, mediocre being, the European today" (BGE 62. GM I 11). – History presents all the violence of culture as the legitimate property of peoples, States and Churches, as the manifestation of *their* force. And in fact, all the procedures of training are employed, but inside-out, twisted, inverted. A morality, a Church, a State are still enterprises of selection, theories of hierarchy. The most stupid laws, the most limited communities, still want to train man and make use of his reactive forces. But to make use of them for what? To carry out what training, what selection? Training procedures are used but in order to turn man into a gregarious, docile and domesticated animal. Training procedures are used but in order to break the strong, to sort out the weak, the suffering or the slaves. Selection and hierarchy are put the wrong way round. Selection becomes the opposite of what it was from the standpoint of activity, it is now only a means of preserving, organising and propagating the reactive life (GM III 13–20 BGE 62).

History thus appears as the act by which reactive forces take possession of culture or divert its course in their favour. The triumph of reactive forces is not an accident in history but the principle and meaning of "universal history". This idea of a historical degeneration of culture occupies a prominent place in Nietzsche's work: it is an argument in Nietzsche's struggle against the philosophy of history and the dialectic. It is the source of Nietzsche's disappointment: culture begins "Greek" but becomes "German" . . . From the *Untimely Meditations* onwards Nietzsche tries to explain how and why culture comes to serve reactive forces which pervert it.[27] More profoundly, Zarathustra develops an obscure symbol: the fire-dog (Z II "Of Great Events"). The fire-dog is the image of species activity, it expresses man's relation to the earth. But, in fact, the earth has two sicknesses, man and the fire-dog itself. For man is domesticated man; species activity is deformed, unnatural activity which serves reactive forces, which becomes mixed up with the Church and the State. – " 'The church?' I answered, 'The church is a kind of State and indeed the most mendacious kind. But keep quiet, you hypocrite dog! You surely know your own kind best! Like you, the state is a hypocrite dog; like you, it likes to speak with smoke and bellowing – to make believe, like you, that it speaks out of the belly of things. For the state wants to be absolutely the most important beast on earth; and it is believed to be so, too!' " (Z II "Of Great Events", p. 154). – Zarathustra appeals to another fire-dog, "This one really speaks from the heart of the earth". Is this still species activity? But, this time, species activity seized in the element of prehistory, to which man corresponds insofar as he is produced in the element of post-history? This interpretation must be taken into consideration, even if it is insufficient. In the *Untimely Meditations* Nietzsche was already putting his trust in "the non-historical and supra-historical element of culture" (what he called the Greek sense of culture) (UM II 10, 8).

In fact there are a certain number of questions which we cannot yet answer. What is the status of this double element of culture? Is it real? Is it anything but one of Zarathustra's "visions"? Culture is inseparable from the history of the movement which perverts it and puts it at the service of reactive forces; but culture is also inseparable from history itself. The activity of culture, man's species activity: is this not a simple idea? If man is essentially (that is to say generically) a *reactive* being, how could he have, or even have had in pre-history, a species *activity*? How could an active man appear, even in a post-history? If man is essentially reactive it seems that activity must concern a being different from man. If man, on the contrary, has a species activity, it seems that it can only be deformed in an accidental way. For the moment we can only list Nietzsche's theses, their precise significance must be considered later: man is essentially reactive; there is nevertheless a species activity of man, but one that is necessarily deformed, necessarily missing its goal, leading to the domesticated man; this activity must be taken up again on another plane, the plane on which it produces, but produces something other than man . . .

It is, however, already possible to explain why species activity necessarily falls in history and turns to the advantage of reactive forces. If the schema of the *Untimely Meditations* is insufficient Nietzsche's work presents other directions in which a solution can be found. The aim of the activity of culture is to train man, that is to say, to make reactive forces suitable for service, for being acted. But throughout the training this suitability for service remains profoundly ambiguous. For at the same time it allows reactive forces to put themselves at the service of other reactive forces, to give these latter forces an appearance of activity, an appearance of justice, to form with them a fiction that gets the better of active forces. It will be recalled that, in *ressentiment*, certain reactive forces prevent other reactive forces from being acted. Bad conscience reaches the same end by almost opposite means: *in bad conscience some reactive forces make use of their suitability for being acted to give other reactive forces an appearance of acting*. There is no less fiction in this procedure than in the procedure of *ressentiment*. *In this way associations of reactive forces are formed under the cover of species activity*. These associations are grafted onto species activity and necessarily divert it from its real sense. Training provides reactive forces with a marvellous opportunity to go into partnership, to form a collective reaction usurping species activity.

14. Bad Conscience, Responsibility, Guilt

When reactive forces are grafted onto species activity in this way they break off its "lineage". Here again, a projection intervenes. It is debt, it is the debtor-creditor relationship, that is projected and that changes its nature in this projection. From the standpoint of species activity man was held responsible for his reactive forces; his reactive forces themselves were considered responsible to an active tribunal. Now, reactive forces take advantage of their training to form a complex association with other reactive forces: they feel responsible to these other forces, these other forces feel themselves to be judges and masters of the former. The association of reactive forces is thus accompanied by a transformation of debt; this becomes a debt toward "divinity", toward "society", toward "the State", toward reactive instances. Everything then takes place between reactive forces. Debt loses the active character by virtue of which it took part in man's liberation: in its new form it is inexhaustible, *unpayable*. "The *aim* now is to preclude pessimistically, once and for all, the prospect of a final discharge; the *aim* now is to make the glance recoil disconsolately from an iron impossibility; the *aim* now is to turn back the concepts 'guilt' and 'duty' – back against whom? There can be no doubt: against the 'debtor' first of all . . . finally they are turned back against the 'creditor' too" (GM II 21 p. 91). Examine what Christianity calls "redemption". It is no longer a matter of discharge from debt, but of a deepening of debt. It is no longer a matter of a suffering through which debt is paid, but of a suffering through which one is shackled to it, through which one becomes a debtor forever. Suffering now only pays the interest on the debt; *suffering is internalised, responsibility-debt has become responsibility-guilt*. So that the creditor himself must accept responsibility for the debt, take upon himself the bulk of the debt. This is Christianity's stroke of genius, says Nietzsche: "God himself sacrifices himself for the guilt of mankind, God himself makes payment to himself, God as the only being who can redeem man from what has become unredeemable for man himself" (GM II 21 p. 92).

We can see a qualitative difference between the two forms of responsibility, responsibility-debt and responsibility-guilt. One originates in the activity of culture; it is only the instrument of this activity, it develops the external sense of pain, it must disappear in the product in order to give way to a beautiful irresponsibility. In the other, everything is reactive: its origin is *ressentiment's* accusation, it grafts itself onto culture and diverts it from its initial direction, it entails a necessary change of direction of *ressentiment* which no longer looks outside for someone to blame. It perpetuates itself at the same time as it internalises pain. – We said: the priest is the one who internalises pain by changing the direction of *ressentiment*; in this way he gives bad conscience form. We asked: how can *ressentiment* change direction whilst keeping its properties of hate and revenge? The lengthy analysis above gives us the elements of an answer:

1) Under the cover of species activity and by usurping this activity, reactive forces constitute associations (herds). Certain reactive forces appear to act, others serve as material: "Wherever there are herds, it is the instinct of weakness that organised it" (GM II 18 pp. 135–6).

2) It is in this milieu that bad conscience is formed. Abstracted from species activity, debt is projected into reactive association. Debt becomes the relation of a debtor who will never finish paying to a creditor who will never finish using up the interest on the debt: "Debt toward the divinity". The pain of a debtor is internalised, responsibility for the debt becomes a feeling of guilt. In this way the priest comes to change the direction of *ressentiment*: we, reactive beings, do not have to look for the guilty ones outside, we are all guilty towards ourselves, toward the Church, toward God (GM II 20–22).

3) But the priest does not only corrupt the herd, he organises it, he protects it. He invents the means which enable us to endure multiplied, internalised pain. He makes it possible to live with the culpability which he introduces. He makes us participate in an apparent activity, in an apparent injustice, the service of God; he *involves* us in association, he awakens in us "the desire to see the community prosper" (GM III 18–19). Our underling insolence serves as an antidote to our bad conscience. But, above all, *ressentiment*, in changing direction, has lost nothing of its sources of satisfaction, of its virulence or its hatred of *others*. "It is my fault", this is the cry of love by means of which we, the new sirens, attract others to us and divert them from their path. By changing the direction of *ressentiment* the men of bad conscience have found the best means to satisfy revenge, to spread the

contagion: "how ready they themselves are at bottom to *make* one pay; how they crave to be *hangmen* . . ."[28]

4) It will be noted in all this that the form of bad conscience, just like the form of *ressentiment*, implies a fiction. Bad conscience rests on the diverting of species activity, on the usurping of this activity, on the *projection* of debt.

15. *The Ascetic Ideal and the Essence of Religion*

Nietzsche sometimes writes as if it were possible to distinguish two and even several types of religion. In this sense religion would not have an essential link with *ressentiment* or bad conscience. Dionysus is a God. "I could hardly doubt that there are numerous varieties of gods. There is no lack of those who seem inseparable from a certain insouciance, a certain halcyonism. Light feet are perhaps one of the attributes of divinity" (VP IV 580). Nietzsche never stops saying that there are active and affirmative Gods, active and affirmative religions. Every selection implies a religion. Following his favourite method Nietzsche recognises a plurality of senses in religion depending on the many forces which can take possession of it: there is therefore a religion of the strong, with a profoundly selective, educative sense. Moreover, if we consider Christ as a personal type – distinguishing him from Christianity as collective type – we must recognise how far he lacked *ressentiment*, bad conscience; he defined himself by glad tidings, he presents to us a life which is not that of Christianity, in the same way that Christianity presents us with a religion which is not that of Christ.[29]

But all these typological remarks risk hiding the main point from us. Not that typology is not the main point, but the only good typology is one that takes the following principle into account: the higher degree or affinity of forces. ("In everything only the higher degrees matter.") Religion has as many senses as there are forces capable of taking possession of it. But religion itself is a force with a greater or lesser affinity for the forces that take possession of it and that it takes possession of itself. Insofar as religion is possessed by forces of a different nature it does not reach its higher degree, the only one that matters, where it would cease to be a means. On the contrary, when it is conquered by forces of the same nature, or when, growing up, it takes possession of these forces and shakes off the yoke of those which dominated it in its infancy, it then discovers its own essence in its higher degree. But, each time that Nietzsche speaks to us of an active religion, a religion of the strong, a religion without *ressentiment* or bad conscience, he is talking of a state in which religion finds itself subjugated by forces of an entirely different nature from its own and cannot unmask itself: religion as "procedure of selection and education in the hands of philosophers" (BGE 62). Even in the case of Christ, religion as belief or faith remains entirely subjugated by the force of a practice which merely gives "the feeling of being divine" (AC 33). On the other hand, when religion comes to "act sovereignly by itself", when other forces have to borrow a mask to survive, a "heavy and terrible price" is always paid, even as religion finds its own essence. This is why, according to Nietzsche, *religion on the one hand and bad conscience on the other have an essential link*. Considered in their raw state *ressentiment* and bad conscience represent the reactive forces which seize the elements of religion in order to free them from the yoke under which active forces hold them. In their formal state *ressentiment* and bad conscience represent the reactive forces which religion itself conquers and develops by exercising its new sovereignty. *Ressentiment* and bad conscience – these are the higher degrees of religion as such. The inventor of Christianity is not Christ but St Paul, the man of bad conscience, the man of *ressentiment*. (The question "which one?" applied to Christianity.[30])

Religion is not merely a force. Reactive forces would never have triumphed, carrying religion to its highest degree, if religion for its part was not animated by a will, a will which leads reactive forces to triumph. Beyond *ressentiment* and bad conscience Nietzsche deals with the third stage – the ascetic ideal. But *the ascetic ideal was also there from the start*. In its initial sense the ascetic ideal designates the complex of *ressentiment* and bad conscience: it crosses the one with the other, it reinforces the one with the other. Secondly, it expresses all the ways in which the sickness of *ressentiment*, the suffering of bad conscience become livable, or rather, are organised and propagated; the ascetic priest is simultaneously gardener, breeder, shepherd and doctor. Finally, and this is its deepest sense, the ascetic ideal expresses the will which makes reactive forces triumph. "The ascetic ideal expresses a will" (GM III 23). We discover the idea of a fundamental complicity (not an identity, but a complicity) between reactive forces and a form of the will to power.[31] Reactive forces would never prevail without a will which develops the projections, which organises the necessary fictions. The fiction of a world-beyond in the ascetic ideal: this is what accompanies the steps of *ressentiment* and bad conscience, this is what permits the depreciation of life and all that is active in it, this is what gives the world a value of appearance or of nought. The fiction of another world was already present in other fictions as the condition of their possibility. Conversely, the will to nothingness needs reactive forces: it is not just that it only tolerates life in reactive form, but it needs the reactive life as a means by which life *must* contradict itself, deny itself, annihilate itself. What would become of reactive forces separated from the will to nothingness? But what would the will to nothingness be without reactive forces? Perhaps it would become something completely different from what we see it as. The sense of the ascetic ideal is thus as follows: to express the affinity of reactive forces with nihilism, to express nihilism as the "motor" of reactive forces.

16. Triumph of Reactive Forces

The Nietzschean typology brings into play a whole psychology of "depths" or "caves". In particular the mechanisms which correspond to each moment of the triumph of reactive forces form a theory of the unconscious which ought to be compared to the whole of Freudianism. We must nevertheless be careful not to give Nietzschean concepts an exclusively psychological significance. It is not just that the type is also a biological, sociological, historical and political reality, not only that metaphysics and the theory of knowledge themselves belong to typology. But that Nietzsche, through this typology, develops a philosophy which must, in his view, replace the old metaphysics and transcendental critique and give a new foundation to the sciences of man: genealogical philosophy, that is to say the philosophy of the will to power. The will to power must not be interpreted psychologically, as if the will to power wanted power because of a motive; just as genealogy must not be interpreted as a merely philosophical genesis (cf. summary table overleaf).

TYPE	VARIETY OF TYPE	MECHANISM	PRINCIPLE	PRODUCT	QUALITY OF THE WILL TO POWER
Active Type: the Master (active forces prevail over reactive forces; reactive forces are acted)	*Dream and Intoxication*	The excitants of life, the stimulants of the will to power	Appollo and Dionysus	*The Artist*	AFFIRM-ATION
	Consciousness: System of the reactive apparatus where reactive forces react to excitations	Distinction between trace and excitation (repression of the memory of traces)	Faculty of forgetting (as regulative principle)	*The Noble*	
	Culture: Generic activity by which reactive forces are trained and tamed	Mechanism of violence; *external meaning* of pain; establishment of the debtor–creditor relationship; responsibility–debt	Faculty of memory; memory of words (as teleological principle)	*The Sovereign Individual, the Legislator*	
		TRIUMPH OF REACTIVE FORCES			
Reactive Type: the Slave (reactive forces prevail over active forces; they triumph without forming a greater force)	Ressentiment	Topological Aspect: *Displacement* (displacement of reactive forces)	Memory of traces; ascent of traces; confusion of excitation and trace	The man who cannot "have done" with anything	NEGATION
		Typological Aspect: *Reversal* (reversal of values or of the relation of forces)	First FICTION: Reactive projection of the reversed image	The perpetual accuser (who is not Noble)	
	Bad Conscience (Internalisation)	Topological Aspect: *Turning back* (internalisation of force)	Active force separated from what it can do	The man who multiplies his pain	
		Typological Aspect: *Changing of direction* (internalisation of pain by changing the direction of *ressentiment*)	Second FICTION: Reactive projection of debt; usurping of culture and formation of the herd	*The guilty man* internal meaning of pain responsi-bility–guilt. *The domesticated man* (who is not Legislator)	
	Ascetic Ideal	Ways of making bad conscience and *ressentiment* bearable	Third FICTION: Setting up of a world-beyond	*The ascetic man* (who is not Artist)	
		Expression of the will to nothingness			

5

The Overman: Against the Dialectic

1. Nihilism

In the word nihilism *nihil* does not signify non-being but primarily a value of nil. Life takes on a value of nil insofar as it is denied and depreciated. Depreciation always presupposes a fiction: it is by means of fiction that one falsifies and depreciates, it is by means of fiction that something is opposed to life (AC 15, the opposition of dream and fiction). The whole of life then becomes unreal, it is represented as appearance, it takes on a value of nil in its entirety. The idea of another world, of a supersensible world in all its forms (God, essence, the good, truth), the idea of values superior to life, is not one example among many but the constitutive element of all fiction. Values superior to life are inseparable from their effect: the depreciation of life, the negation of this world. And if they are inseparable from this effect it is because their principle is a will to deny, to depreciate. We must be careful not to think that higher values form a threshold where the will stops, as if, confronted by the divine, we were released from the constraint of willing. It is not the will that denies itself in higher values, it is higher values that are related to a will to deny, to annihilate life. "Nothingness of the will": this Schopenhauerian concept is only a symptom; it means primarily a will to annihilation, a will to nothingness . . . "but it is and remains a *will!*" (GM III 28 p. 163). Nihil *in "nihilism" means negation as quality of the will to power*. Thus, in its primary and basic sense, nihilism signifies the value of nil taken on by life, the fiction of higher values which give it this value and the will to nothingness which is expressed in these higher values.

Nihilism has a second, more colloquial sense. It no longer signifies a will but rather a reaction. The supersensible world and higher values are reacted against, their existence is denied, they are refused all validity – this is no longer the devaluation of life in the name of higher values but rather the devaluation of higher values themselves. Devaluation no longer signifies life taking on the value of nil, the null value, but the nullity of values, of higher values. The sensational news spreads: there is nothing to be seen behind the curtain, "The characteristics which have been assigned to the 'real being' of things are the characteristics of non-being, of *nothingness*" (TI " 'Reason' in Philosophy" 6 p. 39). Thus the nihilist denies God, the good and even truth – all the forms of the supersensible. Nothing is true, nothing is good, God is dead. The nothingness of the will is no longer merely the symptom of a will to nothingness, but ultimately a negation of all will, a *taedium vitae*. There is no longer any human or earthly will. "Here is snow; here life has grown silent; the last crows whose cries are audible here are called 'wherefore?', 'in vain!', *'nada!'* – here nothing will grow or prosper any longer" (GM III 26 p. 157). This second sense would be familiar but no less incomprehensible if we did not see how it derives from and presupposes the first. Previously life was depreciated from the height of higher values, it was denied in the name of these values. Here, on the contrary, only life remains, but it is still a depreciated life which now continues in a world without values, stripped of meaning and purpose, sliding ever further towards its nothingness. Previously essence was opposed to appearance, life was turned into an appearance. Now essence is denied but appearance is retained: everything is merely appearance, life which is left to us remains for itself an appearance. The first sense of nihilism found its principle in the will to deny as will to power. The second sense, "the pessimism of weakness", finds its principle in the reactive life completely solitary and naked, in reactive forces reduced to themselves. The first sense is a *negative nihilism*; the second sense a *reactive nihilism*.

2. Analysis of Pity

The fundamental complicity of the will to nothingness and reactive forces is due to the fact that it is the will to nothingness that allows reactive forces to triumph. When, under the influence of the will to nothingness, universal life becomes unreal, life as particular life becomes reactive. Life becomes simultaneously unreal as a whole and reactive in particular. In its enterprise of denying life the will to nothingness on the one hand merely tolerates the reactive life but on the other hand has need of it. It tolerates the reactive life as a state of life close to zero, it has need of it as a means by which life is led to deny and contradict itself. In this way victorious reactive forces have a *witness*, or worse, a *leader*. But what happens is that the triumphant reactive forces are less and less tolerant of this leader and witness. They want to triumph alone, they no longer want to owe their triumph to anyone else. Perhaps they dread the obscure goal of its own that the will to power attains through their victory, perhaps they fear that this will to power will turn against them, and destroy them in turn. *The reactive life breaks its alliance with the negative will*, it wants to rule alone. This is why reactive forces project their image, but this time in order to take the place of the will which leads them. How far will they go along this path? It is better to have no "will" at all than this over-powerful, over-lively will. It is better to have stagnant herds than the shepherd who persists in leading us too far. It is better to have only our own strength than a will which we no longer need. How far will reactive forces go? *It is better to fade away passively*! "Reactive nihilism", in a way, prolongs "negative nihilism": triumphant reactive forces take the place of power of denying which led them to their triumph. But "passive nihilism" is the final outcome of reactive nihilism: fading away passively rather than being led from outside.

This story can also be told in another way. God is dead, but what did he die of? *He died of pity*, says Nietzsche. This death is sometimes presented as accidental: old and tired, weary of willing, God "one day suffocated through his excessive pity" (Z IV "Retired from Service" p. 273: The old pope's version). This death is sometimes the effect of a criminal act: " 'His pity knew no shame: he crept into my dirtiest corners. This most curious, most over-importunate, over-compassionate god had to die. He always saw *me*: I desired to take revenge on such a witness – or cease to live myself. The god who saw everything, *even man*: this god had to die! Man could not *endure* that such a witness should live' " (Z IV "The Ugliest Man" pp. 278-9: version of the murderer of God). – What is pity? It is this tolerance for states of life close to zero. Pity is the love of life, but of the weak, sick, reactive life. It is militant and announces the final victory of the poor, the suffering, the powerless and the small. It is divine and gives them this victory. *Who* feels pity? Precisely those who can only tolerate life when it is reactive, those who need this life and this triumph, those who build their temples on the marshy ground of such a life. Those who hate everything which is active in life, those who use life to deny and depreciate life, to oppose it to itself. Pity, in Nietzsche's symbolism, always designates this complex of will to nothingness and reactive forces, this affinity or tolerance of one for the other. "Pity is *practical* nihilism . . . pity persuades to *nothingness*! . . . One does not say 'nothingness": one says 'the Beyond'; or 'God'; or '*true* life'; or Nirvana, redemption, blessedness . . . This innocent rhetoric from the domain of religio-moral idiosyncracy at once appears *much less innocent* when one grasps *which* tendency is here draping the mantle of sublime words about itself: the tendency *hostile to life*" (AC 7 pp. 118–119). Pity for the reactive life in the name of higher values, God's pity for the reactive man: we can guess what kind of will is hidden in this way of loving life, in this God of mercy, in these higher values.

God suffocates from pity: it is as if the reactive life had blocked up his throat. The reactive man puts God to death because he can no longer bear there being a witness, he wants to be alone with his triumph and his strength. *He puts himself in God's place*: he no longer knows any values which are superior to life, but only a reactive life that is satisfied with itself and claims tc secrete its own values. The weapons which God gave him, *ressentiment*, even bad conscience – all the forms of his triumph – are turned against and opposed to God. *Ressentiment* becomes atheistic, but this atheism is still *ressentiment*, always *ressentiment*, always bad conscience.[1] God's murderer is the reactive man, "the ugliest man", "rumbling with bile and full of secret shame" (Z IV "The Ugliest Man"). He reacts against God's pity, "There is also good taste in pity: *that* said at last: Away with *such* a god. Better no god, better to produce destiny on one's own account, better to be a fool, better to be God oneself!" (Z IV "Retired from Service" p. 274). – How far will he go along this road? As far as the great disgust. It is better to have no values at all than higher values, it is better to have no will at all, better to have a nothingness of will than a will to nothingness. It is better to fade away passively. It is the prophet, "prophet of great weariness", who announces the consequences of the death of God: the reactive life left alone with itself, no longer even having the will to disappear, dreaming of a passive extinction. "Everything is empty, everything is past! . . . All our wells have dried up, even the sea has receded. The earth wants to break open, but the depths will not devour us! Alas, where is there still a sea in which one could drown . . . Truly we have grown too weary even to die."[2] *The last man* is the descendant of God's murderer: it is better to have no will at all, better to have a single herd. "Nobody grows rich or poor any more: both are too much of a burden. Who still wants to rule? Who still wants to obey? Both are too much of a burden. *No herdsman and one herd*. Everyone wants the same thing, everyone is the same . . ." (Z Prologue 5 p. 46*).

Told in this way the story still leads to the same conclusion: *negative nihilism* is replaced by *reactive nihilism*, reactive nihilism ends in *passive nihilism*. From God to God's murderer, from God's murderer to the last man. But this outcome is known to the prophet. There are many avatars, many variations on the nihilist theme, before we reach this point. The reactive life strives for a long time to secrete its own values, the reactive man takes the place of God: adaptation, evolution, progress, happiness for all and the good of the community; the God-man, the moral man, the truthful man and the social man. These are the new values that are recommended in place of higher values, these are the new characters proposed in place of God. The last men still say: "We have invented happiness" (Z Prologue 5). Why would man have killed God, if not to take his still warm seat? Heidegger remarks, commenting on Nietzsche, "if God . . . has disappeared from his authoritative position in the suprasensory world, then this authoritative place itself is still always preserved, even though as that which has become empty. The now-empty authoritative realm of the suprasensory and the ideal world can still be adhered to. What is more, the empty place demands to be occupied anew and to have the god now vanished from it replaced by something else".[3] Moreover it is always the same type of life which benefits from the depreciation of the whole of life in the first place, the type of life which took advantage of the will to nothingness in order to obtain its victory, the type of life which triumphed in the temples of God, in the shadow of higher values. Then, secondly, the type of life which puts itself in God's place, which turns against the principle of its own triumph and no longer recognises values other than its own. Finally, the exhausted life which prefers to not will, to fade away passively, rather than being animated by a will which goes beyond it. This still is and always remains the same type of life; life depreciated, reduced to its reactive form. Values can change, be renewed or even disappear. What does not change and does not disappear is the nihilistic perspective which governs this history from beginning to end and from which all these values (as well as their absence) arise. This is why Nietzsche can think that nihilism is not an event in history but the motor of the history of man as universal history. *Negative, reactive* and *passive* nihilism: for Nietzsche one and the same history is marked out by Judaism, Christianity, the reformation, free thought, democratic and socialist ideology etc. Up until the last man.[4]

3. God is Dead

Speculative propositions bring the idea of God into play from the point of view of its form. God does *or* does not exist insofar as the idea of him does or does not imply a contradiction. But the phrase "God is dead" is completely different: it makes the existence of God depend on a synthesis, it synthesizes the idea of God with time, becoming, history and man. It says at one and the same time: God existed *and* he is dead *and* he will rise from the dead, God has become Man *and* Man has become God. The phrase "God is dead" is not a speculative proposition but a dramatic proposition, *the* dramatic proposition *par excellence*. God cannot be made the object of synthetic knowledge without death entering into him. Existence or non-existence cease to be absolute determinations which derive from the idea of God, but rather life and death become relative determinations which correspond to the forces entering into synthesis with or in the idea of God. The dramatic proposition is synthetic, therefore essentially pluralist, typological and differential. Who dies and who puts God to death? "When gods die, they always die many kinds of deaths" (Z IV "Retired from Service" p. 273).

1)*From the point of view of negative nihilism: the moment of the Judaic and Christian consciousness.* The idea of God expresses the will to nothingness, the depreciation of life, "If one shifts the centre of gravity of life *out* of life into the 'Beyond' – into nothingness – one has deprived life as such of its centre of gravity" (AC 43 p. 155). But depreciation, hatred of life in general, entails a glorification of the reactive life in particular. They the evil ones, the sinners . . . we the good; principles and consequence. The Judaic consciousness of the consciousness of *ressentiment* (after the golden age of the kings of Isreal) presents these two aspects: the universal appears as a hatred for life, the particular as a love of life – provided that it is sick and reactive. But for these two aspects to be related as premises and conclusion, as principle and consequence, for love to be the consequence of hate, it is of the greatest importance that it be hidden. The will to nothingness must be made more seductive by opposing one aspect to the other, by making love an antithesis of hate. The Jewish God puts his son to death to make him independent of himself and of the Jewish people. This is the first sense of the death of God.[5] Even Saturn did not have this subtlety of motive. The Judaic consciousness puts God to death in the person of the Son: it invents a God of love who would prefer to *suffer from* hate rather than find his premises and principle there. The Judaic consciousness makes God in his Son independent of Jewish principles themselves. In putting God to death it has found the way of making *its* God a God who is universal "for all" and truly cosmopolitan.[6]

The Christian God is therefore the Jewish God, but the Jewish God becomes cosmopolitan – a conclusion separated from its premises. On the cross God ceases to appear as a Jew. Moreover, on the cross, it is the old God who dies and the new God who is born. He is born an orphan and creates a Father for himself in his own image: God of love, but this love is still that of the reactive life. This is the second sense of the death of God: the Father dies, the Son creates another God for us. The Son asks only that we believe in him, that we love him as he loves us, that we become reactive in order to avoid hate. Instead of a father who makes us afraid, we have a son who asks for a little confidence, a little belief.[7] Apparently detached from its hateful premises the love of the reactive life must be valid in itself and must become the universal for the Christian consciousness.

Third sense of the death of God: St Paul seizes hold of this death, he gives it an interpretation which constitutes Christianity as such. The Gospels had begun and St Paul brought to perfection, a grandiose falsification. In the first place, Christ is said to have died for our *sins*! The creditor is said to have given his own son, to have repaid himself with his own son, so immense was the debtor's debt. The father no longer kills his own son to make him independent, but *for us*, because of us (first element of the interpretation of St Paul, AC 42, 49; VP I 390). God put his son on the cross out of love; we respond to this love to the extent that we feel guilty, guilty of this death, and we redress it by accusing ourselves, by paying interest on the debt. Through the love of God, through the sacrifice of his son, the whole of life becomes reactive. – Life dies but it is reborn as reactive. The reactive life is the content of survival as such, the content of the resurrection. The reactive life alone is God's elect, the reactive life alone finds grace before God, before the will to nothingness. The crucified God *rises from the dead*: this is St Paul's other falsification, the resurrection of Christ and the afterlife for us, the unity of love and the reactive life. It is no longer the father who kills the son, it is no longer the son who kills the father: the father dies in the son, the son is resurrected in the father, for us, because of us. "In fact . . . St Paul could make no use at all of the redeemer's life – he needed the death on the Cross *and* something in addition": the resurrection.[8] – *Ressentiment* is not only hidden in the Christian consciousness, its direction is changed: the Judaic consciousness was consciousness of *ressentiment*, the Christian consciousness is bad conscience. Christian consciousness is the Judaic consciousness reversed, turned round: the love of life, but as reactive life, became the universal; love became the principle, undying hatred appears merely as a consequence of this love, the means to be used against anyone who resists this love. Warrior-Jesus, hateful-Jesus – but for the sake of love.

2) *From the point of view of reactive nihilism: the moment of European consciousness.* Up to this point the death of God has meant the synthesis of the will to nothingness and the reactive life in the idea of God. These elements can be synthesized in many different proportions. But, insofar as the reactive life becomes what is essential, Christianity has a strange result. It teaches us that we put God to death. In this way it secretes its own atheism, an atheism of bad conscience and *ressentiment*. The reactive life instead of the divine will, the reactive Man instead of God, the Man-God replacing the God-Man – the *European Man*. Man killed God, but which man killed God? The reactive man, "the ugliest of men". The divine will, the will to nothingness, can not tolerate any other life but the reactive one and this no longer even tolerates God, it cannot bear God's pity, it takes his sacrifice literally, it suffocates him in the trap of his mercy. It prevents him from rising from the dead, it sits on the coffin-lid. We no longer have the correlation of divine will and reactive life, but rather the displacement of God by the reactive man. This is the fourth sense of the death of God: God suffocates through love of the reactive life, God is suffocated by the ungrateful one whom he loves too much.

3) *From the point of view of passive nihilism: the moment of Buddhist consciousness.* If the falsifications which begin with the Gospels and

which find their definitive form in St Paul are taken into account what is left of Christ, what is *his personal type*, what is the sense of his death? What Nietzsche calls the "gaping contradiction" of the Gospel must guide us. What these texts allow us to guess of the true Christ is as follows; the *glad tidings* that he brings, the *suppression* of the idea of sin, the *absence* of all *ressentiment* and of all spirit of revenge, the consequent *refusal* of all war, the *revelation* of a kingdom of God on Earth as state of the heart and above all *the acceptance of death as the proof of his doctrine*.[9] It is easy to see what Nietzsche is getting at: Christ was the opposite of what St Paul made of him, the true Christ was a kind of Buddha, "a Buddha on a soil very little like that of India".[10] Given his surroundings he was too far ahead of his time, he had already taught the reactive life to die serenely, to fade away passively, he showed the reactive life its true outcome when it was still struggling with the will to power. He gave the reactive life a certain hedonism, the last man a certain nobility, when men were still at the stage of wondering whether they would take God's place. He gave passive nihilism a certain nobility where men were still at the stage of negative nihilism, when reactive nihilism had hardly begun. Beyond bad conscience and *ressentiment* Jesus gave the reactive man a lesson: he taught him to die. He was the gentlest of the decadents, the most interesting (AC 31). Christ was neither Jew nor Christian but Buddhist; nearer the Dalai Lama than the Pope. So far ahead of his country, of his surroundings, that his death had to be deformed, his whole story falsified, moved backward, made to serve preceding stages, turned to the benefit of negative or reactive nihilism. "Reversed by Paul into pagan mystery doctrine which finally learns to treat with the entire state organisation – and wages war, condemns, tortures, swears, hates" (VP I 390/ WP 167): hate became the instrument of this very gentle Christ. For here we have the difference between Buddhism and the official Christianity of St Paul. Buddhism is the religion of passive nihilism, "Buddhism is a religion for the end and fatigue of a civilisation; Christianity does not even find civilization in existence – it establishes civilization if need be" (AC 22 p. 132). It is characteristic of Christian and European history to achieve, by iron and fire, an end which, elsewhere, is already given and naturally attained: the final outcome of nihilism. What Buddhism had come to live as a realised end, as an attained perfection, Christianity saw only as a motor. There is nothing to prevent it from reaching this end; there is nothing to prevent the outcome of Christianity being a "practice" freed from the whole Pauline mythology, there is nothing to prevent it from rediscovering the true practice of Christ. "Buddhism is progressing silently in the whole of Europe" (VP III 87). But how much hate and how many wars would be needed to get to this point? Christ was personally established at this ultimate end, he had attained it with a beat of his wings, bird of the Buddha in surroundings which were not Buddhist. Christianity, on the other hand, has to go through all the stages of nihilism to make this end its own, as the result of a long and terrible politics of revenge.

4. Against Hegelianism

We must not see this philosophy of history and religion as a revival or even a caricature of Hegel's views. The relationship and the difference are deeper. God is Dead, God has become Man, Man has become God: Nietzsche, in contrast to his predecessors, does not believe in this death. He does not bet on this cross. That is to say: he does not make this death an event possessing its meaning in itself. The death of God has as many meanings as there are forces capable of seizing Christ and making him die; but we are still waiting for the forces or the power which will carry this death to its highest point and make it into something more than an apparent and abstract death. In opposition to the whole romantic movement and to every dialectic Nietzsche mistrusts the death of God. With him the age of naive confidence comes to an end, the age which at some times acclaims the reconciliation of man and God, at others the replacement of God by man. Nietzsche has no faith in great resounding events.[11] An event needs silence and time to discover finally the forces which give it an essence. – Of course, for Hegel too, time is necessary for an event to attain its true essence. But this time is only necessary for meaning "in itself" to become "for itself". On Hegel's interpretation the death of Christ stands for superseded opposition, the reconciliation of finite and infinite, the unity of God and individual, of changeless and particular; but the Christian consciousness will have to pass through other figures of opposition in order for this unity to become for itself what it already is in itself. The time that Nietzsche speaks of, on the contrary, is necessary for the formation of the forces which give the death of God a sense that it did not contain in itself, which give it an essence determined as the magnificent gift of exteriority. In Hegel the diversity of senses, the choice of essence and the necessity of time are so many appearances, mere appearances.[12]

Universal and singular, changless and particular, infinite and finite – what are these? Nothing but symptoms. What is this particular, this single, this infinite? And what is this universal, this changeless, this infinite? The former is subject, but which subject, which forces? The latter is predicate or object, but *what will* is it "object" of? The dialectic does not even skim the surface of interpretation, it never goes beyond the domain of symptoms. It confuses interpretation with the development of the uninterpreted symbol. This is why, in questions of change and development, it conceives of nothing deeper than an abstract permutation where the subject becomes predicate and the predicate, subject. But the one that is subject and what the predicate is have not changed, they remain as little determined at the end as they were at the beginning, as little interpreted as possible: everything has happened in the intermediate regions. It is not surprising that the dialectic proceeds by opposition, development of the opposition or contradiction and solution of the contradiction. It is unaware of the real element from which forces, their qualities and their relations derive; it only knows the inverted image of this element which is reflected in abstractly considered symptoms. Opposition can be the law of the relation between abstract products, but difference is the only principle of genesis or production; a principle which itself produces opposition as mere appearance. Dialectic thrives on oppositions because it is unaware of far more subtle and subterranean differential mechanisms: topological displacements, typological variations. This can be seen clearly in one of Nietzsche's favourite examples: his whole theory of bad conscience must be seen as a reinterpretation of the Hegelian unhappy consciousness; this apparently torn consciousness finds its meaning in the differential relations of forces which are hidden beneath sham oppositions. In the same way the relationship of Christianity with Judaism only lets opposition continue to exist as a cover and a pretext. Deprived of all its ambitions, opposition ceases to be formative, impelling and co-ordinating: it becomes a symptom, nothing but a symptom to be interpreted. Deprived of its claim to give an account of difference, contradiction appears for what it is: a perpetual misinterpretation of difference itself, a confused inversion of genealogy. In fact, to the eye of the genealogist, the labour of the negative is only a coarse approximation to the games of the will to power. Considering symptoms abstractly, making the movement of appearance into the genetic law of things and retaining only an inverted image of principle – the whole dialectic operates and moves in the element of *fiction*. How could its solution not be fictitious when its problems themselves are? There is no fiction that it does not turn into a moment of spirit, one of its own moments. One dialectician cannot accuse another of standing on his head – it is the fundamental character of the dialectic itself. How could it still maintain a critical view point in this position? Nietzsche's work is directed against the dialectic for three reasons: it misinterprets sense because it does not know the nature of the forces which concretely appropriate phenomena; it misinterprets essence because it does not know the real element from which forces, their qualities and their relations derive; it misinterprets change and transformation because it is content to work with permutations of abstract and unreal terms.

All these deficiencies have a single origin: ignorance of the question "which one?" There is always the same socratic contempt for the sophist's art. We are informed, in the Hegelian manner, that man and God, religion and philosophy, are reconciled. We are informed, in the manner of Feuerbach, that man takes God's place, that he recuperates the divine as his own property or essence, and that theology becomes anthropology. But *who is Man and what is God? Which is particular and what is universal?* Feuerbach says that man has changed, that he has become God; God has changed, the essence of God has become the essence of man. But he who is Man has not changed: the reactive man, the slave, who does not cease to be slavish by presenting himself as God, always the slave, a machine for manufacturing the divine. What God is has not changed either; always the divine, the supreme Being, a machine for manufacturing the slave. What has changed, or rather, what has exchanged its determinations, is the intermediate concept, the middle terms which can be either subject or predicate of each other: God or Man.[13]

God becomes Man, Man becomes God. But who is Man? He is always the reactive being, the representative, the subject of a weak and depreciated life. What is God? He is always the supreme Being as the means of depreciating life, "object" of the will to nothingness, "predicate" of nihilism. Before and after the death of God man remains "the one that he is" as God remains "what he is": reactive forces and will to nothingness. The dialectic foretells the reconciliation of Man and God. But what is this reconciliation, if not the old complicity, the old affinity of will to nothingness and reactive life? The dialectic foretells the replacement of God by man. But what is this replacement if not the reactive life in place of the will to nothingness, the reactive life now producing its own values? At this point it seems that the whole of the dialectic moves within the limits of reactive forces, that it evolves entirely within the nihilistic perspective. There *is* a standpoint from which opposition appears as the genetic element of force – the standpoint of reactive forces. From the standpoint of reactive forces the differential element is inverted, reflected wrong way up and turned into opposition. There *is* a perspective which opposes fiction to the real, which develops fiction as the means by which reactive forces triumph; it is nihilism, the nihilistic perspective. The labour of the negative serves a will. It is sufficient to ask: "which will is it?" in order to sense the essence of the dialectic. The discovery dear to the dialectic is the unhappy consciousness, the deepening, the re-solution and glorification of the unhappy consciousness and its resources. *It is reactive forces that express themselves in opposition, the will to nothingness that expresses itself in the labour of the negative*. The dialectic is the natural ideology of *ressentiment* and bad conscience. It is thought in the perspective of nihilism and from the standpoint of reactive forces. It is a fundamentally Christian way of thinking, from one end to the other; powerless to create new ways of thinking and feeling. The death of God is a grand, noisy, dialectical event; but an event which happens in the din of reactive forces and the fumes of nihilism.

5. The Avatars of the Dialectic

In the history of the dialectic Stirner has a place apart, the final, extreme place. Stirner was the audacious dialectician who tried to reconcile the dialectic with the art of the sophists. He was able to rediscover the path of the question: "which one?". He knew how to make it the essential question against Hegel, Bauer and Feuerbach simultaneously. "The conceptual question, 'what is man?' has then changed into the personal question 'who is man?'. With 'what' the concept was sought for in order to realise it; with 'who' it is no longer any question at all, but the answer is personally on hand at once in the

asker."[14] In other words, the posing of the question "who?" is sufficient to lead the dialectic to its true result: *saltus mortalis*. Feuerbach
foretold Man in God's place. But *I* am no longer man or species being,
I am no more the essence of man than I am God and the essence of
God. Man and God have been exchanged; but the labour of the
negative, once released, is here to tell us: it is still not You. "I am
neither God nor Man, neither the supreme essence nor my essence,
and therefore it is all one in the main whether I think of the essence as
in me or outside me" (Stirner p. 33), "because Man represents only
another Supreme Being, nothing in fact has taken place but a
metamorphosis in the Supreme Being, and the fear of Man is merely
an altered form of the fear of God" (p. 185). – Nietzsche will say: the
ugliest of men, having killed God because he could not bear his pity, is
still exposed to the pity of Men (Z IV "The Ugliest Man").

The speculative motor of the dialectic is contradiction and its
resolution. But its practical motor is alienation and the suppression of
alienation, alienation and reappropriation. Here the dialectic reveals
its true nature; an art of quibbling beyond all others, an art of
disputing properties and changing proprietors, an art of *ressentiment*.
Stirner penetrates yet again to the truth of the dialectic in the very title
of his great book: *The Ego and His Own*. He thinks that Hegelian
freedom remains an abstract concept; "I have nothing against freedom but I wish you more than just freedom. You should be disen-
cumbered of what you do not want, you should also possess what you
do want, you should not only be a free man, you should also be a
proprietor". But who is appropriated or reappropriated? What is the
reappropriating instance? Is not Hegel's Objective Spirit, his absolute
knowledge, yet another alienation, a spiritual and refined form of
alienation? And cannot the same be said of Bauer's self-consciousness
and pure or absolute human critique and Feuerbach's species being,
man as species, essence and sensuous being? I am *nothing* of all that.
Stirner has no difficulty in showing that idea, consciousness or species
are no less alienations than traditional theology. Relative reappropriations are still absolute alienations. Competing with theology, anthropology makes me the property of Man. But the dialectic cannot be
halted until I finally become a proprietor. Even if it means ending up
in nothingness. – At the same time as the reappropriating instance
diminishes in length, breadth and depth, the act of reappropriation
changes sense, being carried out from a narrower and narrower base.

In Hegel it was a matter of a reconciliation: the dialectic was quick to be reconciled with religion, Church, State and all the forces which nourished it. We know what the famous Hegelian transformations mean: they do not forget to conserve piously. Transcendence remains transcendent at the heart of the immanent. With Feuerbach the sense of "reappropriating" changes, it is less reconciliation that recuperation, human recuperation of transcendent properties. Nothing is conserved however except the human as "absolute and divine being". But this conservation, this final alienation, disappears in Stirner: State and religion, but also human essence are denied in the EGO, which is not reconciled with anything because it annihilates everything, for its own "power", for its own "dealings", for its own "enjoyment". Overcoming alienation thus means pure, cold annihilation, a recovery which lets nothing which it recovers subsist: "it is not that the ego *is* all, but the ego *destroys* all" (Stirner p. 182).

The ego which annihilates everything is also the ego which is nothing: "only the self-dissolving ego, the never-being ego, the *-finite* ego is really I" (Stirner p. 182). "I am *owner* of my might, and I am so when I know myself as *unique*. In the *unique one* the owner himself returns into his creative nothing, of which he is born. Every higher essence above me, be it God, be it man, weakens the feeling of my uniqueness and pales only before the sun of this consciousness. If I found my affair on myself, the unique one, them my concern rests on its transitory, mortal creator, who consumes himself, and I may say: I have founded my affair on nothing" (Stirner p. 366). The interest of Stirner's book is threefold: *a profound analysis of the insufficiency of the reappropriations of his predecessors; the discovery of the essential relation between the dialectic and the theory of the ego, the ego alone being the reappropriating instance; a profound vision of what the outcome of the dialectic was, with the ego, in the ego.* History in general and Hegelianism in particular found their outcome, but also their most complete dissolution, in a triumphant nihilism. Dialectic loves and controls history, but it has a history itself which it suffers from and which it does not control. The meaning of history and the dialectic together is not the realisation of reason, freedom or man as species, but nihilism, nothing but nihilism. *Stirner is the dialectician who reveals nihilism as the truth of the dialectic.* It is enough for him to pose the question "which one?" The unique ego turns everything but itself into nothingness, and this nothingness is precisely its own nothingness, the ego's own nothingness. Stirner is too much of a dialectician to think in any other terms but those of property, alienation and reappropriation – but too exacting not to see where this thought leads: to the ego which is nothing, to nihilism. – This is one of the most important senses of Marx's problem in *The German Ideology*: for Marx it is a matter of stopping this fatal sliding. He accepts Stirner's discovery that the dialectic is the theory of the ego. On one point he supports Stirner: Feuerbach's human species is still an alienation. But Stirner's ego is, in turn, an abstraction, a projection of bourgeois egoism. Marx elaborates his famous doctrine of the conditioned ego: the species and the individual, species being and the particular, social order and egoism are reconciled in the ego conditioned by social and historical relations. Is this sufficient? What is the species and *which one* is the individual? Has the dialectic found its point of equilibrium and rest or merely a final avatar, the socialist avatar before the nihilist conclusion? It is difficult in fact to stop the dialectic and history on the common slope down which they drag each other. Does Marx do anything else but mark the last stage before the end, the proletarian stage?[15]

6. *Nietzsche and the Dialectic*

We have every reason to suppose that Nietzsche had a profound knowledge of the Hegelian movement, from Hegel to Stirner himself. The philosophical learning of an author is not assessed by numbers of quotations, nor by the always fanciful and conjectural check lists of libraries, but by the apologetic or polemical directions of his work itself. We will misunderstand the whole of Nietzsche's work if we do not see "against whom" its principle concepts are directed. Hegelian themes are present in this work as the enemy against which it fights. Nietzsche never stops attacking *the theological and Christian character of German philosophy* (the "Tubingen seminary") – *the powerlessness of this philosophy to extricate itself from the nihilistic perspective* (Hegel's negative nihilism, Feuerbach's reactive nihilism, Stirner's extreme nihilism) – *the incapacity of this philosophy to end in anything but the ego, man or phantasms of the human* (the Nietzschean overman against the dialectic) – *the mystifying character of so-called dialectical transformations* (transvaluation against reappropriation and abstract permutations). It is clear that Stirner plays the revelatory role in all this. It is he who pushes the dialectic to its final consequences, showing what its motor and end result are. But precisely because Stirner still thinks like a dialectician, because he does not extricate himself from the categories of property, alienation and its suppression, he throws himself into the nothingness which he hollows out beneath the steps of the dialectic. He makes use of the question "which one?" but only in order to dissolve the dialectic in the nothingness of the ego. He is incapable of posing this question in anything but the human perspective, under any conditions but those of nihilism. He cannot let this question develop for itself or pose it in another element which would give it an affirmative response. He lacks a method, a typological method which would correspond to the question.

Nietzsche's positive task is twofold: the Overman and Transvaluation. Not "who is man?" but *"who overcomes man?"* "The most cautious peoples ask today: 'How may man still be preserved?' Zarathustra, hoever, asks as the sole and first one to do so: 'How shall man be *overcome*?' The overman lies close to my heart, *he* is my paramount and sole concern – and *not* man: not the nearest, not the nearest, not the poorest, not the most suffering, not the best" (Z IV 'Of the Higher Man", 3, p. 297 – the allusion to Stirner is obvious). Overcoming is opposed to preserving but also to appropriating and reappropriating. Transvaluing is opposed to current values but also to dialectical pseudo-transformations. The overman has nothing in common with the species being of the dialecticians, with man as species or with the ego. Neither ego nor man is unique. The dialectical man is the most wretched because he is no longer anything but a man, having annihilated everything which was not himself. He is also the best man because he has suppressed alienation, replaced God and recuperated his properties. We should not think of Nietzsche's overman as simply a raising of the stakes: he differs in nature from man, from the ego. The overman is defined by *a new way of feeling*: he is a different subject from man, something other than the human type. *A new way of thinking*, predicates other than divine ones; for the divine is still a way of preserving man and of preserving the essential characteristic of God, God as attribute. *A new way of evaluating*: not a change of values, not an abstract transposition nor a dialectical reversal, but a change and reversal in the element from which the value of values derives, a "transvaluation".

All Nietzsche's critical intentions come together in the perspective

of this positive task. Amalgamation, a procedure dear to the
Hegelians, is turned against them. In a single polemic Nietzsche
encompasses Christianity, humanism, egoism, socialism, nihilism
the theories of history and culture and the dialectic itself. Taken
together all this forms the theory of the *higher man*: the object of the
Nietzschean critique. In the higher man disparity manifests itself as
the disorder and indiscipline of the dialectical moments themselves
as the amalgam of human and too-human ideologies. The cry of the
higher man is manifold: "It was a strange, protracted, manifold cry
however, and Zarathustra clearly distinguished that it was composed
of many voices: although, heard from a distance, it might sound like a
cry from a single throat" (Z IV "The Greeting" p. 289; "But it seems
to me you are ill adapted for company, you disturb one another's
hearts, you criers of distress, when you sit here together" p. 290). But
the unity of the higher man is also a critical unity: made up entirely of
bits and pieces that the dialectic has gathered together, its unity is that
of the thread tying them all together, the thread of nihilism and
reaction.[16]

7. Theory of the Higher Man

The theory of the higher man occupies book IV of Zarathustra. This
book is the essence of the published Zarathustra. The characters
which make up the higher man are: the prophet, the two kings, the
man with the leeches, the sorcerer, the last pope, the ugliest man, the
voluntary beggar and the shadow. Now, through this diversity of
characters, we quickly discover what the ambivalence of the higher
man consists in: man's reactive being, but also man's species activity.
The higher man is the image in which the reactive man represents
himself as "higher", and, better still, deifies himself. At the same
time, the higher man is the image in which the product of culture or
species activity appears. – The *prophet* is the prophet of great weariness, representative of passive nihilism, prophet of the last man. He is
looking for a sea to drink, a sea in which to drown himself; but every
death seems to him still too active, we are too tired to die. He wills
death but as a passive extinction (Z II "The Prophet", IV "The Cry of
Distress"). The *sorcerer* is the bad conscience, the "counterfeiter", the
"penitent of the spirit", the "demon of melancholy" who fabricates
his suffering in order to excite pity, in order to spread the contagion.

"You would deck out even your disease if you showed yourself naked to your physician": the sorcerer fakes pain, he invents a new sense for it, he betrays Dionysus, he seizes hold of Ariadne's song, he, the falsely tragic one (Z IV "The Sorcerer"). The *ugliest of men* represents reactive nihilism: the reactive man has turned his *ressentiment* against God, he has put himself in the place of the God that he has killed, but he does not stop being reactive, full of bad conscience and *ressentiment* (Z IV "The Ugliest of Men").

The *two kings* are customs, the morality of customs and the two ends of this morality, the two extremities of culture. They represent species activity grasped in the prehistoric principle of determination of customs but also in the post-historic product where customs are suppressed. They lose hope because they witness the triumph of a "mob": they see forces being grafted onto the customs themselves which distort species activity and deform both its principle and its product (Z IV "Conversation with the Kings"). The *man with leeches* represents the product of culture as science. He is the "conscientious man of the spirit". He wanted certainty and to appropriate science and culture. "Better to know nothing than to half-know many things" (Z IV "The Leech" p. 263). And through this striving for certainty he learns that science is not even an objective knowledge of the leech and of its primary causes, but only a knowledge of the leech's "brain", knowledge which is no longer knowledge because it must identify itself with the leech, think like it and surrender itself to it. Knowledge is life against life, the life which cuts into life, but only the leech cut into life, it alone is knowledge (Z IV "The Leech" – the importance of the brain in Schopenhauer's theories will also be recalled). The *last pope* has turned his existence into a long service. He represents the product of culture as religion. He served God until the end and in doing so lost an eye. The lost eye is undoubtedly the eye which saw active, affirmative gods. The remaining eye followed the Jewish and Christian god through the whole of his history: he saw nothingness, the whole of negative nihilism and the replacement of God by man. The old lackey who depairs because he has lost his master: "I am without master and nevertheless I am not free; neither am I merry except in memories" (Z IV "Retired from Service"). The *voluntary beggar* has gone through the whole human species, from rich to poor. He was seeking the "kingdom of heaven", "happiness on earth", as a recompense but also as the product of human, species and cultural activity. He wanted to know who this kingdom belonged to and what this activity represented; Science, morality or religion? Or something else again, poverty or work? But the kingdom of heaven is no more among the poor than among the rich: everywhere there is the mob, "mob above, mob below"! The voluntary beggar found the kingdom of heaven to be the only recompense and the true product of a species activity: but only among cows, only in the species activity of cows. For cows know how to ruminate and rumination is the product of culture *as* culture (Z IV "The Voluntary Beggar"). The *shadow* is the wanderer himself, species activity itself, culture and its movement. The meaning of the wanderer and of his shadow is that only the shadow wanders. The wandering shadow is species activity, but only insofar as it loses its product and its principle and hunts for them desperately (Z IV "The Shadow"). – The two kings are the guardians of species activity, the man with leeches is the product of this activity as science, the last pope is the product of this activity as religion; the voluntary beggar, beyond science and religion, wants to know what the adequate product of this activity is; the shadow is this activity itself insofar as it loses its aim and searches for its principle.

We have proceeded as if there were two kinds of higher man. But, in fact, each character of the higher man has the two aspects in differing proportions; representing both reactive forces and their triumph, species activity and its product. We must take this double aspect into account in order to understand why Zarathustra treats the higher man in two ways: sometimes as the enemy who will consider any trap, any infamy, in order to divert Zarathustra from his path and sometimes as a host, almost a companion who is engaged in an enterprise close to that of Zarathustra himself.[17]

8. Is Man Essentially "Reactive"?

This ambivalence can only be interpreted correctly if a more general problem is considered: to what extent is man essentially reactive? On the one hand, Nietzsche presents the triumph of reactive forces as something essential to man and history. *Ressentiment* and bad conscience are constitutive of the humanity of man, nihilism is the *a priori* concept of universal history. This is why conquering nihilism, liberating thought from bad conscience and *ressentiment* means the overcoming and destruction of even the best men (Z IV "Of the

Higher Man" 6 p. 299; "More and more, better and better men of our kind must perish"). Nietzsche's critique is not directed against an accidental property of man, but against his very essence; it is in his essence that man is called the skin-disease of the Earth (Z II "Of Great Events" p. 153). Yet, on the other hand, Nietzsche speaks of the masters as a type of human being that the slave has merely conquered, of culture as a human species activity that reactive forces have simply diverted from its course, of the free and sovereign individual as the human product of this activity that the reactive man has only deformed. Even the history of man seems to include active periods (GM I 16). Zarathustra sometimes evokes his true men and announces that his reign is also the reign of man (Z IV "The Sign").

At a deeper level than forces or their qualities there are modes of becoming of forces or qualities of the will to power. To the question "is man essentially reactive?" we must reply that what constitutes man is still deeper. What constitutes man and his world is not only a particular type of force, but a mode of becoming of forces in general, not reactive forces in particular, but the becoming-reactive of all forces. Now, such a becoming of forces always requires, as its *terminus a quo*, the presence of the opposite quality, which in becoming passes into its opposite. The genealogist is well aware that there is a health which only exists as the presupposition of a becoming-sick. The active man is that young, strong, handsome man, whose face betrays the discreet signs of sickness to which he has not yet succumbed, of a contagion which will only affect him tomorrow. The strong must be defended against the weak, but we know the desperate character of this enterprise. The strong man can oppose the weak, but not his own becoming-weak, which is bound to him by a subtle attraction. Each time that Nietzsche speaks of active men, he does so with the sadness of seeing the destiny to which they are predetermined as their essential becoming: the Greek world overthrown by the theoretical man, Rome overthrown by Judea, the Renaissance by the Reformation. There *is* therefore a human activity, there *are* active forces of man; but these particular forces are only the nourishment of all forces which defines man and the human world. In this way Nietzsche reconciles the two aspects of the higher man, his reactive and his active character. At first sight men's activity appears to be generic; reactive forces are grafted onto it, perverting it and diverting it from its course. But more deeply, what is truly generic is the becoming reactive of all forces, activity being only the particular term presupposed by this becoming.

Zarathustra never stops telling his "visitors": you are failures, you are failed natures (Z IV "Of the Higher Men"). This expression must be taken in its strictest sense: it is not man who does not succeed in being a higher man, it is not man who fails or misses his goal, it is not man's activity which misses or fails to achieve its product. Zarathustra's visitors do not experience themselves as false higher men, they experience the higher man that they are as something false. The goal itself is missed, fallen short of, not because of insufficient means, but because of its nature, because of the kind of goal that it is. If it is missed it is not insofar as it is not reached but rather insofar as it is reached it is also missed. The product itself is botched, not because of accidents which happen to it, but because of the activity, the nature of the activity, of which it is the product. Nietzsche wants to say that man's species activity or culture only exists as the presumed end result of a becoming-reactive which turns the principle of this activity into a failed product. The dialectic is the movement of activity as such and it too is essentially failed and fails essentially. The movement of reappropriations, dialectical activity, is nothing more or less than the becoming-reactive *of* man and *in* man. Consider the way in which the higher men are presented: their despair, their disgust, their cry of distress and their "unhappy consciousness". They all know and feel the abortive character of the goal that they attain, the failed nature of the product that they are (for example, the way in which the two kings suffer from the transformation of "good manners" into "mob"). The shadow has lost its goal, not because it has not reached it but because the goal which it has reached is itself a lost goal (Z IV "The Shadow"). Species and cultural activity is a false fire-dog, not because it is an appearance of activity, but because its only reality is to serve as the first term of becoming-reactive (Z II "Of Great Events"). It is in this sense that the two aspects of the higher man are reconciled: the reactive man as the purified or deified expression of reactive forces and the active man as the essentially abortive product of an activity which falls short of its goal essentially. We must reject every interpretation which would have the Overman succeed where the higher man fails. The Overman is not a man who surpasses *himself* and succeeds in surpassing himself. The Overman and the higher man differ in nature; both in the instances which produce them and in the goals that they attain. Zarathustra says, "*You Higher Men, do you think I am here to put*

right what you have done badly?" (Z IV "Of the Higher Man" 6 p. 299).
And neither can we follow an interpretation such as that of Heidegger
who turns the Overman into the realisation and even the determination
of the human essence.[18] For the human essence does not wait for the
Overman in order to be determined. It is determined as human,
all-too-human. Man's essence is the becoming-reactive of forces, this
becoming as universal becoming. The essence of man and of the world
occupied by man is the becoming reactive of all forces, nihilism and
nothing but nihilism. Man and his generic activity – these are the two
skin-diseases of the Earth (Z II "Of Great Events").

We must now ask why species activity, its aim and its product, are
essentially abortive. Why do they only exist as failed? The answer is
simple if we remember that this activity aims to train reactive forces,
to make then suitable for being acted, to make them active themselves. How could this project be viable without the power of affirming which constitutes becoming-active? Reactive forces, for their
part, were able to find the ally that led them to victory – nihilism, the
negative, the power of denying, the will to nothingness which forms a
universal becoming-reactive. Separated from a power of affirming,
active forces can, on their side, do nothing except also become reactive
or turn against themselves. Their activity, their goal and their product
are abortive for all time. They lack a will which goes beyond them, a
quality capable of manifesting and bearing their superiority.
Becoming-active only exists in and through the will to nothingness.
An activity which does not raise itself to the powers of affirming, an
activity which trusts only in the labour of the negative is destined to
failure; in its very principle it turns into its opposite. – When
Zarathustra considers the higher men as hosts, companions and forerunners he thus reveals to us that their project is not without resemblance to his own: becoming active. But we quickly learn that these
declarations of Zarathustra must only be taken half-seriously. They
can be explained by pity. From one end of Book IV to the other the
higher man do not conceal from Zarathustra the fact that they are
laying a trap for him, that they bring him a final temptation. God felt
pity for man, this pity was the cause of his death; pity for the higher
man, – this is Zarathustra's temptation which would, in turn, be the
death of him.[19] That is to say, whatever the resemblance between the
higher man's project and that of Zarathustra himself, a deeper
instance intervenes to make the two enterprises qualitatively distinct.

The higher man remains within the abstract element of activity, he never raises himself, even in thought, to the element of affirmation. The higher man claims to reverse values, to convert reaction into action. Zarathustra speaks of something else: transmuting values, converting negation into affirmation. But reaction will never become action without this deeper conversion: negation must first become a power of affirming. Separated from the conditions which would make it viable, the enterprise of the higher man is abortive, not accidentally but in principle and essence. Instead of forming a becoming-active it nourishes the opposite becoming, becoming-reactive. Instead of reversing values values are changed, made to exchange places while retaining the nihilistic perspective from which they derive. Instead of training forces and making them active they organise associations of reactive forces (Z IV "The Greeting": Zarathustra says to the higher men: "And there is hidden mob in you too"). Conversely the conditions which would make the enterprise of higher man viable are conditions which would change its nature: Dionysian affirmation rather than man's species activity. The element of affirmation is the superhuman element. The element of affirmation is what man lacks – even and above all the higher man. Nietzsche expresses this lack symbolically as the deficiency at the heart of man in four ways:

1) There are things that the higher man does not know how to do: to laugh, to play and to dance.[20] To laugh is to affirm life, even the suffering in life. To play is to affirm chance and the necessity of chance. To dance is to affirm becoming and the being of becoming.

2) The higher men themselves recognise the ass as their "superior". They adore him as if he were a god; through their old theological way of thinking they have an inkling of what it is they themselves lack and what it is that goes beyond them, what the mystery of the ass is, what its bray and its long ears hide: the ass is the animal that says "Ye-a", the affirmative and affirming animal, the Dionysian animal (Z IV "The Awakening" "The Ass Festival").

3) The symbolism of the shadow has a related sense. The shadow is the activity of man, but it needs light as a higher instance; without light it vanishes; with light it is transformed and disappears in another way, changing in nature when it is midday (WS; cf. the dialogues of "Shadow and Wanderer").

4) One of the two fire-dogs is the caricature of the other. One bustles about on the surface, in the din and the fumes. It feeds on the surface,

it makes the mud boil: that is to say its activity only serves to nourish, warm up and maintain a becoming-reactive, a becoming cynical in the universe. But the other fire-dog is an affirmative animal: "Which really speaks from the heart of the earth . . . Laughter flutters from him like a motley cloud" (Z II "Of Great Events" pp. 154–5).

9. Nihilism and Transmutation: the focal point

The kingdom of nihilism is powerful. It is expressed in values superior to life, but also in the reactive values which take their place and again in the world without values of the last man. It is always the element of depreciation that reigns, the negative as will to power, the will as will to nothingness. Even when reactive forces stand up against the principle of their triumph, even when they end up with a nothingness of the will rather than a will to nothingness, it is always the same element which appears in the principle and which, now blends and disguises itself in the consequences or in the effect. No will at all– this remains the final avatar of the will to nothingness. Under the sway of the negative the whole of life is always depreciated and the reactive life in particular triumphs. Activity can do nothing despite its superiority over reactive forces; under the sway of the negative it has no other outlet than to turn against itself; separated from what it can do it becomes reactive itself, it now only serves to nourish the becoming-reactive of forces. And, in fact, the becoming-reactive of forces is also the negative as quality of the will to power. – We know what transmutation or transvaluation means for Nietzsche: not a change of values, but a change in the element from which the value of values derives. Appreciation instead of depreciation, affirmation as will to power, will as affirmative will. As long as we remain in the element if the negative it is no use changing values or even suppressing them, it is no use killing God: the place and the predicate remain, the holy and the divine are preserved, even if the place is left empty and the predicate unattributed. But when the element is changed, then, and only then, can it be said that all values *known or knowable up to the present* have been reversed. Nihilism has been defeated: activity recovers its rights but only in relation and in affinity with the deeper instance from which these derive. Becoming-active appears in the universe, but as identical with affirmation as will to power. The question is: how can nihilism be defeated? How can the element of values itself be changed, how can affirmation be substituted for negation?

Perhaps we are closer to a solution that we might think. It will be noted that, for Nietzsche, all the previously analysed forms of nihilism, even the extreme or passive form, constitute and *unfinished*, *incomplete* nihilism. Is this not to say, conversely, that the transmutation which defeats nihilism is itself the only complete and finished form of nihilism? In fact nihilism is defeated, but defeated by itself.[21] We approach a solution insofar as we understand why transmutation constitutes completed nihilism. – We can suggest an initial reason: it is only by changing the element of values that all those values that depend on the old element are destroyed. The critique of the values known up to the present is only a radical and absolute critique, excluding all compromise, if it is carried out in the name of a transmutation and in its terms. Transmutation would therefore be a completed nihilism because it would give the critique of values a completed, "totalising" form. But such an interpretation does not yet tell us why transmutation is nihilistic, not merely in its consequences but in and of itself.

The values which depend on this old element of the negative, the values which fall under a radical critique, are all the values known or knowable up to the present. "Up to the present" means up to the time of transmutation. But what does "all *knowable* values" mean? Nihilism is negation as a quality of the will to power. Nevertheless, this definition remains insufficient if we do not take the role and function of nihilism into account: the will to power appears in man and makes itself known in him as a will to nothingness. And, in point of fact, our knowledge of the will to power will remain limited if we do not grasp its manifestation in *ressentiment*, bad conscience, the ascetic ideal and the nihilism which forces us to know it. The will to power is spirit, but what would we know of spirit without the spirit of revenge which reveals strange powers to us? The will to power is body, but what would we know of the body without the sickness which makes it known to us? Thus nihilism, the will to nothingness, is not only a will to power, a quality of the will to power, but the *ratio cognoscendi of the will to power in general*.[22]* All known and knowable values are, by nature, values which derive from this *ratio*. – If nihilism makes the will to power known to us, then conversely, the latter teaches us that it is known to us in only one form, in the form of the negative which constitutes only one of its aspects, one of its *qualities*. We "think" the will to power in a form distinct from that in which we know it. (Thus the *thought* of the eternal return goes beyond all the laws of our *knowledge*.) This is a distant survival of themes from Kant to Schopenhauer: what we in fact know of the will to power is suffering and torture, but the will to power is still the unknown joy, the unknown happiness, the unknown God. Ariadne sings in her complaint: "I bend and twist myself, tormented by all the eternal martyrs, struck by you, the most cruel hunter, you, the God-unknown . . . Speak, finally, you who hide behind the lightning? Unknown! Speak! What do you want . . .? O come back, my unknown God! my pain! my last happiness" (DD "Ariadne's Complaint"). The other side of the will to power, the unknown side, the other quality of the will to power, the unknown quality, is affirmation. And affirmation, in turn, is not merely a will to power, a quality of the will to power, it is the *ratio essendi of the will to power in general*.[23*] It is the *ratio essendi* of the will to power as a whole and therefore the *ratio* which expels the negative from this will, just as negation was the *ratio cognoscendi* of the whole will to power (thus the *ratio* which does not fail to eliminate the affirmative from the knowledge of this will). New values derive from affirmation: values which were unknown up to the present, that is to say up to the moment when the legislator takes the place of the "scholar", *creation takes the place of knowledge itself* and affirmation takes the place of all negations. – Thus we can see that the relation between nihilism and transmutation is deeper than was initially suggested. Nihilism expresses the quality of the negative as *ratio cognoscendi* of the will to power; but it cannot be brought to completion without transmuting itself into the opposite quality, into affirmation as *ratio essendi* of this same will. A Dionysian transmutation of pain into joy, which Dionysus announces in reply to Ariadne in a suitably mysterious way "Must we not first of all hate ourselves if we have to love ourselves?" (DD "Ariadne's Complaint"). That is to say: must you not know me as negative if you are going to experience me as affirmative, espouse me as the affirmative, think of me as affirmation?

But why is transmutation nihilism brought to its conclusion if it is true that it is content to substitute one element for another? A third reason must be taken into account, a reason which risks passing unnoticed, so subtle or scrupulous do Nietzsche's distinctions become. Let us reconsider the history of nihilism and its successive stages: negative, reactive and passive. Reactive forces owe their triumph to the will to nothingness: once this triumph is established they break off their alliance with it, they want to assert their own values on their own account. *This* is the great resounding event: the reactive man in place of God. We know what the result of this is – the last man, the one who prefers a nothingness of will, who prefers to fade away passively, rather than a will to nothingness. But this result is a result for the reactive man, not for the will to nothingness itself. The will to nothingness continues its enterprise, this time in silence, beyond the reactive man. *Reactive forces break their alliance with the will to nothingness, the will to nothingness, in turn, breaks its alliance with reactive forces*. It inspires in man a new inclination: for destroying himself, but destroying himself actively. What Nietzsche calls self-destruction, active destruction, must not, above all, be confused with the passive extinction of the last man. We must not confuse, in Nietzsche's terms, "the last man" and "the man who wants to perish."[24] One is the final product of becoming reactive, the final way in which the reactive man who is tired of willing, preserves himself. The other is the product of a selection which undoubtedly passes through the last men but does not stop there. Zarathustra praises the man of active destruction: he wants to be overcome, he goes beyond the human, already on the path of the overman, "crossing the bridge", father and ancestor of the overman. "I love him who lives for knowledge and who wishes to know that one day the Overman may live. *And thus he wills his own downfall*" (Z Prologue 4 p. 44*). Zarathustra wants to say: I love the one who makes use of nihilism as the *ratio cognoscendi* of the will to power, but who finds in the will to power a *ratio essendi* in which man is overcome and therefore nihilism is defeated.

Active destruction means: the point, the moment of transmutation in the will to nothingness. Destruction becomes *active* at the moment when, with the alliance between reactive forces and the will to nothingness broken, the will to nothingness is converted and crosses over to the side of *affirmation*, it is related to a *power of affirming* which destroys the reactive forces themselves. Destruction becomes active to the extent that the negative is transmuted and converted into affirmative power: the "eternal joy of becoming" which is avowed in an instant, the "joy of annihilation", the "*affirmation* of annihilation and destruction" (EH "Birth of Tragedy" 3). This is the "decisive point" of Dionysian philosophy: the point at which negation expresses an affirmation of life, destroys reactive forces and restores the rights of activity. The negative becomes the thunderbolt and lightning of a power of affirming. *Midnight*, the supreme focal or transcendent point which is not defined by Nietzsche in terms of an equilibrium or a reconciliation of opposites, but in terms of a conversion. Conversion of the negative into its opposite, conversion of the *ration cognoscendi* in the *ratio essendi* of the will to power. We asked: why is transformation the completion of nihilism? It is because, in transmutation, we are not concerned with a simple substitution, but with a conversion. Nihilism reaches its completion by passing through the last man, but going beyond him to the man who wants to perish. In the man who wants to perish, to be overcome, negation has broken everything which still held it back, it has defeated itself, it has become of affirming, a power which is already superhuman, a power which announces and prepares the Overman. "You could transform yourselves into forefathers and ancestors of the Overman: and let this be your finest creating" (Z II "On the Blissful Islands" p. 110'*). Negation *sacrifices* all reactive forces, becoming "relentless destruction of everything that was degenerating and parasitical", passing into the service of an *excess* of life (EH III "Birth of Tragedy" 3–4): only here is it completed.

10. Affirmation and Negation

Transmutation or transvaluation means:

1) *Change of quality in the will to power*. Values and their value no longer derive from the negative, but from affirmation as such. In place of a depreciated life we have life which is affirmed – and the expression "in place of" is still incorrect. It is the place itself which changes, there is no longer any place for another world. The element of values changes place and nature, the value of values changes its principle and the whole of evaluation changes character.

2) *The transition from the ratio cognoscendi to the ratio essendi in the will to power*. The *ratio* in terms of which the will to power is known is not the *ratio* in terms of which it exists. (*La raison sous laquelle la volonté de puissance est connue n'est pas la raison sous laquelle elle est.*) We will only think the will to power as it *is*, we will only think it as having being, if we use the *ratio* for knowing as a quality which passes into its opposite and find in this opposite the *ratio* for being unknown.

3) *Conversion of the element in the will to power*. The negative becomes a power of affirming: it is subordinated to affirmation and passes into the service of an excess of life. Negation is no longer the form under which life conserves all that is reactive in itself, but is, on the contrary, the act by which it sacrifices all its reactive forms. In the man who wants to perish, the man who wants to be overcome, negation changes sense, it becomes a power of affirming, a preliminary condition of the development of the affirmative, a premonitory sign and a zealous servant of affirmation as such.

4) *Reign of affirmation in the will to power*. Only affirmation subsists as an independent power; the negative shoots out from it like lightning, but also becomes absorbed into it, disappearing into it like a soluble fire. In the man who wants to perish the negative announces the superhuman, but only affirmation produces what the negative announces. There is no other power but affirmation, no other quality, no other element: the whole of negation is converted in its substance, transmuted in its quality, *nothing remains of its own power or autonomy*. This is the conversion of heavy into light, of low into high, of pain into joy. This trinity of dance, play and laughter creates the transubstantiation of nothingness, the transmutation of the negative and the transvaluation or change of power of negation. What Zarathustra calls "the Communion".

5) *Critique of known values*. The values known up to the present lose all their value. Negation reappears here but always in the form of a power of affirming, as the inseparable consequence of affirmation and transmutation. Sovereign affirmation is inseparable from the destruction of all known values, it turns this destruction into a total destruction.

6) *Reversal of the relation of forces*. Affirmation constitutes becoming-active as the universal becoming of forces. Reactive forces are denied, all forces become active. The reversal of values and the establishment of active values are all operations which presuppose the transmutation of values, the conversion of the negative into affirmation.

We are now perhaps in a position to understand Nietzsche's texts concerning affirmation, negation and their relations. In the first place, negation and affirmation are opposed as two qualities of the will to power, two *ratios* of the will to power. They are both opposites, but also wholes which exclude their opposite. We can say that negation has dominated our thought, our ways of feeling and evaluating, up to the present day. In fact it is constitutive of man. And with man the whole world sinks and sickens, the whole of life is depreciated, everything known slides towards its own nothingness. Conversely, affirmation is only manifested above man, outside man, in the Overman which it produces and in the unknown that it brings with it. But the superhuman, the unknown, is also the whole which drives out the negative. The Overman as species is in fact "the superior species of *everything that is*". Zarathustra says yes and *amen* in a "tremendous and unbounded way", he is himself "the eternal affirmation of *all things*" (EH III "Thus Spoke Zarathustra" 6). "I, however, am one who blesses and affirms if only you are around me, you pure, luminous sky! You abyss of light! – then into all abysses do I carry my consecrating affirmation" (Z III "Before Sunrise" pp. 185–6). While the negative reigns it is vain to seek a speck of affirmation, either in earth or in the other world: what we call affirmation is a sad, grotesque phantom, shaking the chains of the negative.[25] But, at the moment of transmutation, negation is dissipated, *nothing remains of it as independent power*, neither as quality nor *ratio*: "Supreme constellation of being, that no wish reaches, that no negation can soil, eternal affirmation of being, eternally I am your affirmation" (DD "Glory and Eternity").

But why then does Nietzsche present affirmation as inseparable from a preliminary negative condition and also from a proximate negative consequence? "I know the pleasure in destroying to a degree that accords with my powers to destroy" (EH IV 2 p. 327).

1) There is no affirmation which is not *immediately followed* by a negation no less tremendous and unbounded than itself. Zarathustra rises to this "supreme degree of negation". *Destruction as the active destruction of all known values* is the trail of the creator: "Look at the good and the just! What do they hate the most? The one who breaks their tables of values, the destroyer, the criminal: but it is he, the creator."

2) There is no affirmation which is not preceded by an immense negation: "One of the essential conditions of affirmation is negation and destruction." Zarathustra says: "I have become the one who blesses and affirms, and I have long struggled for this." The lion becomes a child but the child's "holy yes" must be preceded by the lion's "holy no" (Z I "Of the Three Metamorphoses"). *Destruction as the active destruction of the man who wants to perish and to be overcome*

announces the creator. Separated from these two negations is nothing, incapable of affirming itself.[26]

It might be thought that the ass, the animal which says "Ye-a", was the Dionysian animal *par excellence*. In fact, this is *not* the case; its appearance is Dionysian but its reality is wholly Christian. It is only fit to be used as a God by the higher men: it does represent affirmation as the element which goes beyond the higher man but it disfigures it in their image and for their needs. It always says yes, *but does not know how to say no*. "I honour the obstinate, fastidious tongues and stomachs that have learned to say 'I' and 'Yes' and 'No'. But to chew and digest everything – that is to have a really swinish nature! Always to say "Ye-a" – only the ass and those like him have learned that" (Z III "Of the Spirit of Gravity" p. 212). Dionysus once said jokingly to Ariadne that her ears were too small: he means that she does not yet know how to affirm or to develop affirmation.[27] But, in reality, Nietzsche himself boasts of having small ears: "This is of no small interest to women – it seems to me that they may feel I understand them better. – I am the *anti-ass par excellence* and thus a world historical monster. I am, in Greek, and not only in Greek, the *Antichrist*" (EH III 2 p. 263). Ariadne and Dionysus himself have small ears, small circular ears favouring the eternal return. For long pointed ears are not the best: they are not able to pick up "the shrewd word" or give it its full echo (DD "Ariadne's Complaint": "Dionysus: You have small ears, you have my ears, 'put a shrewd word there' "). The shrewd word is yes, but it is preceded and followed by an echo which is no. The ass' yes is a false yes: a yes which is not able to say no, without echo in the ass' ears, affirmation separated from the two negations which should surround it. The ass can no more articulate affirmation than its ears can pick up – it and its echoes. Zarathustra says: "My verse is not suited to everyone's ears. I long ago unlearned consideration for long ears" (Z IV "Conversation with the Kings" I p. 259* and Z IV "Of the Higher Man", "The long ears of the mob").

There is no contradiction at this point in Nietzsche's thought. On the one hand Nietzsche announces the Dionysian affirmation that no negation can defile. On the other hand he denounces the affirmation of the ass who does not know how to say no, that contains no negation. In the one case affirmation does not let negation remain *as an autonomous power or primary quality*: the negative is completely expelled from the constellation of being, from the circle of the eternal return, from the will to power itself and from the *ratio* of its being. But in the other case affirmation would never be real or complete if it were not preceded and followed by the negative. Here we are concerned with negations, but with negations *as powers of affirming*. Affirmation would never be itself affirmed if negation had not broken its alliance with reactive forces and become an affirmative power in the man who wants to perish; and if negation had not then united, totalised all reactive values in order to destroy them from an affirmative perspective. *In these two forms the negative ceases to be a primary quality and an autonomous power*. The whole of the negative has become a power of affirming, it is now only *the mode of being* of affirmation as such. This is why Nietzsche is so insistent on the distinction between *ressentiment* (power of denying which is expressed by reactive forces) and aggression (the active way of being of a power of affirming – EH I 6 and 7). From one end of *Zarathustra* to the other Zarathustra himself is followed, imitated, tempted and compromised by his "ape", his "buffoon", his "dwarf" and his "demon".[28] The demon is nihilism: because he denies everything, despises everything, he also believes he is taking negation to its supreme degree. But living off negation as an independent power, having no other quality but the negative, he is merely a creature of *ressentiment*, hate and revenge. Zarathustra says to him: "I despise your contempt . . . My contempt and my bird of warning shall ascend from love alone; not from the swamp" (Z III "Of Passing By" p. 197). This means that it is only as power of affirming (love) that the negative attains its higher degree (the bird of warning which precedes and follows affirmation). Insofar as the negative is its own power or quality it is in the swamp and is itself a swamp (reactive forces). It is only under the sway of affirmation that the negative is raised to its higher degree at the same time as it defeats itself: it is no longer a power and a quality but the mode of being of the one who is powerful. Then, and only then, the negative is aggression, negation becomes active, joyful destruction (EH III "The Birth of Tragedy", "Thus Spoke Zarathustra").

We can see what Nietzsche is driving at and what he is opposed to. He is opposed to every form of thought which trusts in the power of the negative. He is opposed to all thought which moves in the element of the negative, which makes use of negation as a motor, a power and a quality. Just as other ways of thinking are maudlin, such a way of thinking is tearfully destructive, tearfully tragic: it is and remains the thought of *ressentiment*. *Two negations are necessary to turn a thought like this into an affirmation*, that is to say an appearance, a phantom of affirmation. (Thus *ressentiment* needs its two negative premisses in order to conclude with the so-called positivity of its sequel. Either the ascetic ideal needs *ressentiment* and bad conscience as two negative premisses in order to conclude with the so-called positivity of the divine. Or man's species activity needs the negative twice in order to conclude with the so-called positivity of reappropriations.) In this thought represented by Zarathustra's buffoon everything is false and sad, activity here is only a reaction, and affirmation is only a phantom. Zarathustra opposes pure affirmation to the buffoon: *affirmation is necessary and sufficient to create two negations, two negations form part of the powers of affirming which are modes of being of affirmation as such*. And, in a different way, as we will see, two affirmations are necessary to turn the whole of negation into a mode of affirming. The aggression of the Dionysian thinker as against the *ressentiment* of the Christian thinker. To the famous positivity of the negative Nietzsche opposes his own discovery: the negativity of the positive.

11. The Sense of Affirmation

According to Nietzsche affirmation includes two negations: but in exactly the opposite way to the dialectic. One problem remains: why is it necessary for pure affirmation to contain these two negations? Why is the affirmation of the ass a false affirmation insofar as it does not know how to say no? – Let us return to the litany of the ass as sung by the ugliest man (Z IV "The Awakening" pp. 321-2). Two elements can be distinguished here: on the one hand the apprehension of affirmation as what the higher men lack ("What hidden wisdom it is, that he wears long ears and says only Yea and never Nay . . . Your kingdom is beyond good and evil"). But on the other hand a misinterpretation (which the higher men are likely to make) of the nature of affirmation: "He bears our burden, he has taken upon himself the likeness of a slave, he is patient from the heart and he never says Nay" (Z IV "The Awakening" p. 321).

In this way the ass is also a camel. At the beginning of the first book Zarathustra presents the "courageous spirit" which demands the heaviest burdens with the characteristics of the camel (Z I "Of the Three Metamorphoses"). The strengths of the ass and those of the camel are very similar: humility, acceptance of pain and sickness, patience towards the chastiser, taste for truth even if given acorns to eat and love of the real even if this real is a desert. Once again Nietzsche's symbolism must be interpreted and cross-checked with other texts.[29] The ass and the camel do not only have the strength to carry the heaviest burdens, they have a back for estimating and evaluating their weight. These burdens seem to them to have the weight of the *real*. The real as such – this is how the ass experiences its load. This is why Nietzsche presents the ass and the camel as impervious to all forms of seduction and temptation: they are only sensitive to what they have on their backs, to what they call real. Thus we can guess the meaning of the ass' affirmation, of the yes which does not know how to say no: *this kind of affirming is nothing but bearing, taking upon oneself*, acquiescing in the real as it is, taking reality as it is upon oneself.

The idea of the real in itself is an ass' idea. The ass feels the weight of the burdens that it has been loaded with, that it has taken up, as the positivity of the real. What happens is this: the spirit of gravity is the spirit of the negative, the combined spirit of gravity is the spirit of the negative, the combined spirit of nihilism and reactive forces; the practised eye has no trouble in discovering the reactive in all the Christian virtues of the ass, in all its strengths which are useful for bearing; the prudent eye sees the products of nihilism in all the burdens that it carries. But the ass only ever grasps consequences separated from their premisses, products separated from the principle of their production and forces separated from the spirit which animates them. Its burdens therefore seem to it to have the positivity of the real, like the strength with which it is endowed, positive qualities which correspond to an acceptance of life and the real. "Almost in the cradle are we presented with heavy words and values: this dowry calls itself 'Good' and 'Evil' . . . And we – we bear loyally what we have been given upon hard shoulders over rugged mountains! And when we sweat we are told: 'Yes, life is hard to bear!' " (Z III "Of the Spirit of Gravity" 2 p. 211). First of all the ass is Christ: it is Christ who takes up the heaviest burdens, it is he who bears the fruits of the negative as if they contained the positive mystery *par excellence*. Then, when man takes the place of God, the ass becomes a free thinker. He appropriates everything that is put on his back. There is no longer any need to load him, he loads himself. He recuperates the State, religion etc. as his own powers. He has become God: all the old values of the other world now appear to him as forces which control this world, as his own forces. The heaviness of the burden becomes confused with the heaviness of his tired muscles. He accepts himself in accepting the real, he accepts the real in accepting himself. With this frightening sense of responsibility the whole of morality returns at the gallop. But the real and its acceptance remain what they are, false positivity and false affirmation. Faced with "the men of the present" Zarathustra says: "the unfamiliar things of the future and whatever frightened stray birds, are truly more familiar and more genial than your 'reality'. For thus you speak: 'We are complete realists and without belief or superstition': thus you thump your chests – alas, even without having chests! But how should you be *able* to believe, you motley-spotted men! – you who are paintings of all that has ever been believed! . . . *Unworthy of belief*: that is what *I* call you, you realists! . . . You are unfruitful . . . You are half-open doors at which grave-diggers wait. And that is *your* reality . . ." (Z II "Of the Land of Culture" p. 143). The men of the present still live under an old idea: that everything heavy is real and positive, that everything that carries it is real and affirmative. But this reality which unites the camel and its burden to the point of confusing them in a single mirage is only the desert, the reality of the desert, nihilism. Zarathustra has already said of the camel: "As soon as it is laden it hastens towards the desert." And of the courageous, "vigorous and patient" spirit: "now life seems to him a desert!" (Z I "Of the Three Metamorphoses" and III "Of the Spirit of Gravity"). The real, understood as the object, aim and limit of affirmation; affirmation understood as acquiescence in or adhesion to the real: this is the meaning of braying. But this affirmation is an affirmation of a consequence, the consequence of eternally negative premises, an answering yes, answering the spirit of gravity and all its solicitations. The ass does not know how to say no; but first and foremost he does not know how to say no to nihilism itself. He gathers all its products, he carries them into the desert and there christens them: the real as such. This is why Nietzsche can denounce the yes of the ass: the ass is *not* opposed to Zarathustra's ape, he does not develop a power different from the power of denying, he answers faithfully to this power. He does not know how to say no, he always answers yes, but answers yes each time nihilism opens the conversation.

In this critique of affirmation as acceptance of responsibility Nietzsche is not thinking simply nor distantly of stoic conceptions.

The enemy is closer to hand. Nietzsche is engaged in a critique of all conceptions of affirmation which see it as a simple function, a function of being or of what is. This applies however this being is conceived: as true or as real, whether as noumenon or phenomenon, and however this function is conceived: whether as development, exposition, unveiling, revelation, realisation, grasping in consciousness or knowledge. *Philosophy since Hegel appears as a bizarre mixture of ontology and anthropology, metaphysics and humanism, theology and atheism, theology of bad conscience and atheism of ressentiment.* For, insofar as affirmation is presented as a function of being, man himself appears as the functionary of affirmation: being is affirmed in man at the same time as man affirms being. Insofar as affirmation is defined by an acceptance, that is to say an acceptance of responsibility, it establishes a supposedly fundamental relation between man and being, an athletic and dialectical relation. Once again, and for the last time, there is no difficulty in identifying Nietzsche's enemy: it is the dialectic which confuses affirmation with the truthfulness of truth or the positivity of the real; and this truthfulness, this positivity, are primarily manufactured by the dialectic itself with the products of the negative. The being of Hegelian logic is merely 'thought' being, pure and empty, which affirms itself by passing into its own opposite. But this being was never different from its opposite, it never had to pass into what it already was. Hegelian being is pure and simple nothingness; and the becoming that this being forms with nothingness, that is to say with itself, is a perfectly nihilistic becoming; and affirmation passes through negation here because it is merely the affirmation of the negative and its products. Feuerbach took the refutation of Hegelian being a long way. For a merely 'thought' truth he substituted the truth of the sensuous. For abstract being he substituted sensuous, determined, real being, "the real in its reality", "the real as real". He wanted real being to be the object of real being: the total reality of being as the object of the real and total being of man. He wanted thought to be affirmative and understood affirmation as the positing of that which is.[30] But the real in itself in Feuerbach preserves all the attributes of nihilism as the predicate of the divine; the real being of man preserves all the reactive properties as the strength and taste for accepting this divine. In "the men of the present", in "the realists", Nietzsche denounces the dialectic and the dialectician: a portrayal of all that has ever been believed.

Nietzsche wants to say three things:

1) Being, the true and the real are the avatars of nihilism. Ways of mutilating life, of denying it, of making it reactive by submitting it to the labour of the negative, *by loading it with the heaviest burdens*. Nietzsche has no more belief in the self-sufficiency of the real than he has in that of the true: he thinks of them as the manifestations of a will, a will to depreciate life, to oppose life to life.

2) Affirmation conceived of as acceptance, as affirmation of that which is, as truthfulness of the true or positivity of the real, is a false affirmation. It is the yes of the ass. The ass does not know how to say no because he says yes to everything which is no. The ass or the camel is the opposite of the lion; in the lion negation becomes a power of affirming, but in them affirmation remains at the service of the negative, a simple power of denying.

3) This false conception of affirmation is still a way of preserving man. As long as being is a burden the reactive man is there to carry it. Where could being be better affirmed than in the desert? And where could man be better preserved. "The last man lives the longest." Beneath the sun of being he loses even the taste for dying, disappearing into the desert to dream at length of a passive extinction.[31] – Nietzsche's whole philosophy is opposed to the postulates of being, of man and of acceptance. "Being: we have no other representation of it than the fact of living. How could that which is dead have being?" (VP II 8). The world is neither true nor real but living. And the living world is will to power, *will to falsehood*, which is actualised in many different powers. To actualise the will to falsehood under any power whatever, to actualise the will to power under any quality whatever, is always to evaluate. To live is to evaluate. There is no truth of the world as it is thought, no reality of the sensible world, all is evaluation, even and above all the sensible and the real. "The will to appearance, to illusion, to deception, to becoming and change (to objectified deception) here counts as more profound, primeval, 'metaphysical', than the will to truth, to reality, to mere appearance: – the last is itself merely a form of the will to illusion" (VP IV 8/WP 853 III p. 453 – "here" refers to BT). Being, truth and reality are themselves only valid as evaluations, that is to say as lies. But, in this capacity, as means of actualising the will through one of its powers, they have, up to now served the power or quality of the negative. Being, truth and reality itself are like the divine in which life is opposed to life. The

ruler is then negation as quality of the will to power which, opposing life to life, denies the whole of it and makes it triumph as reactive in particular. By contrast, the other quality of the will to power is a power through which willing is adequate to the whole of life, a higher power of the false, a quality through which the whole of life and its particularity is affirmed and has become active. To affirm is still to evaluate, but to evaluate from the perspective of a will which enjoys its own difference in life instead of suffering the pains of the opposition to this life that it has itself inspired. *To affirm is not to take responsibility for, to take on the burden of what is, but to release, to set free what lives*. To affirm is to unburden: not to load life with the weight of higher values, but *to create* new values which are those of life, which make life light and active. There is creation, properly speaking, only insofar as we make use of excess in order to invent new forms of life rather than separating life from what it can do. "And you yourselves should create what you have hitherto called the World: the World should be formed in your image by your reason, your will and your love!" (Z II "On the Blissful Islands" p. 110). But this task is not completed in man. Going as far as he can man raises negation to a power of affirming. But *affirming in its full power, affirming affirmation itself – this is beyond man's strength*. "To create new values – even the lion is incapable of that: but to create itself freedom for new creation – that the lion can do" (Z I "Of the Three Metamorphoses" p. 55). The sense of affirmation can only emerge if these three fundamental points in Nietzsche's philosophy are borne in mind: not the true nor the real but evaluation; not affirmation as acceptance but as creation; not man but the Overman as a new form of life. Nietzsche attaches so much importance to art because art realises the whole of this programme: the highest power of the false, Dionysian affirmation or the genius of the superhuman (VP IV 8/WP 853).

Nietzsche's argument can be summarised as follows: the yes which does not know how to say no (the yes of the ass) is a caricature of affirmation. This is precisely because it says yes to everything which is no, because it puts up with nihilism it continues to serve the power of denying – which is like a demon whose every burden it carries. The Dionysian yes, on the contrary, knows how to say no: it is pure affirmation, it has conquered nihilism and divested negation of all autonomous power. But it has done this because it has placed the negative at the service of the powers of affirming. To affirm is to create, not to bear, put up with or accept. A ridiculous image of thought is formed in the head of the ass. " 'Thinking' and 'taking something seriously', giving it 'weighty consideration' – to them these things go together: that is the only way they have 'experienced' it" (BGE 213 p. 126).

12. The Double Affirmation: Ariadne

What is affirmation in all its power? Nietzsche does not do away with the concept of being. He proposes a new conception of being. Affirmation is being. Being is not the object of affirmation, any more than it is an element which would present itself, which would give itself over to affirmation. Affirmation is not the power of being, on the contrary. Affirmation itself is being, being is solely affirmation in all its power. Thus it is not surprising that Nietzsche neither analyses being for itself nor nothingness for itself. It should not be assumed that in this respect, Nietzsche had not delivered his final thought. *Being and nothingness are merely the abstract expression of affirmation and negation as qualities (qualia) of the will to power.*[32] But the whole question is: in what sense is affirmation being?

Affirmation has no object other than itself. To be precise it is being insofar as it is its own object to itself. Affirmation as object of affirmation – this is being. In itself and as primary affirmation, it is becoming. But it is being insofar as it is the object of another affirmation which raises becoming to being or which extracts the being of becoming. This is why affirmation in all its power is double: affirmation is affirmed. It is primary affirmation (becoming) which is being, but only as the object of the second affirmation. The two affirmations constitute the power of affirming as a whole. Nietzsche expresses the fact that this power is necessarily double in texts rich with important symbolic implications:

1) *Zarathustra's two animals, the eagle and the serpent.* Interpreted from the point of view of the eternal return the eagle is like the great cycle, the cosmic period, and the serpent is like the individual destiny inserted into this great period. But this precise interpretation is nevertheless insufficient, because it presupposes the eternal return and says nothing about the preconstituent elements from which it derives. The eagle flies in wide circles, a serpent wound round its neck, "not like a prey but like a friend" (Z Prologue 10 p. 53): we see

here the necessity for the proudest affirmation to be accompanied, paralleled, by a second affirmation which takes it as its object.
2) *The divine couple, Dionysus-Ariadne.* "Who besides me knows what Ariadne is!" (EH III "Thus spoke Zarathustra" 8 p. 308). The mystery of Ariadne has, without doubt, a plurality of senses. Ariadne loved Theseus. Theseus is a representation of the higher man: he is the sublime and heroic man, the one who takes up burdens and defeats monsters. But what he lacks is precisely the virtue of the bull, that is to say the sense of the earth when he is harnessed and also the capacity to unharshness, to throw off burdens.[33] As long as woman loves man, as long as she is mother, sister, wife of man, even if he is the higher man, she is only the feminine image of man: the feminine power remains fettered in man (Z III "Of the Virtue that Makes Small"). As terrible mothers, terrible sisters and wives, femininity represents the spirit of revenge and the *ressentiment* which animates man himself. But Ariadne, abandoned by Theseus, senses the coming of a transmutation which is specific to her: the feminine power emancipated, become beneficient and affirmative, the Anima. "Let the flash of a star glitter in your love! Let your hope be: May I bear the Overman" (Z I "Of Old and Young Women" p. 92*). Moreover: in relation to Dionysus, Ariadne-Anima is like a second affirmation. The Dionysian affirmation demands another affirmation which takes it as its object. Dionysian becoming is being, eternity, but only insofar as the corresponding affirmation is itself affirmed: *"Eternal affirmation of being, eternally I am your affirmation"* (DD "Glory and Eternity"). The eternal return "is the closest approximation of being and becoming", it affirms the one of the other (VP II 130/WP 617); a second affirmation is still necessary in order to bring about this approximation. This is why the eternal return is itself a wedding ring (Z III "The Seven Seals"). This is why the Dionysian universe, the eternal cycle, is a wedding ring, a wedding mirror which awaits the soul (*anima*) capable of admiring itself there, but also of reflecting it in admiring itself (VP II 51: another development of the image of betrothal and the wedding ring). This is why Dionysus wants a fiancée: "Is it me, me that you want? The whole of me?. . ." (DD "Ariadne's Complaint"). (Here again it will be noticed that, depending on the point at which one is placed, the wedding changes sense or partners. For, according to the constituted eternal return, Zarathustra himself appears as the fiancé and eternity as the woman loved. But according

to the constitution of the eternal return Dionysus is the first affirmation, becoming and being, more precisely the becoming which is only being as the object of a second affirmation; Ariadne is this second affirmation, Ariadne is the fiancée, the loving feminine power.)

3) *The labyrinth or the ears.* The labyrinth is a frequent image in Nietzsche. It designates firstly the unconscious, the self; only the Anima is capable of reconciling us with the unconscious, of giving us a guiding *thread* for its exploration. In the second place, the labyrinth designates the eternal return itself: circular, it is not the lost way but the way which leads us back to the same point, to the same instant which is, which was and which will be. But, more profoundly, from the perspective of the constitution of the eternal return, the labyrinth is becoming, the affirmation of becoming. Being comes from becoming, it is affirmed of becoming itself, in as much as the affirmation of becoming is the object of another affirmation (Ariadne's thread). As long as Ariadne remained with Theseus the labyrinth was interpreted the wrong way round, it opened out onto higher values, the thread was the thread of the negative and *ressentiment*, the moral thread.[34] But Dionysus teaches Ariadne his secret: the true labyrinth is Dionysus himself, the true thread is the thread of affirmation. "I am your labyrinth."[35] Dionysus is the labyrinth and the bull, becoming and being, but becoming is only being insofar as its affirmation is itself affirmed. Dionysus not only asks Ariadne to hear but to affirm affirmation: "You have little ears, you have my ears: put a shrewd word there." The ear is labyrinthine, the ear is the labyrinth of becoming or the maze of affirmation. The labyrinth is what leads us to being, the only being is that of becoming, the only being is that of the labyrinth itself. But Ariadne has Dionysus' ears: affirmation must itself be affirmed so that it can be the affirmation of being. Ariadne puts a *shrewd word* into Dionysus' ear. That is to say: having herself heard Dionysian affirmation, she makes it the object of a second affirmation heard by Dionysus.

If we understand affirmation and negation as qualities of the will to power we see that they do not have a univocal relation. Negation is *opposed* to affirmation but affirmation *differs* from negation. We cannot think of affirmation as "being opposed" to negation: this would be to place the negative within it. Opposition is not only the relation of negation with affirmation but the essence of the negative as such. Affirmation is the enjoyment and play of its own difference, just as negation is the suffering and labour of the opposition that belongs to it. But what is this play of difference in affirmation? Affirmation is posited for the first time as multiplicity, becoming and chance. For multiplicity is the difference of one thing from another, becoming is difference from self and chance is difference "between all" or distributive difference. Affirmation is then divided in two, difference is reflected in the affirmation of affirmation: the moment of reflection where a second affirmation takes the first as its object. But in this way affirmation is redoubled: as object of the second affirmation it is affirmation itself affirmed, redoubled affirmation, difference raised to its highest power. Becoming is being, multiplicity is unity, chance is necessity. The affirmation of becoming is the affirmation of being etc. – but only insofar as it is the object of the second affirmation which raises it to this new power. Being ought to belong to becoming, unity to multiplicity, necessity to chance, but only insofar as becoming, multiplicity and chance are reflected in the second affirmation which takes them as its object.[36*] It is thus in the nature of affirmation to return or of difference to reproduce itself. Return is the being of becoming, the unity of multiplicity, the necessity of chance: the being of difference as such or the eternal return. If we consider affirmation as a whole we must not confuse (except for ease of expression) the existence of two powers of affirming with the existence of two distinct affirmations. Becoming and being are a single affirmation, which only passes from one power to the other insofar as it is the object of a second affirmation. The first affirmation is Dionysus, becoming. The second affirmation is Ariadne, the mirror, the fiancée, reflection. But the second power of the first affirmation is the eternal return or the being of becoming. The will to power as the differential element that produces and develops difference in affirmation, that reflects difference in the affirmation of affirmation and makes it return in the affirmation which is itself affirmed. Dionysus developed, reflected, raised to the highest power: these are the aspects of Dionysian willing which serve as principles for the eternal return.

13. Dionysus and Zarathustra

The lesson of the eternal return is that there is no return of the negative. The eternal return means that being is selection. Only that which affirms or is affirmed returns. The eternal return is the reproduction of becoming but the reproduction of becoming is also the production of becoming active: child of Dionysus and Ariadne. In the eternal return being ought to belong to becoming, but the being of becoming ought to belong to a single becoming-active. Nietzsche's speculative teaching is as follows: becoming, multiplicity and chance do not contain any negation; difference is pure affirmation; return is the being of difference excluding the whole of the negative. And this teaching would perhaps remain obscure without the practical clarity in which it is steeped. Nietzsche exposes all the mystifications which disfigure philosophy: the apparatus of bad conscience, the false marvels of the negative which turn multiplicity, becoming, chance and difference itself into so many misfortunes of consciousness itself and turn misfortunes of consciousness into so many moments of formation, reflection or development. Nietzsche's practical teaching is that difference is happy; that multiplicity, becoming and chance are adequate objects of joy by themselves and that only joy returns. Multiplicity, becoming and chance are the properly philosophical joy in which unity rejoices in itself and also in being and necessity. Not since Lucretius has the critical enterprise which characterises philosophy been taken so far (with the exception of Spinoza). Lucretius exposes the trouble of the soul and those who need it to establish their power – Spinoza exposes sorrow, all the causes of sorrow and all those who found their power at the heart of this sorrow. – Nietzsche exposes *ressentiment*, bad conscience and the power of the negative which serves as their principle: the "untimeliness" of a philosophy which has liberation as its object. There is no unhappy consciousness which is not also man's enslavement, a trap for the will and an opportunity for all basenesses of thought. The reign of the negative is the reign of powerful beasts, Churches and States, which fetter us to their own ends. The murderer of God committed a sad crime because his motivation was sad: he wanted to take God's place, he killed in order to "steal", he remained in the negative whilst taking on the attributes of divinity. The death of God needs time finally to find its essence and become a joyful event. Time to expel the negative, to exorcise the reactive – the time of a becoming-active. This time is the cycle of the eternal return.

The negative expires at the gates of being. Opposition ceases its labour and difference begins its play. But is there any being which does not belong to another world and how is the selection made?

Nietzsche calls the point of conversion of the negative *transmutation*. The negative loses its power and quality. Negation ceases to be an autonomous power, that is to say a quality of the will to power. Transmutation relates the negative to affirmation in the will to power, it is turned into a simple mode of being of the powers of affirming. Instead of the labour of opposition or the suffering of the negative we have the warlike play of difference, affirmation and the joy of destruction. The no stripped of its power, transformed into the opposite quality, turned affirmative and creative: such is transmutation. This transmutation of values is what essentially defines Zarathustra. If Zarathustra passes through the negative as his disgusts and temptations show, it is not in order to make use of it as a motor, nor to take on its burden or product, but to reach the point where the motor is changed, the product surmounted and the whole of the negative vanquished or transmuted.

Zarathustra's whole story is contained in his relationship with nihilism, that is to say with the demon. The demon is the spirit of the negative, the power of denying which plays several, apparently opposed roles. Sometimes *he gets man to carry him*, suggesting to him that the weight he is burdened with is positivity itself. Sometimes, on the contrary, *he jumps over man*, taking all forces and will from him. [37] The contradiction is only apparent: in the first case man is the reactive being who wants to seize power, to substitute his own strength for the power which dominates him. But in fact the demon finds the opportunity here to get himself carried, to get himself taken on, to pursue his task, disguised by a false positivity. In the second case, man is the last man: still a reactive being, he no longer has the strength to take possession of willing, the demon takes all man's strength and leaves him without strength or will. In both cases the demon appears as the spirit of the negative which, through all the avatars of man, *preserves his power and keeps his quality*. He stands for the will to nothingness which makes use of man as a reactive being which gets itself carried by him but which, at the same time, does not fuse with him and "jumps over". From all these points of view transmutation differs from the will to nothingness, just as Zarathustra differs from his demon. With Zarathustra negation loses its power and quality: beyond the reactive man, there is *the destroyer of known values*; beyond the last man there is *the man who wants to perish or to be overcome*. Zarathustra stands for affirmation, the spirit of affirmation as the power which turns the negative into a mode and man into an active being who wants to be overcome (not "jumped-over"). Zarathustra's sign is the sign of the lion: the first book of Zarathustra opens with the lion and the last closes with it. But the lion is precisely the "holy no" become creative and affirmative, this no which only affirmation knows how to say, in which the whole of the negative is converted, transmuted in power and quality. With transmutation, the will to power ceases to be fettered to the negative as the *ratio* by which it is known to us, it reveals its unknown face, the unknown *raison d'être* which makes the negative a simple mode of being.

Zarathustra has, moreover, a complex relation to Dionysus, as transmutation does to the eternal return. In a certain way Zarathustra is cause of the eternal return and father of the Overman. The man who wants to perish, the man who wants to be overcome, is the ancestor and father of the Overman. The destroyer of all known values, the lion of the holy no prepares its final metamorphosis: it becomes a child. And, with his hands thrust into the lion's fleece, Zarathustra feels that his children are near or that the Overman is approaching. But in what sense is Zarathustra father of the overman and cause of the eternal return? In the sense of a precondition. In another way the eternal return has an unconditioned principle to which Zarathustra himself is subject. From the perspective of the principle which conditions it, the eternal return depends on transmutation but, from the perspective of its unconditioned principle, transmutation depends more profoundly on the eternal return. Zarathustra is subject to Dionysus: "Who and *I*? I await one who is more worthy; I am not worthy even to break myself against him" (Z II "The Stillest Hour", p. 167*). In the trinity of the Antichrist – Dionysus, Ariadne and Zarathustra – Zarathustra is Ariadne's conditional fiancé, but Ariadne is Dionysus' unconditioned fiancée. This is why Zarathustra is always in an inferior position in relation to the eternal return and the Overman. He is the cause of the eternal return, but a cause which delays producing its effect. A prophet who hesitates to deliver his message, who knows the vertigo and the temptation of the negative, who must be encouraged by his animals. Father of the Overman, but a father whose products are ripe before he is ripe for his products, a lion who still lacks a final metamorphosis.[38] In fact the eternal return and the Overman are at the crossing of two genealogies, of two unequal genetic lines.

On the one hand they relate to Zarathustra as to the conditioning principle which "posits" them in merely hypothetical manner. On the other hand, they relate to Dionysus as the unconditioned principle which is the basis of their apodictic and absolute character. Thus in Zarathustra's exposition it is always the entanglement of causes or the connection of moments, the synthetic relation of moments to each other, which determines the hypothesis of the return of the same moment. But, from Dionysus' perspective by contrast, it is the synthetic relation of the moment to itself, as past, present and to come, which absolutely determines its relations with all other moments. The return is not the passion of one moment pushed by others, but the activity of the moment which determined the others in being itself determined through what it affirms. Zarathustra's constellation is the constellation of the lion, but that of Dionysus is the constellation of being: the yes of the child-player is more profound than the holy no of the lion. The whole of Zarathustra is affirmative: even when he who knows how to say no, says no. But Zarathustra is not the whole of affirmation, nor what is most profound in it.

Zarathustra relates the negative to affirmation in the will to power. It is still necessary for the will to power to be related to affirmation as its *raison d'être*, and for affirmation to be related to the will to power as the element which produces, reflects and develops its own *ratio*. This is the task of Dionysus. All affirmation finds its condition in Zarathustra but its unconditioned principle in Dionysus. Zarathustra determines the eternal return, moreover he determines it to produce its effect, the Overman. But this determination is the same as the series of conditions which finds its final term in the lion, in the man who wants to be overcome, in the destroyer of all known values. Dionysus' determination is of another kind, identical to the absolute principle without which the conditions would themselves remain powerless. And this is Dionysus' supreme disguise – to subject his products to conditions which are themselves subject to him, conditions that these products themselves surpass. The lion becomes a child, the destruction of known values makes possible a creation of new values. But the creation of values, the yes of the child-player, would not be formed under these conditions if they were not, at the same time, subject to a deeper genealogy. It is no surprise, therefore, to find that every Nietzschean concept lies at the crossing of two unequal genetic lines. Not only the eternal return and the Overman, but laughter, play and dance. In relation to Zarathustra laughter, play and dance are affirmative powers of transmutation: dance transmutes heavy into light, laughter transmutes suffering into joy and the play of throwing (the dice) transmutes low into high. But in relation to Dionysus dance, laughter and play are affirmative powers of reflection and development. Dance affirms becoming and the being of becoming; laughter, roars of laughter, affirm multiplicity and the unity of multiplicity; play affirms chance and the necessity of chance.

Conclusion

Modern philosophy presents us with amalgams which testify to its vigour and vitality, but which also have their dangers for the spirit. A strange mixture of ontology and anthropology, of atheism and theology. A little Christian spiritualism, a little Hegelian dialectic, a little phenomenology (our modern scholasticism) and a little Nietzschean fulguration oddly combined in varying proportions. We see Marx and the Pre-Socratics, Hegel and Nietzsche, dancing hand in hand in a round in celebration of the surpassing of metaphysics and even the death of philosophy properly speaking. And it is true that Nietzsche *did* intend to "go beyond" metaphysics. But so did Jarry in what, invoking etymology, he called "pataphysics". We have imagined Nietzsche withdrawing his stake from a game which is not his own. Nietzsche called the philosophers and philosophy of his time "the portrayal of all that has ever been believed". He might say the same of today's philosophy where Nietzscheanism, Hegelianism and Husserlianism are the scraps of the new gaudily painted canvas of modern thought.

There is no possible compromise between Hegel and Nietzsche. Nietzsche's philosophy has a great polemical range; it forms an absolute anti-dialectics and sets out to expose all the mystifications that find a final refuge in the dialectic. What Schopenhauer dreamed of but did not carry out, caught as he was in the net of Kantianism and pessimism, Nietzsche carries out at the price of his break with Schopenhauer, setting up a new image of thought, freeing thought from the burdens which are crushing it. Three ideas define the dialectic: the idea of a power of the negative as a theoretical principle manifested in opposition and contradiction; the idea that suffering and sadness have value, the valorisation of the "sad passions", as a practical principle manifested in splitting and tearing apart; the idea of positivity as a theoretical and practical product of negation itself. It is no exaggeration to say that the whole of Nietzsche's philosophy, in its polemical sense, is the attack on these three ideas.

If the speculative element of the dialectic is found in opposition and contradiction this is primarily because it reflects a false image of difference. Like the eye of the ox it reflects an inverted image of difference. The Hegelian dialectic is indeed a reflection on difference, but it inverts its image. For the affirmation of difference as such it substitutes the negation of that which differs; for the affirmation of self it substitutes the negation of the other, and for the affirmation of affirmation it substitutes the famous negation of the negation. – But this inversion would be meaningless if it were not in fact animated by forces with an "interest" in doing so. The dialectic expresses every combination of reactive forces and nihilism, the history or evolution of their relations. Opposition substituted for difference is also the triumph of the reactive forces that find their corresponding principle in the will to nothingness. *Ressentiment* needs negative premises, two negations, in order to produce a phantom of affirmation; the ascetic ideal needs *ressentiment* itself and bad conscience, like the conjuror needs his marked cards. Everywhere there are sad passions; the unhappy consciousness is the subject of the whole dialectic. The dialectic is, first of all, the thought of the theoretical man, reacting against life, claiming to judge life, to limit and measure it. In the second place, it is the thought of the priest who subjects life to the labour of the negative: he needs negation to establish his power, he represents the strange will which leads reactive forces to triumph. Dialectic in this sense is the authentically Christian ideology. Finally, it is the thought of the slave, expressing reactive life in itself and the becoming-reactive of the universe. Even the atheism that it offers us is a clerical atheism, even its image of the master is a slavish one. – It is not surprising that the dialectic only produces a phantom of affirmation. Whether as overcome opposition or as resolved contradiction, the image of positivity is radically falsified. Dialectical positivity, the real in the dialectic, is the yes of the ass. The ass knows how to affirm because it takes things upon itself, but it only takes on the products of the negative. For the demon, Zarathustra's ape, it is sufficient to jump on our shoulders; those who carry are always tempted to think that by carrying they affirm and that the positive is assessed by weight. The ass in a lion's skin – this is what Nietzsche calls the "man of the present".

Nietzsche's greatness was to know how to separate these two plants, *ressentiment* and bad conscience. If this were its only aspect Nietzsche's philosophy would be of the greatest importance. But in his work polemic is only the aggression which derives from a deeper, active and affirmative instance. Dialectic emerged from Kantian critique, from false critique. Carrying out a true critique implies a philosophy which develops itself for itself and only retains the negative as a mode of being. Nietzsche reproaches the dialecticians for going no further than an abstract conception of universal and particular; they were prisoners of symptoms and did not reach the forces or the will which give to these sense and value. They moved within the limits of the question "What is . . .?", the contradictory question *par excellence*. Nietzsche creates his own method: dramatic, typological and differential. He turns philosophy into an art, the art of interpreting and evaluating. In every case he asks the question "Which one?" The one that . . . is Dionysus. That which . . . is the will to power as plastic and genealogical principle. The will to power is not force but the differential element which simultaneously determines the relation of forces (quantity) and the respective qualities of related forces. It is in this element of difference that affirmation manifests itself and develops itself as creative. The will to power is the principle of multiple affirmation, the donor principle or the bestowing virtue.

The sense of Nietzsche's philosophy is that multiplicity, becoming and chance are objects of pure affirmation. The affirmation of multiplicity is the speculative proposition, just as the joy of diversity is the practical proposition. The player only loses because he does not affirm strongly enough, because he introduces the negative into chance and opposition into becoming and multiplicity. The true dicethrow necessarily produces the winning number, which *re*-produces the dicethrow. We affirm chance and the necessity of chance; becoming and the being of becoming; multiplicity and the unity of multiplicity. Affirmation turns back on itself, then returns once more, carried to its highest power. Difference reflects itself and repeats or reproduces itself. The eternal return is this highest power, the synthesis of affirmation which finds its principle in the will. The lightness of that which affirms against the weight of the negative; the games of the will to power against the labour of the dialectic; the affirmation of affirmation against that famous negation of the negation.

Negation, it is true, appears primarily as a quality of the will to power. But in the sense that reaction is a quality of force. More profoundly, negation is only one face of the will to power, the face by which it is known to us, insofar as knowledge itself is the expression of reactive forces. Man inhabits only the dark side of the Earth, of which he only understands the becoming-reactive which permeates and constitutes it. Which is why the history of man is that of nihilism, negation and reaction. But the long story of nihilism has a conclusion: the full stop where negation turns back on reactive forces themselves. This is the point of transmutation or transvaluation; negation loses its own power, it becomes active, it is now only the mode of being of the powers of affirming. The negative changes quality, passes into the service of affirmation; it is now only valid as a preliminary offensive or a subsequent aggression. Negativity as negativity *of the positive* is one of Nietzsche's anti-dialectic discoveries. This is the same as saying that transmutation is a condition of the eternal return, or rather, that it depends on the eternal return from the standpoint of a deeper principle. Because the will to power only makes what is affirmed return: it is the will to power which both transforms the negative and reproduces affirmation. That the one is *for* the other, that the one is *in* the other, means that eternal return is being but being is selection. Affirmation remains as the sole quality of the will to power, action as the sole quality of force, becoming-active as the creative identity of power and willing.

Notes

1. The Tragic

1*. *Translator's note*. The French word élément has a range of senses very close to the English word "element". But its sense here is uncommon in English, taking in both "environment" and "grounds for existence".

2*. *Translator's note*. *Ressentiment* is one of Nietzsche's technical terms. It is discussed at length in his writings, for example, GM I 10. He always uses the French word – the English translation of which is "resentment" – and I retain the French throughout.

3*. *Translator's note*. The French word *force* can be translated as either "force" or "strength". I have rendered it as "force" almost always, even in contexts when this strains the English text, because of the importance of retaining the unity of this key Deleuzian notion.

4. Nietzsche asks which force gives religion the chance of acting "in its own right and as *sovereign*" (BGE 62 p. 69).

5. TI "The Problem of Socrates" 3–7. VP I 70: "It is the slave that triumphs in the dialectic . . . The dialectic can only serve as a defensive weapon."

6. Against the idea that the will to power is will to have oneself "recognised", therefore to have current values attributed to oneself; BGE 261, D 113.

7. On the opposition of the mediate image and the symbol (sometimes called "immediate image of willing") cf. BT 5, 16 and 17.

8. VP IV 556: "At bottom I was only striving to guess why Greek Apollonianism had to arise from a Dionysian sub-soil, why the Dionysian Greek necessarily had to become Apollonian."

9. On the "manufacture of the ideal", cf. GM I 14.

10. This was already Feuerbach's general reproach to the Hegelian dialectic, its taste for fictitious antitheses to the detriment of real

coordinations (cf. Feuerbach, "Contribution to the Critique of the Hegelian Philosophey" trans. Althusser, *Manifestes Philosophiques*, PUF). Similarly, Nietzsche will say "coordination instead of cause and effect" (VP II 346).

11. NW 5. It will be noticed that not all intoxication is Dionysian; there is a Christian intoxication which is opposed to that of Dionysus.

12. cf. Zarathustra's anguish and disgust regarding the eternal return. As early as the *Untimely Meditations* Nietzsche says that in principle "All existence which can be denied is also worthy of being denied; true being, this equivalent to believing in an existence which could absolutely not be denied and which is itself true and without deception" (UM III "Schopenhauer Educator" 4).

13. As early as the *Birth of Tragedy* Nietzsche attacks the Aristotelian conception of tragedy-catharsis. He points out the two possible interpretations of *catharsis*: moral sublimation and medical purging (BT 22). But, whichever way it is interpreted, catharsis sees the tragic as the exercise of depressive passions and "reactive" feelings. cf. VP IV 460.

14. M. Jeanmaire; *Dionysos* (Payot); "Joy is one of the most marked traits of his personality and contributes to imparting to him this dynamism to which one must always return in order to understand the power of expansion of his cult" (27). "One essential trait of the conception one gets of Dionysus is the one that arouses the idea of an essentially mobile divinity in perpetual displacement, a mobility in which a cortège participates, this is both the model and the image of the congregations or thiases in which his followers are grouped" (273–4). "Born of a woman, escorted by women who are the emulators of his mythical nurses, Dionysus is a god who continues to associate with mortals to whom he communicates the feeling of his immediate presence which raises them up to himself much more than he goes down towards them etc." (339 ff.).

15. BT & p. 71: "Thus the very first philosophical problem produces a powerful and irresolvable contradiction between man and god and moves it before the gate of every culture like a huge boulder. The best and highest mankind can acquire is obtained by sacrilege and must be paid for with consequences that involve the

whole flood of sufferings and sorrows with which the offended divinities have to inflict the nobly aspiring race of men." We see the extent to which Nietzsche is still a "dialectician" in the *Birth of Tragedy*: he makes Dionysus accountable for the criminal acts of the Titans of which he is nevertheless the victim. He turns Dionysus' death into a kind of crucifixion.

16. EH III "Thus Spoke Zarathustra" 8 p. 308: "Who besides me knows what Ariadne is?"

17. Thus, if we bring together the theses of the *Birth of Tragedy* that Nietzsche later abandons or transforms we see that there are five of them: a) Dionysus interpreted in the perspectives of contradiction and its solution will be replaced by an affirmative and multiple Dionysus. b) The Dionysus/Apollo antithesis will be toned down in favour of the Dionysus/Ariadne complementary. c) The Dionysus/Socrates opposition will be less and less adequate and will prepare the deeper Dionysus/Crucified opposition. d) The dramatic conception of tragedy will give way to a heroic conception. e) Existence will lose its criminal character in order to become radically innocent.

18. VP III 458: "The whole cannot be judged nor measured nor compared nor above all denied."

19. For all that follows concerning Heraclitus cf. PTG.

20. Nietzsche nuances his interpretation. On the one hand Heraclitus has not completely disengaged himself from the perspectives of punishment and guilt (cf. his theory of total combustion by fire). On the other hand he had only a foreboding of the meaning of eternal return. This is why Nietzsche, in PTG, only makes allusions to the eternal return and in EH (III "The Birth of Tragedy") his judgment is not without reservations.

21. PTG: "The *Dike* or immanent gnome; the *Polemos* which is its place, the whole envisaged as a game; and judging the whole, the creative artist, himself identical with his work."

22. It should not be thought that, according to Nietzsche, chance is *denied* by necessity. In an operation like transmutation many things are denied or abolished, for example the spirit of heaviness is denied by the dance. Nietzsche's general formula is: everything which *can* be denied (that is to say, the negative itself, nihilism and its expressions). But chance is not – unlike the spirit of gravity – an expression of nihilism, it is the object of

pure affirmation. There is, in transmutation itself, a correlation of affirmations: chance and necessity, becoming and being, multiplicity and unity. What is correlatively affirmed should not be confused with what is denied or supressed by the transmutation.

23.　In two texts of the *Will to Power* Nietzsche presents the eternal return in a probabilistic perspective and as being deduced from a large number of throws: "If we assume an enormous mass of cases the fortuitous repetition of a single dicethrow is more probable than absolute non-identity" (VP II 324); if the world has a definite magnitude of force and time has an infinite duration then "every possible combination would be realised at least once, moreover it would be realised an infinite number of times" (VP II 329). But, 1) these texts only give a "hypothetical" exposition of the eternal return; 2) they are "apologetic" in a sense close to that sometimes given to Pascal's wager. It is a question of taking mechanism at its word, of showing that mechanism arrives at a conclusion which "is not necessarily mechanistic"; 3) they are "polemical" in an aggressive way, it is a question of defeating the *bad player* on his own ground.

24.　It is only in this sense that Nietzsche speaks of "fragments" as "terrible chances" (Z II "Of Redemption").

25.　Z I "Of Voluntary Death": "Believe it my brothers! He died too early; he himself would have recanted his teaching had he lived to my age!"

26.　VP II 38 (on the steam engine), 50, 60, 61 (on the releasing of forces "Man proves that there are unheard of forces which can be put into action by a small being of a composite nature . . . *Beings who play with the stars*". "Inside the molecule explosions and changes of direction of all the atoms are produced and sudden unleashings of forces. All our solar system could, in a single brief instant, experience an excitation comparable to that which the nerve exercises on the muscle.")

27.　Thibaudet, in *La Poésie de Stéphane Mallarmé*, p. 424, points this out. He rightly ruled out all question of influence.

28.　Thibaudet, in a strange passage (433), does point out that, according to Mallarmé, the die is only thrown once; but he seems to regret it, finding the principle of several dicethrows clearer: "It is exceedingly doubtful that the development of his meditation would have led him to write a poem on the theme; several dicethrows abolish chance. This is nevertheless certain and clear. We should remember the law of large numbers . . ." It is clear above all that the laws of large numbers would not introduce any development of the meditation but only a misrepresentation. M. Hyppolite has a deeper vision when he compares the Mallarmean dicethrow not with the law of large numbers but with the cybernetic machine (cf. *Études Philosophiques*, 1958). The same comparison would be valid for Nietzsche following what has been said above.

29. When Nietzsche spoke of the "ascetic justification of existence" it was, on the contrary, a question of art as "stimulant of life": art affirms life, life is affirmed in art.

30. Heidegger stresses these points. For example: "Nihilism moves history like a fundamental process, hardly recognised in the destiny of the peoples of the West. Nihilism is therefore not one historical phenomenon among others, nor a spiritual current which, in the framework of western history, is encountered along with other spiritual currents." "The Word of Nietzsche: 'God is Dead' ", in *The Question Concerning Technology*, (Harper and Row, 1977).

31. EH IV 1: "I am the opposite of a negative spirit. I am a bringer of glad tidings like noone before me."

32. VP I 406: "What do we attack in Christianity? That it wishes to break the strong, to discourage their courage, to use their bad hours and their wearinesses, to transform their proud assurance into uneasiness and torment of conscience . . . A horrible disaster of which Pascal is the most illustrious example."

33. Z III "Of Old and New Law Tables", 4: "Man is something that must be overcome. There are diverse paths and ways to overcoming: just look to it! But only a buffoon thinks: 'Man can also be leapt over'." Z Prologue 4: "I love him who is ashamed when the dice fall in his favour and who then asks: Am I then a cheat?"

34. "The movement of Pascal: *un monstre et un chaos*, consequently something to be denied" (VP III 42/WP 83*).

2. Active and Reactive

1. Spinoza, *Ethics*, III 2 Proof: "I have already shown that they know not what a body can do, or what can be deduced from mere

contemplation of its nature, and that they have known of many things which happen merely by reason of the laws of nature, which they have believed to happen save by the direction of the mind."

2. VP II 173/WP 659: The human body is "a more astonishing idea than the old soul". VP II 226: "What is most surprising is rather the body; one never ceases to be amazed at the idea that the human body has become possible."

3. On the false problem of a beginning of life, VP II 66 and 68. On the role of chance, VP II 25 and 334.

4. The originality of Nietzsche's pluralism is found here. In his conception of the organism he does not limit himself to a plurality of constituent forces. What interests him is the diversity of active and reactive forces and the investigation of active forces themselves. Compare this with Butler's pluralism which is admirable but contents itself with memory and habit.

5. VP II 86 and 87: "In the chemical world the sharpest perception of the difference between forces reigns. But a protoplasm, which is a multiplicity of chemical forces, has only a vague and uncertain perception of a strange reality." "To admit that there are perceptions in the inorganic world, and perceptions of an absolute exactitude; it is here that truth reigns! With the organic world imprecision and appearance begin."

6. cf. The judgments on Mayer in the letters to Gast.

7. PTG 4 p. 50: "But then Anaximander sees another question: Why hasn't all that come-to-be passed away long since, since a whole eternity of time has passed? Whence the ever renewed stream of coming-to-be? And from this question he can save himself only by a mystic possibility."

8. The account of the eternal return in terms of the passing moment is found in Z III "Of the Vision and the Riddle".

9. VP II 334: "Where would the diversity inside a cycle come from? . . . By admitting that there exists an equal concentration of energy in all the centres of force in the universe, we have to ask how the least suspicion of diversity could arise . . ."

10. VP II 23/WP 692: "My proposition is: that the will of psychology hitherto is an unjustified generalisation, that this will *does not exist at all*, that instead of grasping the idea of the development of one definite will into many forms, one has eliminated

the character of the will by subtracting it from its content, its 'whither?' – this is in the highest degree the case with *Schopenhauer*: what he calls 'will' is a mere empty word."

11. Z II "Of Self-Overcoming" p. 137: "How has this come about? Thus I asked myself what persuades the living creature to obey and to command and to practise obedience even in commanding? Listen now to my teaching you wisest men! Test in earnest whether I have crept into the heart of life itself and down to the roots of its heart!
     Where I found a living creature, there I found will to power; and even in the will of the servant I found the will to be master" (cf. VP II 91).

12*. (*Translator's note*: The word *divers* which is translated here as "diversity" could also be translated by the word used by Kant's English translators – "manifold" – in "Kantian" contexts such as the present one. I have retained "diversity" which is more appropriate in most contexts but the Kantian connotation should be borne in mind.)
     On these problems which are posed following Kant, cf. M. Guéroult, *La Philosophie Transcendental de Salomon Maimon*, *La Doctrine de la Science chez Fichte*, and M. Vuillemin, *L'Heritage Kantien et la revolution Copernicienne*.

13. GM Preface 6 p. 20: "We need a *critique* of moral values, *the value of these values themselves must first be called in question.*"

14. The theory of values moves further and further away from its origins insofar as it loses sight of the principle "to evaluate = to create". The Nietzschean inspiration is revived in researches like those of M. Polin concerning the creation of values. However, from Nietzsche's point of view, the correlative of the creation of values can, in no case, be their contemplation but must be rather the radical critique of all "current" values.

15. GM I 10 p. 36: Instead of affirming themselves and having denial as a simple consequence, reactive forces begin by denying what is different from themselves, from the start they are opposed to whatever is not part of themselves.

16. On the English conception of genealogy as evolution: GM Preface 7 and I 1–4. On the mediocrity of this kind of English thought: BGE 253. On the German conception of genealogy as evolution and its mediocrity: GS 357 and BGE 244.

17. VP II 85: "We note that in chemistry every body extends its power as far as it is able." VP II 374/WP 634: "There is no law: every power draws its ultimate consequence at every moment." VP II 369/WP 630: "I beware of speaking of chemical 'laws': that savours of morality. It is far rather a question of the absolute establishment of power relationships."

18. If our interpretation is accurate Spinoza saw, before Nietzsche, that a force is inseparable from a capacity for being affected and that this capacity expresses its power. Nietzsche is nevertheless critical of Spinoza, but on another point: Spinoza was not able to elevate himself to the conception of a will to power. He confused power with simple force and conceived of force in a reactive way (cf. *conatus* and conservation).

19. VP II 171/WP 712: "This highest force, which, turning against itself when it no longer has anything left to organise, expends its force on disintegration."

20. VP II 170/WP 617: "Instead of 'cause and effect' the mutual struggle of that which becomes, often with the absorption of one's opponent; the number of becoming elements are not constant."

21. GM I 6 p. 33: "It was on the soil of this *essentially dangerous* form of human existence, the priestly form, that man first became an *interesting animal*, that only here did the human soul in a higher sense acquire *depth* and become *evil* . . ." On the ambivalence of the priest, GM III 15 p. 126*: "He must be sick himself, he must be profoundly related to the sick – how else would they understand each other? – but he must also be strong, master of himself even more than of others, *above all unshakeable in his will to power*, so as to be trusted and feared by the sick . . ."

22. Z III "Of the Virtue that makes small" p. 191; II, "Of the Compassionate" p. 113: "But worst of all are petty thoughts. Truly, better even to have done wickedly than to have thought pettily! To be sure, you will say: 'Delight in petty wickedness spares us many a great evil deed.' But here one should not wish to be spared."

3. Critique

1. GM III 23–25. On the psychology of the scholar, BGE 206–207.

2*. *Translator's note*: The expression translated here as "means" is *veut dire*, literally "wants or wills to say". The French sentence reads "un mot ne veut dire quelque chose que dans la mesure où celui qui le dit veut quelque chose en le disant", relating "willing to say" to "willing something" in a way which cannot be simply translated into English. Throughout this translation I have used both "wills" and "wants" for *vouloir* and its derivatives.

3*. *Translator's note*: Deleuze's exposition of Nietzsche's change in the "form of the question" is central to his interpretation. The change hinges on the difference, in French, between the questions *qu'est-ce que?* and *qui?* This would usually be translated as the difference between the questions "what?" and "who?" But the word *qui?* has a wider sense than the English "who?", picking out particulars of all kinds not just persons. Deleuze suggested translating *qui?* as "which (one)?" since "it is never a person" that is being asked for. He discusses "the form of the question" in the Conclusion and also in the Preface to the English translation.

4. WS Sketch for a Preface, 10 (French translation, Albert, p. 226).

5*. *Translator's note*: The French word *instance* has a range of senses rather different from the English word – including both "insistence" and "authority" and excluding the sense of "example" which the word has in English. The different senses have been played on by a number of recent French philosophical writers in ways which are very difficult to translate and it has become common practice to retain the word in English.

6. This is always Nietzsche's method, in all his books. It is presented in an especially systematic manner in GM.

7. Z Prologue 3 p. 42: "The Overman is the meaning of the earth. Let your will say: The Overman *shall be* the meaning of the Earth!" Z III "Of the Spirit of Gravity" p. 210: "He who will one day teach men to fly will have moved all boundary stones; all boundary stones will themselves fly into the air to him, he will baptise the earth anew – as 'the weightless' ".

8. BGE 261. On the "aspiration to distinction" cf. D 113: "He who aspires to distinction has his eye ceaselessly on his neighbour and wants to know what his feelings are; but the sympathy and

abandon which this penchant needs to satisfy itself are far from being inspired by innocence, compassion or benevolence. On the contrary, one wants to perceive or guess in what way the neighbour *is suffering*, internally or externally to our sight, how he is losing power over himself and giving way to the impression that our hand or sight make on him."

9. VP IV 522: "How impossible is it for a demagogue to clearly represent a *higher nature* to himself. As if the essential trait and the true value of higher men consisted in their aptitude to stir up the masses, in short, in the effect that they produce. But the higher nature of the great man resides in the incommunicable thing that differentiates him from others of a different rank." (Effect that they produce = demagogic representation that they make of themselves = established values that are attributed to them.)

10. EH II 9 p. 255: "No trace of *struggle* can be demonstrated in my life: I am the opposite of a heroic nature. 'Willing' something, 'striving' for something, envisaging a 'purpose', a 'wish' – I know none of this from experience."

11. Z III "Of the Three Evil Things" p. 97: "Desire for power: but who shall call it *desire* . . . Oh who shall find the rightful baptismal and virtuous name for such a longing! 'Bestowing virtue' – that is the name Zarathustra once gave the unnameable."

12. cf. Nietzsche's judgments on Flaubert: he discovered stupidity but not the baseness of the soul which it presupposes (BGE 218).

13. There can be no preestablished values here to decide which is *better than*; cf. VP II 530. "I distinguish an ascendent type of life and a type of decadence, decomposition, weakness. Is it thought that the question of precedence between these two types is still in balance?"

14. Z Prologue 9: "the destroyer, the criminal – but he is the creator"; Z I 15 "whoever creates must always destroy".

15. GM II 18: "contradictory concepts such as *selflessness*, *self-denial, self-sacrifice* . . . their delight is tied to cruelty", p. 88*.

16. The source of antinomy is the bad conscience (GM II). Antinomy is expressed as the opposition of morality and life (VP I 304, PTG II, GM III).

17. AC 10 p. 121: "Among Germans one will understand immediately when I say that philosophy has been corrupted by theologian blood. The Protestant pastor is the grandfather of German philosophy, Protestantism itself is its original sin . . . Kant's success is merely a theologian's success".

18. GS 345 p. 285: "the more refined . . . uncover and criticise the perhaps foolish opinions of a people about their morality, or of humanity about all human morality – opinions about its origin, religious sanction, the superstition of free will and things of that sort – and then suppose that they have criticised the morality itself".

19. VP I and II (cf. knowledge defined as "error which becomes organic and organised").

20. Chestov, "La Seconde Dimension de la Pensée", *NRF*, Sept. 1932.

21. VP I 78/WP 414 – analogous passage, AC 12.

22. UM I "David Strauss" 1; III "Schopenhauer Educator" 1: the opposition of private and public thinker (the public thinker is a "cultivated philistine", representing reason). An analogous theme is found in Kierkegaard, Feuerbach and Chestov.

23. VP I 107: "In order to be able to imagine a world of truth and being it was first necessary to create the veracious man (including the fact that he believes himself *veracious*)."

24. "We the seekers after knowledge". Likewise, Nietzsche will say that the masters are "veracious" men in a different sense (GM I 15).

25. Apollo already appeared in this form in the *Birth of Tragedy*: he traces limits round individuals, "by again and again calling these to mind as the most sacred laws of the world, with his demands for self-knowledge and measure" (BT 9 p. 72).

26*. *Translator's note*: This translates the French word *raison*; see note 22, Chapter 5.

27. WS Sketch for a Preface, 6: "This is not the world as thing-in-itself (this is empty, empty of sense and worthy of a homeric laugh) it is the world as error that is so rich in meaning, so profound, so marvellous" (VP I 453). "Art is given to us to prevent us dying of truth". GM III 25 pp. 153–4: "Art, in which precisely the *lie* is sanctified and the *will to deception* has a good conscience, is much more fundamentally opposed to the ascetic

ideal than is science."

28. TI " 'Reason' in Philosophy" 6: " 'Appearance' here signifies reality *once more*, only selected, strengthened, corrected. The tragic artist is *not* a pessimist – it is precisely he who *affirms* all that is questionable and terrible in existence, he is *Dionysian* . . ." p. 38.

29. HH 146: "The artist has, as to knowledge of the truth, a weaker morality than the thinker; he absolutely does not want to let brilliant interpretations of life be taken away . . ."

30. UM III "Schopenhauer Educator" 8: "Diogenes objected, when they praised a philosopher in front of him: What has he to show that is great, he who has given himself up to philosophy for so long without ever making anyone *grieve*? Indeed it would be necessary to put as an epitaph on the tomb of university philosophy: it has made noone grieve." GS 328 p. 258: ancient philosophers gave a sermon against stupidity. "Let us not decide here whether this sermon against stupidity had better reasons on its side than did the sermon against selfishness: what is certain is that it deprived stupidity of its good conscience; these philosophers *harmed* stupidity".

31. PTG UM III 'Schopenhauer Educator" 7: "Nature sends the philosopher into humanity like an arrow; it does not aim, but it hopes that the arrow will remain caught somewhere."

32. AC 38 p. 149: "With regard to the past I am, like all men of knowledge, of a large tolerance, that is to say a *magnanimous* self-control . . . But my feelings suddenly alter, burst forth, immediately I enter the modern age, *our* age."

33. Plato, *Republic* VII: cf. not only the myth of the cave but also the famous passage on the "fingers" (distinction between that which forces us to think and that which does not force us to think). Plato then develops an image of thought which is very different from that which appeared in other texts. These other texts present us with a conception that is already dogmatic: thought as love and desire for the true, the beautiful, the good. Is there not a place for opposing these two images of thought in Plato, only the second being particularly Socratic? Is it not something of this kind that Nietzsche has in mind when he advises "Trying to characterise Plato without Socrates"? (cf. PTG).

34. GM II 3 p. 61; TI "What the Germans lack" 7 p. 65; BGE 188, pp. 92–3.
35. cf. a) VP II 226: "At this moment Ariadne lost patience . . . 'But sir,' she said, 'you speak German like a pig!' 'Like a German,' I said without getting angry, 'Nothing but a German.' " b) WS Sketch for a Preface, 10: "The God appeared before me, the God whom I had known for a long time, and he began to speak, 'Well, rat catcher, what have you come to do here? You who are half-jesuit and half-musician and almost a German?' " c) It will be recalled that the admirable poem *Ariadne's Complaint* is attributed, in Zarathustra, to the *Enchanter*, but the enchanter is a mystifier, a "counterfeiter" of culture.

4. *From* Ressentiment *to the Bad Conscience*

1*. *Translator's note*. Deleuze uses the verb *agir*, to act, in a transitive sense, which sounds as odd in French as it does in English. On his advice I retained this oddity in translation.
2. Freud, *The Interpretation of Dreams*. Article on "The Unconscious" of 1915, *Beyond the Pleasure Principle*.
3. GM II 1 and GM I 10. It will be noted that there are several kinds of unconscious in Nietzsche, but this unconscious must not be confused with that of reactive forces.
4. GM II 1 p. 57 and GM I 10 – a theme already present in UM II "Use and Abuse of History" 1.
5. *Note on Nietzsche and Freud*: Must we conclude, from the above, that Nietzsche influenced Freud? According to Jones, Freud absolutely denied this. The coincidence of Freud's topical hypothesis with the Nietzschean schema is sufficiently explained by the "energetic" presuppositions common to both writers. We should be all the more sensitive to the fundamental differences that separate them. We can imagine what Nietzsche would have thought of Freud: once again he would have denounced a too "reactive" conception of psychic life, an ignorance of true "activity", and inability to conceive and provoke the true "transmutation". We can imagine it with all the more credibility because Freud had an authentic Nietzschean among his disciples. Otto Rank criticised the "flat and dull idea of sublimation" in Freud. He accused Freud of not knowing how

to free the *will* from bad conscience or guilt. He wanted to rely on the active forces of the unknown unconscious of Freudianism and to replace sublimation by a *creative and artistic* will. Which led him to say; "I am to Freud what Nietzsche is to Schopenhauer". cf. Rank, *La Volonté de Bonheur*.

6. This second memory of consciousness is founded on speech and is manifested as a *faculty of promising*: cf. GM II 1. In Freud there is also a conscious memory dependent on "verbal traces" that are distinguished from mnemonic traces "and probably corresponds to a special transcription" (cf. "The Unconscious" and *The Ego and the Id*).

7. EH II 1 p. 238 and p. 240: "The German spirit is an indigestion: it does not finish with anything . . . All prejudices come from the intestines. The sedentary life – as I have said once before – is the real *sin* against the holy spirit." GM I 6; on the "intestinal debility" of the man of *ressentiment*.

8. An expression common in Jung when he denounces the "objectivist" character of Freudian psychology. It is Nietzsche whom Jung admires for having been the first to place psychology on the plane of the subject, that is to say, for having conceived it as a true *typology*.

9. Jules Vallès, "active" revolutionary, insisted on this necessity of respecting the causes of misfortune (*Tableau de Paris*).

10. GS 21 p. 94: "The 'neighbour' praises selflessness *because it brings him advantages*. If the neighbour himself were 'selfless' in his thinking he would repudiate this diminution of strength, this mutilation for *his* benefit; he would work against the development of such inclinations, and above all he would manifest his selflessness by *not* calling it *good*! This indicates the fundamental contradiction in the morality that is very prestigious nowadays: the motives of this morality stand opposed to its principle."

11. BGE 260 p. 176 (cf. will to power as "the virtue that bestows").

12. GM I 13 pp. 44–5; " 'These birds of prey are evil; and whoever is least like a bird of prey, but rather its opposite, a lamb – would he not be good?' "

13. cf. TI "The Four Great Errors"; a detailed critique of causality.

14. Nietzsche summarises his interpretation of the history of the Jewish people in AC 24, 25, 26: the Jewish priest is already the one who deforms the tradition of the Kings of Israel and the Old Testament.

15. AC 18 p. 128: "In God a declaration of hostility towards life, nature, the will to life! God, the formula for every calumny of 'this world', for every lie about 'the next world'! In God nothingness deified, the will to nothingness sanctified!. . ." AC 26 p. 137: "The *priest* abuses the name of God: he calls a state of society in which the priest determines the value of things 'the kingdom of God'; he calls the means by which such a state is achieved and perpetuated 'the will of God' ".

16. AC 24 p. 135 – GM I 6, 7, 7; this priest is not identical to the slave but forms a special caste.

17. *Oeuvres Posthumes*, trans. Bolle, Mercure.

18. Letters to Fritsch, 23 and 29 March 1887. On all these points, on the falsifications of Nietzsche by the Nazis, cf. P. M. Nicolas' book, *De Nietzsche à Hitler* (Fasquelle, 1936), where the two letters to Fritsch are reproduced. A good case of a Nietzschean text used by the anti-semites when its sense is exactly the opposite can be found in BGE 251.

19. BGE 52 pp. 61–2 "the taste for the Old Testament is a touchstone in regard to 'great' and 'small' . . . To have glued this New Testament, a species of rococo taste in every respect, on to the Old Testament to form a *single* book, as 'bible' as the 'book of books': that is perhaps the greatest piece of temerity and 'sin against the spirit' that literary Europe has on its conscience."

20. cf. BGE 251 (well-known text on the Jews, the Russians and the Germans).

21. GM II 1: "This necessarily forgetful animal, for whom forgetting is a force and the manifestation of a robust health, creates for itself a contrary faculty, memory, by which, *in certain cases*, it holds forgetting in check."

22. GM II 1: On this point the resemblance between Freud and Nietzsche is confirmed. Freud attributes verbal traces to the preconscious, these are distinct from the mnemonic traces peculiar to the unconscious system. This distinction permits him to reply to the question "How to render repressed elements (pre-) conscious?" The reply is: "By restoring these intermediary preconscious elements which are verbal memories." Nietzsche's question would be stated in this way: how is it possible to "act" reactive forces?

23. GM II 8 p. 70: It was in the debtor-creditor relationship "that

one person first encountered another person, that one person first *measured himself* against another".

24. GM II 6 pp. 65–6: "Whoever clumsily interposes the concept of 'revenge' does not enhance his insight into the matter but further veils and darkens it (for revenge merely leads us back to the same problem: 'how can making suffer constitute a compensation?')". This is what is lacking in the majority of theories: showing from what point of view "making suffer" gives pleasure.

25. GM II 11 p. 75: "The law represents on earth . . . the struggle against the reactive feelings, the war conducted against them on the part of the active and aggressive powers."

26. GM II 10 p. 73: Justice "ends, as does every good thing on earth, by *overcoming itself*".

27. UM III "Schopenhauer Educator", 6: Nietzsche explains the diverting of culture by invoking the "three egoisms", the egoism of *acquirers*, the egoism of the *State*, the egoism of *science*.

28. GM III 14 p. 123: "They walk among us as embodied reproaches, as warnings to us – as if health, well-constitutedness, strength, pride and the sense of power were in themselves necessarily vicious things for which one must pay some day, and pay bitterly: how ready they themselves are at bottom to *make* one pay; how they crave to be *hangmen*. There is among them an abundance of the vengeful disguised as judges, who constantly bear the word 'justice' in their mouths like poisonous spittle, always with pursed lips, always ready to spit upon all who are not discontented but go their way in good spirits."

29. The religion of the strong and its selective significance (BGE 61). Affirmative and active religions which are opposed to nihilistic and reactive religions (VP I 332 and AC 16). Affirmative sense of paganism as a religion (VP IV 464). Active sense of Greek gods (GM II 23). Buddhism, a nihilistic religion but without the spirit of revenge or the feeling of guilt (AC 20–23, VP I 342–343). Christ's personal type, absence of *ressentiment*, of bad conscience and the idea of sin (AC 31–35, 40–41). The famous formula by which Nietzsche summarises his philosophy of religion; "Really only the *moral* God is refuted" (VP III 482, III 8). Commentators who want to make Nietzsche's atheism

into a temperate atheism, or even want to reconcile Nietzsche with God, rely on all these texts.

30. AC 42: "On the heels of the 'glad tidings' came the *worst of all*: those of Paul. In Paul was embodied the antithetical type to the 'bringer of glad tidings', the genius of hatred, of the vision of hatred, of the logic of hatred. *What* did this dysangelist not sacrifice to his hatred! The redeemer above all: he nailed him to *his* Cross." – It is St Paul who "invented" the sense of guilt: he "interpreted" the death of Christ as if Christ died *for our sins* (VP I 366 and 390).

31. It will be remembered that the active priest does not become mixed up with reactive forces: he leads them, he makes them triumph, he turns them to account, he breathes a will to power into them (GM III 15 and 18).

5. *The Overman: Against the Dialectic*

1. On the atheism of *ressentiment*: VP III 458; cf. EH II 1: how Nietzsche opposes his own *aggression* towards religion to the atheism of *ressentiment*.

2. Z II "The Prophet" pp. 155–6. GS 125 p. 181: "Are we not straying as through an infinite nothing? Do we not feel the breath of empty space? Has it not become colder? Is not night continually closing in on us?"

3. M. Heidegger, "The Word of Nietzsche: 'God is Dead' ", in, *The Question Concerning Technology and Other Essays*, trans. W. Lovitt, Harper and Row, 1977, p. 69.

4. Nietzsche is not confining himself to European history. Buddhism seems to him a religion of passive nihilism; Buddhism gives even passive nihilism nobility. Thus Nietzsche thinks that the East is in advance of Europe: Christianity still remains at the negative and reactive stages of nihilism (cf. VP I 343, AC 20–23).

5. GM I 8 p. 35: "Was it not part of the secret black art of truly *grand* politics of revenge, of a farseeing, subterranean, slowly advancing and premeditated revenge, that Israel must itself deny the real instrument of its revenge before all the world as a mortal enemy and nail it to the cross, so that "all the world", namely all the opponents of Israel, could unhesitatingly swallow just this bait?"

6. AC 17 pp. 127–8: "Formerly . . . [God] had only his people, his 'chosen' people. In the meantime, just like his people itself, he has gone abroad, gone wandering about; since then he has sat still nowhere: until at last he is at home everywhere, the great cosmopolitan."

7. The theme of the death of God, interpreted as the death of the Father, is dear to Romanticism; for example Jean Paul (*Choix de Rêves*, trans. Béguin). Nietzsche gives an admirable example of this in WS 84; the prison guard being absent a prisoner leaves the ranks and says in a loud voice: "I am the son of the warder and I can get anything I like from him. I can save you – nay, I will save you. But, remember this: I will only save those of you who *believe* that I am the son of the prison warder." Then the news spreads that the prison guard "has just died suddenly". The son speaks again: "I told you, I will set free all who believe in me, as surely as my father still lives". Nietzsche often denounces this Christian demand for believers; Z II "Of the Poets", p. 149: "Belief does not make me blessed . . . least of all belief in myself." EH IV 1 p. 326: "I *want* no 'believer'; I think I am too malicious to believe in myself; I never speak to masses – I have a terrible fear that one day I will be pronounced *holy*."

8. AC 42 p. 155. Second element of the interpretation of St Paul, AC 42, 43; VP I 390.

9. AC 33, 34, 35, 40. The true Christ, according to Nietzsche, does not appeal to belief, he provides a practice: "The Saviour was nothing else than this practice, his death too was nothing else . . . He does not resist, he does not defend his rights, he takes no steps to avert the worst that can happen to him – more, *he provokes it*. And he entreats, he suffers, he loves *with* those, *in* those who are doing evil to him . . . *Not* to defend oneself, *not* to grow angry, not to make responsible . . . But not to resist even the evil man – to *love* him . . . Jesus himself could have desired nothing by his death but publicly to offer the sternest test, the *proof* of his teaching."

10. AC 31 p. 143 – AC 42: "a new, an absolutely primary beginning to a Buddhistic peace movement". VP I 390/WP 167: "Christianity: a naive beginning to a Buddhistic peace movement in the very seat of *ressentiment*."

11. Z II "Of Great Events" pp. 53–4: "I have unlearned belief in

'great events', whenever there is much bellowing and smoke about them . . . And just confess! Little was ever found to have happened when your noise and smoke dispersed" (cf. also GS 125).

12. On the death of God and its meaning in Hegel's philosophy cf. the important commentaries by M. Wahl (*La Malheur de la Conscience dans la Philosophie de Hegel*) and M. Hyppolite (*Genèse et Structure de la Phénomenologie de l'Ésprit*). And also the important article by M. Birault ("L'Ontothéo-logique hégélienne et la dialectique", in *Tijdschrift voor Philosophie*, 1958).

13. Criticised by Stirner, Feuerbach admits this: I let the predicates of God continue to exist; "but I have to let them continue to exist, for without them (I) could not even let nature and man continue to exist; for God is a being composed of realities, that is to say of predicates of nature and humanity" (cf. "The essence of Christianity in its relation to the Ego and its own", *Manifestes Philosophiques*, trans. Althusser, PUF).

14. M. Stirner, *The Ego and His Own*, trans. S. T. Byington, ed. Martin, Dover, 1973, p. 366. On Stirner, Feuerbach and their relations cf. the books of M. Avron: *Aux Sources de L'Existentialisme: Max Stirner*; *Ludwig Feuerbach ou la transformation du Sacre* (PUF).

15. M. Merleau-Ponty wrote a fine book on *The Adventures of the Dialectic*. Among other things he denounces the objectivist adventure which rests on "the illusion of a negation realised in history and its content" (p. 123 original edition) or which "concentrates the whole of negativity in an existing historical formation, the proletarian class" (p. 278). This illusion necessarily entails the formation of a qualified body, "the functionaries of the negative" (p. 184). But it is doubtful whether, in wanting to maintain the dialectic on the terrain of a mobile subjectivity and inter-subjectivity, one escapes from this organised nihilism. There are figures of consciousness which are already functionaries of the negative. The dialectic has fewer adventures than avatars; naturalist or ontological, objective or subjective, it is, Nietzsche would say, nihilistic in principle; and the image that it gives of positivity is always a negative or inverted one.

16. cf. Z II "Of the land of Culture". *The man of the present* is at once

the representation of the higher man and the portrait of the dialectician. "You seem to be baked from colours and scraps of paper glued together . . . But how should you be *able* to believe, you motley-spotted man – you who are paintings of all that has ever been believed" pp. 142–3.

17. Z IV "The Greeting" p. 293: "It is not for *you* that I have been waiting in these mountains . . . you are not my right arm . . . With you I should still spoil every victory . . . You yourselves are not those to whom my heritage and name belong." Z IV "The Song of Melancholy" p. 307; "All these Higher Men – do they perhaps not *smell* well?" On the trap that they hold out to Zarathustra cf. Z IV "The Cry of Distress", "The Sorcerer", "Retired from Service", "The Ugliest Man", Z IV "The Greeting" p. 291. "This is my kingdom and my domain: but what is mine shall be yours for this evening and this night. My animals shall serve you: let my cave be your resting place!" Higher Men are called "bridges", "steps", "forerunners"; "from your seed there may one day grow for me a genuine son and perfect heir" p. 293.

18. Heidegger, *What is Called Thinking?* (trans. Wieck and Gray, Harper and Row, 1968), pp. 57–64.

19. Z IV "The Cry of Distress" p. 255:" 'The ultimate sin that is reserved for me – perhaps you know what it is called?' 'Pity!' answered the prophet from an overflowing heart, and raised both hands aloft – 'O Zarathustra, I come to seduce you to your ultimate sin!' " Z IV "The Ugliest Man", p. 278: " 'You yourself, however – warn yourself too against *your* pity! . . . I know the axe that fells you' " And, Z IV "The Sign", one of Zarathustra's last words is " '*Pity, Pity for the Higher Man*! . . . *Very* well! *That* has had its time' ".

20. Z IV "Of the Higher Man", 14, p. 303; *Play*, "A *throw* you made had failed. But what of that, you dice throwers! You have not learned to play and mock as a man ought to play and mock." *Dance*, 19 p. 305: "Even the worst thing has good dancing legs: so learn you higher men, how to stand on your own proper legs." *Laughter*, 20 p. 306: "I have canonised laughter; you Higher Men, *learn* – to laugh!"

21. VP Book III – VP I 22: "Having pushed nihilism in itself to its final limit, he puts it behind him, outside him."

22*. *Translator's note*: *Ratio cognoscendi* is the being of a thing in the mode of object known. The scholastic term *ratio* is variously rendered into English as: reason, nature, relation, ground, argument, definition, principle. Here it is used in the last of these senses – principle. The French translation of *ratio* in this sense is *raison*, as in *raison d'être*. I have used the Latin word *ratio* for Deleuze's word *raison*, to avoid losing the range of the original scholastic term. The word *ratio* was once used in this sense in English.

23*. *Translator's note*: *Ratio essendi* – the essence or "formal reason" of a thing, the definition of it or its essential attributes as they are conceived by us, that is they are abstracted from particular conditions. This scholastic term can be translated as *raison d'être*.

24. On active destruction VP III 8 and 102. For the way in which Zarathustra opposes "the man who wants to perish" to the last man or the "preachers of death" see Z Prologue 4 and 5, and Z I "Of Voluntary Death".

25. VP IV 14: "We will have to assess with all possible justice the aspects which were, until then, alone in *affirming* existence; understand where this affirmation comes from and how unconvincing it is as a Dionysian evaluation of existence comes into being."

26. cf. EH: how negation *follows* affirmation – III "Beyond Good and Evil", 1 p. 310: "After having accomplished the affirmative part of this task, it was the turn of the negative part . . ." How negation *precedes* affirmation – EH III "Thus Spoke Zarathustra", 8 and EH IV 2 and 4.

27. TI "Expeditions of an Untimely Man" 19 p. 78: " 'O Dionysus, divine one, why do you pull my ears?' Ariadne once asked her philosophical lover during one of those celebrated dialogues on Naxos. 'I find a kind of humour in your ears, Ariadne: why are they not longer?' "

28. Z Prologue 6, 7, 8. First meeting with the buffoon, who says to Zarathustra, "You spoke like a buffoon" 8. Z II "The Child with the Mirror": Zarathustra dreams that, looking at himself in a mirror, he sees the face of a buffoon, "Truly, I understand the dream's omen and warning all too well: my doctrine is in danger, weeds want to be called wheat! My enemies have grown power-

ful and have distorted the meaning of my doctrine" p. 107. Z III
"Of the Vision and the Riddle": second meeting with the
dwarf-buffoon, near the gateway of the eternal return. Z III "Of
Passing By": third meeting – "But your foolish teaching is
harmful to *me*, even when you are right!"

29. Two texts take up and explain the theme of the burden and the
desert: Z II "Of the Land of Culture" and III "Of the Spirit of
Gravity".

30. Feuerbach, "Contribution to Critique of the Philosophy of
Hegel", and "Principles of the Philosophy of the Future" (*Manifestes Philosophiques*, trans. Althusser, PUF).

31. Heidegger gives an interpretation of Nietzschean philosophy
closer to his own thought than to Nietzsche's. Heidegger sees, in
the doctrine of the eternal return and the overman, the determination of "the relation of Being to the being of man as relation of
this being to Being". (cf. *What is Called Thinking?*) This
interpretation neglects all that Nietzsche fought against.
Nietzsche is opposed to every conception of affirmation which
would find its foundation in Being, and its determination in the
being of man.

32. Finding the very roots of being and nothingness in affirmation
and negation is not new; this thesis belongs to a long philosophical tradition. But Nietzsche reviews and overturns this tradition with his conception of affirmation and negation, with his
theory of their relation and transformation.

33. Z II "Of the Sublime Man": "To steal with relaxed muscles and
unharnessed wills: that is the most difficult thing for all of you,
you sublime men!" p. 141.

34. VP III 408: "We are particularly curious to explore the
labyrinth, we strive to make the acquaintance of Mr Minotaur of
whom such terrible things are told; what do they matter to us,
your path which *ascends*, your thread which leads *out*, which
leads to happiness and to virtue, which leads towards you, I am
afraid of it . . . can you save us with the help of this thread? And
we, we beg you straight away, hang yourself with this thread!"

35. DD "Ariadne's Complaint"; "Be prudent Ariadne! You have
little ears, you have my ears: Put a shrewd word there! Is it not
first necessary to hate oneself if one has to love oneself? . . . I am
your labyrinth . . ."

36*. *Translator's note*. The first part of this sentence reads "l'être se dit du devenir". The translation given was suggested by Professor Deleuze.

37. On the first aspect of the demon cf. the theory of the ass and the camel. But also, Z III "Of the Vision and the Riddle" where the demon (the spirit of gravity) is sitting on the shoulders of Zarathustra himself. And IV "Of the Higher Man", 10 p. 301: "If you want to rise high, use your own legs! Do not let yourselves be carried up, do not sit on the backs and heads of strangers!" On the second aspect of the demon, cf. the famous scene of the Prologue where the buffoon catches up with the tightrope walker and jumps over him. This scene is explained in III "Of Old and New Law Tables", 4 p. 216: "There are diverse paths and ways to overcoming: just look to it! But only a buffoon thinks: Man can also be jumped over."

38. Z II "The Stillest Hour" p. 169. " 'O Zarathustra, your fruits are ripe but you are not ripe for your fruits.' " On Zarathustra's hesitations and evasions about the eternal return cf. II "Of Great Events" and above all "The Stillest Hour" ("It is beyond my strength"); III "The Convalescent".